FAITH IN CHRIST
AND THE
WORSHIP OF CHRIST

FAITH IN CHRIST
AND THE
WORSHIP OF CHRIST

New Approaches to Devotion to Christ

Johann Auer • Walter Baier • Hans Urs von Balthasar
Joachim Becker • Joseph Heer • Felix Heinzer
Norbert Hoffmann and Anton Mattes

Edited by Leo Scheffczyk

Translated by Graham Harrison

IGNATIUS PRESS, SAN FRANCISCO
†
INTERNATIONAL INSTITUTE OF
THE HEART OF JESUS, MILWAUKEE

Papers presented at a Symposium
sponsored by the
International Institute of the Heart of Jesus
April 8–11, 1980

Originally published in German under the title
Christusglaube und Christusverehrung:
Neue Zugänge zur Christusfrömmigkeit,
Paul Pattloch Verlag, Aschaffenburg ©1982

Cover design by Darlene Lawless
Cover art by Carol Townsend

CONTENTS

IN PLACE OF A PREFACE

INTRODUCTION TO THE SYMPOSIUM, APRIL 8–11, 1980

At the start of our symposium I welcome you all most warmly, and I also welcome you in the name of our eminent Patron, Cardinal Ratzinger. In doing so I would also like to express my thanks for your interest in this theological dialogue, and for the sacrifice of time and labor that it has meant. First among our participants I would like to welcome the Most Reverend Bishop of Regensburg, Dr. Rudolf Graber, a teacher of systematics, a pastorally committed theologian and bishop, who himself has done work on our topic. Notwithstanding the burden of his many obligations he would let nothing deter him from honoring this congress with his presence, and for this our special thanks are due to him.

Next, allow me to turn to our foreign guests, and first among them to those who have come the furthest distance: Fr. Roger Vekemans and Juan Cordero from Bogotá, representing the International Institute of the Heart of Jesus which made the congress possible. They have come to this symposium with many expectations, and we hope they will not be disappointed. The same applies to our guest from the United States, Professor Dr. Anton Morgenroth from Erlanger, Kentucky, a North American of German descent, who has already contributed a great deal to our subject. We wish him much joy as he renews his acquaintance with Germany and hope that he will enjoy meeting his German colleagues at this Congress.

Near to us, both in geography and approach, are our colleagues from Belgium and the Netherlands. I welcome Professor Dr. van Calster, President of the John XXIII Seminary in Louvain, our colleagues J. Becker and N. Hoffmann from Simpelveld, and our colleagues from Rolduc, the liturgist Professor J. L. Hermans and Professor L. Elders and J. Ambaum, who, as well as contributing to our congress topic (Professor Elders on Thomas Aquinas for example), will also report to us on their particular problems. Halfway between Germany and the Low Countries, so to speak, we have Professor Dr. W. Paschen who lives in Cologne and teaches New Testament in Rolduc. Thus in him and in one of our speakers, Dr. J. A. Heer from Stuttgart, we can welcome two exegetes.

Coming from an area closer to our congress location, are our Swiss friends and colleagues: H. Urs von Balthasar, who was hard-pressed to find the time but who in the end did not disappoint us; similarly Dr. F. Heinzer of Zurich

7

who will read us a paper on the subject of his dissertation, Maximus the Confessor, and his teacher, the dogmatician C. von Schönborn of Freiburg. We thank them for coming and for being willing to undertake a contribution to our topic.

From Austria I welcome Dr. B. Wenisch. As for our German colleagues, they are nicely balanced between north and south. From the north I give a warm welcome to Monsignor J. Auda, Bochum; Dr. W. Averbeck, Osnabrück; H. M. Köster and F. Courth of the Vallendar Academy of Philosophy and Theology and Professor Dr. K. Wittkemper from Oeventrop.

Last but not least, I welcome our colleagues from the west and southwest, H. Riedlinger and J. Schumacher from Freiburg; also J. Auer from Regensburg who, even more since becoming emeritus, is a mine of knowledge and experience and will share some of it with us here.

Then in close proximity to us we have our colleagues G. Söll from Benediktbeuren, J. Stöhr from Bamberg, F. X. Bantle and Dr. W. Baier from Augsburg, Director Dr. A. Mattes of Eichstätt, Dr. S. Horn from Passau and, from Munich, my colleague J. Finkenzeller.

And now to our aim and our program: strictly speaking, this is a private event; inclination, rather than official duty, has brought us together, this fact is connected with our topic, which is not very popular today in theology and dogmatics.

In all the endless gyrating around the historical Jesus, theology seems to lose the figure of Christ entirely. While some hold aloof from the historical Jesus in favor of the Christ of the kerygma, others commit themselves completely to the former and then deduce the whole of Christianity from the way of life of the historical Jesus. Dogmatic theology, caught up in the maze of problems of "Christology from below" or "from above", no longer seems to come to grips with that center that unites the historical and the suprahistorical, which puts the "from below" in touch with the "from above"; namely, the center of the divine-human mystery of Jesus Christ.

Unless this center is found there can be no devotion to the Person of Jesus Christ. The existentialist will see it as a distraction from the only valid vocation, authenticity of human existence; the apologist for a pragmatic Christianity will take offense at Jesus' elevation to the level of a "divine Icon" and, thus, at the distortion of this "disturber of history" and his dangerously provocative social prophecy (Schillebeeckx, *Jesus*, 671).

The subject of our congress, however, is informed by the conviction that we must regain this christological center, and that the path to this encounter can be prepared, in part, precisely by devotion to Christ in his continuing mystery. Yet we cannot be properly in touch with this mystery as an object of devotion unless it is at the same time made accessible by dogmatics. The topic "Christology and the devotion to Christ", in fact, could once again provide the context for a meeting of dogmatic and spiritual theology, of technical theology and of that pneumatic theology that is animated by spirituality and prayer. No one doubts that our theology today is particularly in need of a leaven of this kind, if it is not to become simply pure historical criticism on the one hand and a mere religious philosophy of the Christian phenomenon on the other.

It is also true that in the present theological situation, characterized first and foremost by the question of hermeneutics and the anthropological perspective, external stimuli are also required for common theological work of this kind, what Paul calls "the mystery of our reverence" (*sacramentum pietatis*: 1 Tim 3:16).

Our external stimulus came to us in the form of a proposal from the International Institute of the Heart of Jesus, and particularly from its Latin American branch, represented by Fr. Roger Vekemans from Bogotá, Colombia. When Cardinal Ratzinger visited Ecuador in 1978, Fr. Vekemans began to explore possibilities, resulting in the idea of trying to interest German theologians in this matter of the devotion to Christ, which, in the form of the cult of the Heart of Jesus, is still a firmly rooted mode of spirituality among the faithful of Latin America. There is a not unreasonable hope that, by cultivating and deepening this spirituality, a counterweight can be set against the limiting and one-sided view of the political Christ, which, though it is to some extent understandable, we cannot regard as generally valid. We see no future in it. So our aim must be to break out of these restrictions by returning to that center that alone can give meaning and relevance to the political field, that is, the concrete Jesus Christ in whom to be divine and to be human is a harmonious thing and who thus can be the object of a unique devotion.

Thus our Latin American friends, including Cardinal Muñoz Duque, Archbishop of Bogotá, approached us for a kind of spiritual assistance. And indeed, in today's Church, which is under pressure everywhere, this kind of aid ought to be available, especially as we know that material help alone is not enough.

We were honored by this proposal, which evinced a great confidence in German theology in spite of all the contrary indications. But taking up the proposal has not been without its problems. It would have been inappropriate in fact and totally unjustifiable to take on this task as if we were dispensing some of our supposed theological surplus to a needy part of the Church, as if it were a case of intellectual almsgiving in which the giver were not inwardly involved.

The preacher knows that it is a dubious business to try to communicate something to others without being involved himself. Fortunately we are not in such a precarious situation. It is not easy to say what part is played, in our own context today, by devotion to Christ in the form of devotion to the

Heart of Jesus, for instance. But one can surmise that, compared with the period between the two World Wars, there has been a great deterioration. Under the pretext of greater authenticity of Christian existence, and of liturgical life too, people have imagined that they could do without the accidental forms and expressions of faith. This renunciation not only runs counter to the requirements of religious psychology but also contradicts the basic law of the central Christ-event, which summons all man's abilities and possibilities and seeks to draw them into its dynamic movement. "Getting at the fundamentals" of faith and its shape in our lives can easily result in its reduction. This, it seems, is what has happened to our spirituality.

In theology, however, the situation seems a little different. In spite of the opposition to a linking of theoretical and spiritual theology, such as we have mentioned, there are and have always been currents within German theology, as elsewhere, that make the link possible; thus, in working on this subject, we are also ministering to our own needs and interests.

There exists a doctrine of the "mysteries of the life of Jesus" that has worked out an understanding of our union with Christ and that can be adapted to spirituality. There exists a whole "theological aesthetics" that opens up revelation to man's mind and senses as form and radiance, revealing new approaches to the worship of the mystery of Christ. Dogmatics too points to the "inner correspondence between ecclesial and personal faith" and has devoted much attention to the theme of experience (J. Auer). Furthermore there has been a wealth of biblical, patristic and historical investigation in the field of spiritual theology and Christology. These materials are at our disposal.

This being the case, it is not entirely rash to tie around these subjects the one thread that unites them all, particularly with regard to the mystery of Christ and the spirituality centered on him. This is the aim of our symposium. We do not imagine that we can straightway produce an integrated unity of the doctrine of Christ and of Christ-centered spirituality, such as was last achieved, in all probability, by the French school of Pierre Bérulle (d. 1629). All the same we are surely right in hoping to take a few steps forward that will give us some intimation of the mystery in its totality.

Our path must start from the biblical basis; on the way we shall profit from various insights we find in Patristics, Scholasticism and the more recent history of spirituality; we shall conclude by facing a number of systematic questions that arise especially from our current concern, such as the theology of conversion and expiation and its relation to the devotion to the Heart of Jesus.

In detail the program looks like this: first we shall hear an introductory exposition of principles from Hans Urs von Balthasar on the single and indivisible mission of Jesus, in which his deeds and sufferings, action and Passion, solidarity with the "poor" and acting on behalf of sinners all form a unity. Then we shall search for the biblical origins of a faith that is open to the veneration of Christ: J. Becker's consideration of the fundamental word "heart" in the language of the Bible will shed light on the central biblical message as to what being human really means, a message that is directly expressed, in terms of Christology and soteriology, in the Johannine image of the pierced Savior (J. Heer). This image generates the basic ideas of the Johannine doctrine of redemption, which, through faith's beholding of this symbol, releases a never-ending stream of impulses of "new life".

In the papers on the soteriology of Maximus the Confessor (F. Heinzer) and on the inner life of the man Jesus according to St. Thomas Aquinas (L. Elders) we shall see how deeply this believing, worshipping contemplation of the mystery of the divine-human Redeemer has etched itself on the tradition. They also show how a spirituality directed toward the veneration of Christ's humanity potently countered the allegedly Monophysite tendencies of traditional faith in Christ and promoted the existential link between the life of Jesus and the life of man.

It is true that these results show that worship of the humanity of Christ was originally directed less toward particular parts than toward the whole incarnate life of Jesus. Research has never really dealt adequately with the transition from the more broadly conceived "Passion" spirituality of the Fathers to the concentration on the "Heart" as a cultic object. These aspects are taken up anew in the papers on "Key Issues in medieval Sacred Heart Piety" (W. Baier) and on "Devotion to the Heart of Jesus in Modern Times: The Influence of Saint Margaret Mary Alacoque" (A. Mattes).

These studies, manifesting as they do the continuity of the stream of tradition as well as the wealth of its changing forms, are not meant merely as an exercise in freshening what is old: the purpose of the systematic contributions is to show that new ideas can be drawn from the tradition and new connections can be discovered in it. Thus the discussion of "Devotion to the Sacred Heart and the Theology of Conversion" (J. Auer) shows that this devotion, in its context of *metanoia* and penance, is an essential structure of the Christian life, while light is shed on a further aspect of this spirituality by the basic principle of Christ our "Representative" (N. Hoffmann). In conclusion we discuss the fundamental importance of cultic worship of Christ for that experience of Jesus that people everywhere are seeking today.

If we succeed, with this loose array of ideas and topics, in becoming once again a little more aware of the ideal, namely the unity of Christology and the devotion to Christ, with special reference to the cult of the Heart of Jesus, it will be our way of contributing to the concern that our Latin American friends have shared with us. It may also be possible to arrange publication of a book, primarily to be seen as a gift to the priests in those countries. But as I have already indicated, this kind of spiritual gift would not involve the recipient only. It would also enrich us, the donors, and have an effect on our own theological and spiritual needs, which are, after all, not so essentially different from those of Latin America for we live in a world that is growing together more and more. What is at stake everywhere today is that, in her efforts to exert a formative influence on the world, the Church should not lose her originality but on the contrary, by accepting the challenge issued by the world, should sharpen her profile.

I conclude my introductory remarks, therefore, by hoping that our modest undertaking will succeed, and I have the pleasure to open the study sessions.

Leo Scheffczyk

HANS URS VON BALTHASAR

THE WORK AND SUFFERING OF JESUS:
DISCONTINUITY AND CONTINUITY

1. The Unity of the Mission of Jesus

a. A proclaimed unity

We have no access to the earthly life of Jesus, let alone to his consciousness, other than the faith of the primitive Church as expressed in the writings of the New Testament. However diverse the perspectives in which these writings see the Person of Jesus, in one point they are absolutely united: God's mission, carried out by Jesus, is one, indivisible, and embraces his earthly activity as well as his suffering and Resurrection. Ultimately it is a gift to the Church by the Holy Spirit, who inspires and communicates this very unity: the Church's mission is a prolongation of the mission of Jesus, but it is also a suffering and dying together with him, and a being raised with him as a "new man". Nowhere in the Church's entire preaching is there the slightest room for a consideration of the earthly deeds of Jesus in isolation, as if, separated from his Passion and Resurrection, they could provide a coherent meaning.

The witnesses openly admit that they in no way grasped this unity of life-death-Resurrection during Jesus' earthly life; only from the end, looking back, did the single, total meaning of the whole mission become clear to them. In Luke it is Jesus himself who makes this unity plain to the Emmaus disciples, and subsequently to those assembled in Jerusalem, after his Resurrection. Paul is clear about it from the first, and in many places (not in all) John does not hesitate to impute this understanding to the disciples even prior to the Passion. It is plain, too, that the synoptic writers are writing from the perspective of this unity, but here the question is to what extent they ascribe an awareness of this concrete unity to the earthly Jesus. For them, initially, did not Jesus simply proclaim the advent of the Kingdom of God and try to instill new life into faith in God? Was it not later, perhaps shortly before his Passion, when he realized that he would have to embrace death for the sake of his mission and that, in a mysterious way, this death could have something to do with its fulfillment?

b. *A unity known to Jesus*

If we try to get nearer to Jesus' consciousness of his mission, the first thing that strikes us is the difference between him and the Baptist. The latter feels that he is the last of the prophets, preparing the way for the final Day of the Lord. Jesus confirms the Baptist's eschatological sense by comparing him to "Elijah who will come", calling him the greatest of the prophets and receiving baptism from him: this is the signal that the threshold to the promised fulfillment has been crossed. When, in prison, John has doubts, Jesus confirms that the fulfillment has come.

Jesus' conviction of his definitive and all-embracing mission is whole, intact and free from all doubt on his part. For it is the Father's mission, the implementation of the will "of him who sent me" (Jn 6:29), not some personal enthusiasm of his own. And the Kingdom of God, which he proclaims to be near, to be on the very threshold, is first of all the Kingdom of *God*, of the Father. On the other hand, it would be both precipitate and wrong to conclude from this that Jesus only proclaimed the Kingdom, not himself. For in everything he says and does it is clear that the Kingdom has come near in *him* and only in him. "But if it is by the Spirit of God that *I* cast out demons, then the Kingdom of God has come upon you" (Mt 12:28). The expressions "I am", "but I say unto you" and "I am come" all point in the same direction. This "I" has only one analogue in the Bible, the "I" of Yahweh. No prophet speaks of himself in this way; he only transmits the "Word of the Lord".

Although it remains so mysterious, the proclaimed Kingdom that has come near in the Person of Jesus is not restricted to particular people, places and times. It is universal. So Jesus' mission of bringing the Kingdom near in his Person is also universal in principle, since it shares in the absoluteness of God himself. If he does not identify himself explicitly with the Kingdom, and in this sense does not preach himself, it is evidently because he himself is still in the act of arriving; his vocation and his whole destiny are not yet complete. Origen's "*autobasileia*" applies to Jesus only after Easter. The mission of Jesus has only just begun; like the coming of the Kingdom, it is only now coming into its stride.

This coming, however, will never be detached from the coming of his own Person and mission. Only on this account can Jesus summon men to follow him unreservedly, as he indubitably has done, in contrast to what prophets or even rabbis required of their disciples. According to John, even the Baptist does not bind his disciples to his own person but points them to the Lamb of God, rejoicing that he is to decrease so that Jesus, the Bridegroom, may increase (Jn 3:27ff.). If men can be bound in this way, called to leave all else behind, it means that they are fit for the Kingdom of God (Lk 9:62) and worthy of Jesus (Mt 10:37).

To be able to "conscript" men in this way—men who, as Jews, believe in their own God—means that Jesus implicitly identifies himself with this God, as John explicitly puts it: "I and the Father are one" (Jn 10:30). Jesus is aware, not only that he embodies the Father in the way an ambassador in a foreign land embodies his sovereign, not only that he is carrying out the Father's will on earth with full authority, but also that he is acting in the role of God himself, "making him present" in the strongest sense of the words. Indeed, that is the main accusation against him, that "You, being a man, make yourself God" (Jn 10:33).

This becomes conclusive where he lays equal claim to that undivided love that, according to the First Commandment, the man of the Old Testament owes to God alone. Such passages are frequent in John. To the Jews he says: "If God were your Father, you would love me, for I proceeded and came forth from God" (8:42). To the disciples: "If you love me, keep my commandments" (Jn 14:15). "He who has my commandments and keeps them, he it is who loves me; and he who loves me will be loved by my Father, and I will love him" (14:21). "If a man loves me, he will keep my Word. . . . He who does not love me does not keep my Word" (14:23–24). "If you loved me, you would have rejoiced, because I go to the Father" (14:28). And at the end of the farewell discourses: "The Father himself loves you, because you have loved me and have believed that I came from the Father" (16:27). Correspondingly we read in the Letter of John: "Everyone who loves the parent loves the child" (1 Jn 5:1). But, someone may object, this is subsequent Johannine reflection, this is spirituality not found at an earlier period. But it is there. Paul ends the First Letter to the Corinthians with these words in his own hand beside his signature: "If anyone has no love for the Lord [Jesus Christ], let him be accursed" (1 Cor 16:22), possibly an acclamation well known to the community from their Liturgy. And for Paul the surrender of his whole life, in faith, is an answer of love to the Son of God, "who loved me and gave himself for me" (Gal 2:20). But in the synoptic writers, too, the same absolute love for Jesus is demanded: "He who loves father and mother more than me is not worthy of me." And, "He who does not take his cross and follow me is not worthy of me" (Mt 10:37–38; cf. Lk 14:26). In our particular context it is immaterial whether the Lucan "cannot be my disciple" is more original than the Matthaean "is unworthy of me". The issue is the unqualified nature of discipleship, which applies equally to service of the Kingdom, and hence of the will of God, and to devotion to Jesus and his way, wherever it may lead. If this summons is heard in the context of the Old Covenant, it presupposes a prior, absolute gesture of love from the gracious God. The Johannine "the Father loves you" is made concrete by Jesus' whole existence on behalf of men, without Jesus needing to make personal avowals of love: his message and his actions speak loudly enough. Only in that final,

farewell hour he tells his disciples: "As the Father has loved me, so have I loved
you. . . . Love one another as I have loved you. Greater love has no man than
this, that a man lay down his life for his friends" (Jn 15:9–13). According to
Paul these "friends" are in fact still enemies (Rom 5:10). And once again this
self-surrendering love is identical with God's, for he loved the world so much
that he gave his only Son for its sake (Jn 3:16; Rom 8:32).

From this vantage point Paul's universal affirmation "God was in Christ
reconciling the world to himself" (2 Cor 5:19) seems both justified and
necessary. But if, as we began by saying, this kind of universalism is intelligible when seen in retrospect, do we not encounter great difficulties when we
come to examine the mission of Jesus in the historical succession of its phases?

2. The Disproportionate Mission

a. Israel's Messiah

Jesus knows that he is the fulfiller of the Law and the Prophets, and in the two
great discourses in Matthew (5–7) and Luke (4:14–30) he speaks expressly
as such. The Law is not to be abolished, but fulfilled and taken beyond
fulfillment. According to Isaiah, the Spirit of the Lord rests upon the
Anointed One, who has been sent "to bring good tidings to the poor . . .
release for the captives . . . liberty for the oppressed". The primary meaning
of this is doubtless non-political, although it certainly includes the social
dimension (powerfully in evidence in Amos) of poverty, captivity and oppres-
sion. But, long before Jesus, in the spirituality of the *anawim* there had been a
predominant spiritual dimension to addressing the poor, the widows and or-
phans. They are the ones who are not regarded, who are discounted, who are
powerless, and who are therefore open to God's laws and promises. Similarly
"captives" are now seen in a deeper sense as those who are in the chains of sin,
held by the bonds of Satan, like the woman who had been bent for eighteen
years (Lk 13:16); the "oppressed", too, are now also those who are margin-
alized by the "pure" who establish the norm: tax collectors (politically speaking among the oppressors) and prostitutes, who are both guaranteed priority
over the self-righteous in the order of entering the Kingdom of God.

In all this Jesus reveals himself as Israel's Messiah. He fulfills the Law and
the Prophets by revealing them again and then going beyond them to reach
their goal. His central concern is to gather together the scattered and lost
sheep of the House of Israel (Mt 10:6). This "gathering of the scattered" is a
basic concept of the prophets; Jesus understands it, not in a geographical, but
in a spiritual sense: the people are ignorant; their learned men and leaders

have gone astray. Contact with heathen territories and their inhabitants remains sporadic and peripheral, even as regards the Samaritans, although —
true to the Old Testament pattern — these strangers are more often presented
to the Jews as an example of faith or active love of neighbor. Jesus is the
Shepherd, sent by God, the Shepherd of Israel (Ez 34) to seek the abandoned
sheep of Israel (Mk 6:34) and bring them back to the fold. Jesus' chosen
"Twelve" associates surely indicate, in number, the totality of Israel.

This messianic work with the Chosen People, which was not to be cut
short in favor of a universal mission to all people, was big enough and burden
enough for one life, especially if it was only taken up at the age of thirty. But,
one must ask, was it feasible at all? What was called for was a conversion of
the people as such to God, not in the vague manner of the Old Covenant,
where, after falling away and being punished, they would again turn back to
God, but in the much more radical manner put forward by Jesus in terms of
God's mercy and God's challenge: to forget and deny oneself, to take up one's
cross daily — something Jesus may indeed have said even before his own Cross
was in sight — to live in the spirit of the Beatitudes.

It is unthinkable that Jesus should ever have entertained the illusion that
the old Israel, which had over a thousand years of tragic history behind it and
which had in any case been scattered to the winds for half a millennium and
had never completely returned, could become the new Israel of God without
a miracle, the miracle of an eschatological transformation. And the wider
Jesus' missionary activity became, the clearer became his lack of success: people
were not willing to give what he demanded; they took offense at his central
message, which was inseparable from hard criticism of the scale of values
adhered to by people of influence. The more he revealed the Father's merciful
love, the more entrenched became their rejection. At the end of his active life
Jesus has to hide. His death is certain; he is a wanted man (Jn 11:54–57). Was
this mission — to reconcile the world with God — to fail, when not merely
some prophet, but the Father's only Son, had come to carry it out?

b. The hour of the Father and of darkness

Nothing that a mortal man can do — even if he were the Messiah — can overcome sin, death, the Prince of this world. If this is to happen, some other
work must be set in motion, beyond the bounds of what can actively be
"done". One cannot "do" this work — for it is beyond one's own strength
— one can only suffer it. The rejection which Jesus encountered, which he actually brought out and polarized through carrying out his mission, was not
something he could accept himself: it had to be laid upon him as an imposi-
tion, totally exceeding human capacity.

The concept of the scapegoat, which people are wont to adduce nowadays as an explanation of the Passion of Jesus, will not suffice. It is not a matter of men looking for a victim, loading it with their sins and letting it bear the terrible consequences of their guilt. It goes much deeper: this terrible, raging darkness is transported into the very spirit and heart of the victim. Beholding how Jesus is forsaken by God on the Mount of Olives and on the Cross, we perceive the abyss between action and Passion; the two are utterly discontinuous. The farewell discourses and even the singing of psalms on the way to the Mount are the finale of the action; then suddenly there comes the headlong fall into the night of impotence, of the impossibility of drinking this cup to the dregs—this cup of the wrath of Yahweh with which he had threatened both Babylon and Jerusalem.

It is the Father's hour, and what it contains remains secret to him; there can be no anticipation of it, no training for it. Jesus does not tamper with the future; he lets it overtake him unprepared and unprotected. But he knows that it will come. He is so sure of this that he lives for this "hour" and can even call it his (Jn 2:4). He *can* speak of it as the baptism with which he is to be baptized and for which he yearns. He *must* speak of it to his accompanying disciples, so that they have no illusions about the coming Kingdom, their part in it, and the meaning of their discipleship. He *must* do this although they do not understand even the external outlines he shows them, let alone the inner content of this hour. Jesus *did* speak of it, even if the evangelists may have added some details in light of their knowledge of the Passion; there can be no doubt that he knew in advance that the conclusive breakthrough would not happen "today and tomorrow" (Lk 13:32) but on a mysterious "third day". That is why he does not speak of it as one of his saving acts; the abyss between such acts "today and tomorrow" and the "fulfillment" on the third day is much too vast for that. It is a petty, comfortable illusion to say, under the pretext of trying to plumb the psyche and psychology of Jesus, that he did not know that this hour and what it held was to be the completion of his mission, in the midst of earthly defeat.

We can leave it open whether he himself used the word "ransom" (λύτρον: Mk 10:45; Mt 20:28)—deliberately recalling the Servant of Deutero-Isaiah bearing the sins of the people and of the "many"—but the words of institution at the Eucharist, which cannot be denied to be his, speak in favor of it. For how could mere gestures, unaccompanied by words, have caused the disciples to understand what he wanted to give them through bread and wine? And if they did not understand him then, how could they have subsequently put such words into his mouth? This perfect gift of himself, of his substance, can only take place in connection with the impending torture of his body under the scourge and by the nails of the Cross, and the shedding of his blood, including the piercing by the lance, as the "wondrous exchange", of which the Liturgy will later speak, between the world's darkness which encroaches on his sphere of light and the light that shines in the darkness.

c. Discontinuity in continuity

Two extreme approaches confront each other in theology, and we must get beyond them, or rather harmonize the one with the other. On the one hand there is the idea expressed by many Fathers, and even by Anselm, that ultimately Jesus became man only in order to die on behalf of sinners. Tertullian put it in a nutshell, *forma moriendi causa nascendi est* (Carn 6,6), and since then many have filled out the details. Here the work of Jesus among the People of Israel is practically of no account; his solemn words and actions as Messiah sink to the level of mere ethical teaching. Nowadays this theory—in a liberalist guise—is only put forward by extreme apocalypticists, who think that Jesus' sole expectation was of the Last Judgment and that therefore he only preached an interim ethics.

However, the other extreme is in fashion today, that is, seeing the Passion only as the last step and consequence of Jesus' action. According to this view his action consisted essentially in his solidarity with the poor, prisoners, the oppressed and all the underprivileged; sinners, too, are seen as a kind of "poor". This solidarity on Jesus' part is in this view a demonstration to the world of the solidarity of God himself with the poor and deprived. Furthermore, to show how dead-seriously Jesus took this demonstration, he chose to be crucified in solidarity with two criminals. Not only avowed liberation theolgians but also a whole host of exegetes and theologians influenced by them take this line. For them, solidarity, not "representation", is the ultimate concept. For them, "the hour" that was the goal of Jesus' life introduces nothing qualitatively different and new over and above what he had done in his active life. They affirm God's "*pro nobis*", which for them attains its final visibility in the Passion, but they do not affirm the "*pro nobis*" of Jesus, or the "*Agnus Dei qui tollit peccata mundi*". We need to ask them if the Cross, understood like this, is really a clarification and not rather an obscuring of the fact that God is for us. The Cross is not an obvious symbol for this—unless one has unconsciously imported the content of propitiation theology into the theology of mere solidarity.

One can agree completely with James M. Robinson when he says: "The Cross would be misunderstood if its chronological distinctness from the public ministry were looked upon as a basic theological separation from the public ministry. . . . On the contrary, the Cross must be interpreted as Jesus' climactic actualization of his message."[1] Continuity is provided by the act of the Cross, not only in the sense that Jesus continually accepted his death because he wanted to break with the present evil eon (as Robinson thinks), nor even merely in the sense that he lived for the hour that would see the longed-for totality of his fragmentary earthly activity, but in the sense that

---

[1] James M. Robinson, *A New Quest of the Historical Jesus* (London: SCM Press, 1959), 89.

Jesus' entire teaching, what he promised to men and demanded of them, was fulfilled in it. That is why there is no liberation theology that is not relative to the Cross of Christ, however necessary and relevant its teaching and activity may be—in the event, that is, that such theology continues to teach and act within the horizon of the Passion (and, beyond it, of the Resurrection).

For it is only in this way that a Christian meaning, indeed ultimately *the* decisive meaning, can be found in all those things that cannot be achieved by active and (in the widest sense) "liberating" Christian effort—continuing suffering, continuing injustice, continuing sin, continuing death. We must begin with the active liberation; Jesus' programmatic discourse in Luke said as much. And, as the quoted words of Isaiah implied, what is envisaged is not merely an ethical and social liberation, but, more deeply, a religious liberation; even at that moment what was sought was a "year of the Lord's favor". In following the path of the real, propitiatory destiny of Jesus, liberation theology is no longer restricted to the kind of solidarity that can heroically embrace death (a death that is of no use to those who need liberating): this discipleship can be propitiatory on behalf of another, as Paul assures us explicitly. At the end, he who had been such an outstanding exponent of activity is sitting manacled in prison, abandoned to his suffering like his Lord, yet working for the community in a new way: "Now I rejoice in my sufferings for your sake, and in my flesh I complete what is lacking in Christ's afflictions for the sake of his body, that is, the Church" (Col 1:24).

d. The pierced side, the Eucharist, the Heart of God

The idea of propitiation, as a taking away of the sin of the world, presupposes that Jesus is the Son of God in the strongest sense, that is, that he himself is God. No mere creature could undergo, out of love, the whole darkness of the world's guilt, let alone get beyond it. Only the only begotten Son of the Father is able to plumb the experience of what it means to be abandoned by the eternal Father. Thus the experience of the Cross cannot really be described as an experience of hell; since it is a Trinitarian experience, it embraces all possible hells. Yet this Trinitarian experience is only possible because of the Incarnation; Christ cannot be a propitiation on behalf of sinners unless he is in communion with them.

The apparently indifferent piercing of the dead Jesus' side becomes a concrete symbol of what has happened, in all its inscrutable mystery. The apparently inaccessible substance of him (who took all that is ours into himself and bore it) is now released and made available to the redeemed; it becomes their hidden dwelling-place: *in tua vulnera absconde me*. Thomas, putting his hand into the marks of the Wounds, is the first to seek out this dwelling, only he must do so in faith and not want to see and experience it. The

Eucharist is less our taking Jesus' flesh and blood into us than our being taken up through him into his eternal, open humanity. Having passed through the Dark Night, it now has room for everything; it can embrace the world. Not until all this is complete — life, death and Resurrection — is the open Heart of the God-Man the place where we are given the gift of God's completely open Heart.

JOACHIM BECKER, SS.CC.

THE HEART IN THE LANGUAGE OF THE BIBLE

Many people, particularly priests and theologians, find it embarrassing to talk about the Heart of Jesus. It is not a matter of actual problems of faith; it is a human problem—which makes it serious enough.

In many areas of life impartiality and cool objectivity are demanded. Whether lovers still use the language of the heart is a question we can leave open. But writers rarely use the word and when they do, it is mostly in hackneyed phrases. And of course there is no point looking in technical literature, since that concentrates on things, not on the human being.

But in the treasury of our [German] language a wealth of expressions is available, and it is worthwhile to become aware of them. For instance, we give "hearty" greetings and "hearty" welcomes. I speak "from the bottom of my heart", and we speak of "brave", "good" and "true hearts". I may do something "with all my heart"; I have something on my "heart"; we "pour out our hearts"; we "take something to heart"; we "set our heart on" something; we know "heartbreak"; we say that someone "wins another's heart", "loses" or "gives" his heart; we "take heart", "take our heart in our hands", "wear our heart on our sleeves". Something "goes to our heart"; we are "heartily" sorry; indeed, our heart "bleeds" for someone. We go through life with a "heavy" or "light heart", a "merry" or a "sad heart". This by no means exhaustive catalogue shows that our language is certainly not so heartless. Nor has the symbol of the heart lost any of its expressive power. Tests may have shown that traffic signs can be ambiguous, but every child knows what a heart carved on a tree means. All the same it is a fact that the heart has been relegated to an idyllic realm; it is kept for special occasions. "Real" life—or what we think is real—speaks a different language.

We could put the problem, deliberately in general terms, like this: How ought we really to speak of ourselves, of others and to one another? This is important, because the way we speak "co-responds" to our attitude and behavior. Most of all, however, the way we speak of and to men will be carried over when we speak to the Lord. If in the interpersonal sphere the heart is only taken seriously in medical terminology, we cannot wonder that an expression like "Heart of Jesus" and the attitude it evinces seems out of place. We are bold to suggest that it is not the language of the Church's piety that is distorted, but our way of being human—a daring challenge, this, to our time, which regards "what is" as normative. But let us ask the Book that was written for the men of all times. Even the statistics are revealing: in the Old Testament the word "heart" occurs roughly one thousand times and in the New Testament about a hundred and fifty times.[1] Not even a romantic novel could compete with this! Even more illuminating is the way the word is used. Nothing sentimental or "pretty" here! It is the authentic expression of real life.

The language of the Bible includes archetypal words like heart, soul, spirit, name, hand, foot, eye, ear, face, way. It prefers to say "My heart rejoiced" rather than "I rejoiced". Typical of the Bible are sentences like "My soul magnifies the Lord and my spirit rejoices in God my Saviour"; "The Lord's hand has done wonders"; "He guides our feet into the way of peace"; "My eyes have seen thy salvation"; "Let your ears be open to my cry and my entreaty"; ". . . that I may behold the face of God"; "Praised be the name of the Lord". Language of this kind may strike us as primitive and ponderous, but in fact it is graphic, warm, close to nature—in a word, human. Strictly speaking it is not biblical but oriental. The Bible arose in the privileged world of the orientals. We do not, however, wish to make any value judgments at this point; first let us review a representative number of biblical examples of the use of the word "heart".[2]

In what contexts does the word appear? Surprisingly often where it is a matter of thinking, considering, understanding, getting insight, knowledge and wisdom. Straightway it gets to the most vital center of man's personal life. According to Deuteronomy 29:3 (cf. also Is 6:10; Mt 13:15; Jn 12:40; Acts 28:27) man has eyes for seeing, ears for hearing and a heart—for understanding, rather than for loving. How often we read "He said in his heart", that is, he thought to himself. It is in the heart that doubts arise (Lk 24:38). Jesus is set for the fall and rising of many in Israel, and Mary's soul will be pierced by a sword, so that the thoughts of many hearts may be revealed (Lk 2:34f.). Mary pondered all these things in her heart (Lk 2:19, 51). In the Bible a "man of heart" is characteristically a wise and perceptive man.

---

[1] Modern translations often sacrifice the word "heart" for the sake of "contemporary" language. Thus the New English Bible says merely that Mary "ponders" (Lk 2:19) and "many hearts" become simply "many" (Lk 2:35).

[2] For an exhaustive treatment of the concept, including details of earlier exegetical work, see F. H. von Meyenfeldt, *Het hart (leb, lebab) in het Oude Testament* (Leiden, 1950). In addition to the more routine articles in dictionaries of philosophy and biblical theology, the following show that there is continued interest in the subject: Helga Rusche, "Das menschliche Herz nach biblischem Verständnis", *Bibel und Leben* 3 (1962): 201–206; J. B. Bauer, *"De 'cordis' notione biblica et judaica"*, *Verbum Domini* 40 (1962): 27–32; H. Schlier, "Das Menschenherz nach dem Apostel Paulus", *Lebendiges Zeugnis* 1/2 (1965): 1–15, reprinted in *Das Ende der Zeit: Exegetische Aufsätze und Vorträge*, 3 (Freiburg-Basel-Vienna, 1971): 184–200; H. W. Wolff, *Menschliches: Vier Reden über das Herz, den Ruhetag, die Ehe und den Tod im Alten Testament* (Munich, 1971), 9–31; idem, *Anthropologie des Alten Testaments* (Munich, 1973), 68–95.

Job insists to his friends that he has a heart as they have, meaning that he is as intelligent as they (Jb 12:3). The prophet Hosea compares Ephraim to a simple dove, silly and without "heart", or sense (Hos 7:11), for looking for help from Egypt and Assyria. Wine has taken away the people's "heart", understanding (Hos 4:11). When we speak of "stealing a person's heart" we have something very different in mind from the biblical meaning, which is to "cheat, outwit", as in the case of Jacob's outwitting of his father-in-law Laban by concealing his departure from him (Gn 31:20, 26), and as Absalom did to the men of Israel, seducing them with dissembling promises into rebellion against his father David (2 Sm 15:6). So too we can easily misunderstand the bridegroom in the Song of Songs when he says that his bride has stolen his heart[3] with a single glance of her eyes, with a single one of her necklaces (Sg 4:9), for what he means is that her beauty has robbed him of his reason. To tell others one's innermost thoughts is to reveal one's "heart", as Samson did to his cost. He betrayed the secret of his strength to his Philistine wife Delilah, and she knew at once that this time he had not deceived her (Jgs 16:17ff.). Judges and those who deal with criminals can tell whether the accused person is telling the whole truth or not. When the heart is really open, there is no mistaking it. The sage Sirach, a perceptive judge of men, warns us not to let everyone look into our heart (Sir 8:19). In another place he says: "The heart of fools is in their mouth; the mouth of the wise reveals their heart" (Sir 21:26), that is, the fool says the first thing that comes into his head, but the words of the wise man are as choice as the thoughts of his heart.

If it is the heart's business to understand and know, then faith also will be a matter of the heart. And so it is. Romans 10:10 says explicitly that "man believes with his heart and confesses with his lips". Of course, the things of faith cannot be grasped by merely natural powers, for they are "what no eye has seen, nor ear heard, nor the heart of man conceived" (1 Cor 2:9). But God causes the light of the knowledge of faith to shine in our hearts so that we see the glory of God in the face of Jesus Christ (2 Cor 4:6). He enlightens the eyes of the heart (Eph 1:18). By faith Christ dwells in our hearts (Eph 3:17). The Jews remain unbelieving because their hearts are covered with a veil whenever Moses is read to them (2 Cor 3:15). Eventually, after the darkness of this life, in which the prophetic word serves as our lantern, the day will dawn and the morning star will rise in our hearts (2 Pt 1:19).

Holy Scripture has no illusions about the human heart. It is above all the source and dwelling-place of evil thoughts (Mt 15:19; Mk 7:21). "The thoughts of his heart are evil continually"—this is God's verdict prior to his sentence in the form of the Flood (Gn 6:5), and after the Flood he simply has to resign himself to the fact that the imaginations of a man's heart are evil from his youth (Gn 8:21). "Their senseless hearts were darkened", says Paul

---

[3] The form of the Hebrew lebab, "heart", here is probably the so-called "Piel privatiuum".

of the heathen (Rom 1:21). He prays tirelessly, even for believers, that God may establish their hearts (1 Thes 3:13; 2 Thes 2:17; 3:5; Phil 4:7). Man's heart is an abyss of wickedness (cf. Jer 17:9; Ps 64:7), but nothing is hidden from God. He is the "cardiognost", he who "knows the heart" (Acts 1:24; 15:8; cf. Rom 8:27). "Sheol and Abaddon lie open before the Lord, how much more the hearts of men!" (Prv 11:15). "He searches the depths of the sea, he searches the heart" (Sir 42:18). "He is greater than our heart" (1 Jn 3:20), that is, he knows it perfectly.[4] No wonder, for he has fashioned all hearts (Ps 33:15). When he returns on the Day of Judgment the Lord will reveal the purposes of the heart (1 Cor 4:5). But in his earthly life, too, he perceives the thoughts of hearts (Mk 2:6, 8; Lk 5:22; 9:47; 24:38).

If the heart is the seat of evil thoughts, it must involve a cooperation of reason and will. The two form an inseparable unity. The direction of the will is determined in the heart, the center of the person; this is where the real decisions are made. Most tellingly, the Hebrew expression "to have something on one's heart" (1 Sm 14:6; 2 Sm 7:3) means "to intend something". "Everyone who looks at a woman lustfully has already committed adultery with her in his heart" (Mt 5:28). The decisions of the frail human heart are not final. Often, as in the case of adultery, the heart follows the eyes (Jb 31:7; cf. Nm 15:39; Sir 5:2) and lets itself be enticed (Jb 31:9; cf. Sir 9:9). In general the heart is always drawn to what seems good, beautiful and desirable. "For where your treasure is, there will your heart be also" runs one of Jesus' proverbial sayings (Mt 6:21; Lk 12:34). It all depends on which treasure the heart has freely chosen.

Where decisions are made, there must also be responsibility. So the heart is where knowledge of one's guilt is registered. The Hebrew of the Old Testament has no abstract concept of "conscience". Instead we find the splendid simplicity of the word "heart". When David had cut off the border of Saul's cloak, his heart smote him (1 Sm 24:6)—the sign of a guilty conscience. The biblical author is hardly thinking of the tense situation and the danger of David being discovered: he is expressing the accusation of David's conscience, for in the ancient East particular powers were ascribed to the border of a garment, and in this case the Lord's Anointed was involved. This interpretation is confirmed in another context. When David had carried out a census against the will of God, his heart smote him again (2 Sm 24:10). The clever Abigail pointed out to him that a bloody deed against her husband would be a "stumbling-stone for his heart", that is, occasioning permanent remorse (1 Sm 25:31). Every man knows of the secret "affliction of his heart" for which he entreats God's forgiveness (1 Kgs 8:38). Sin itself is "written with a pen of iron; with a point of diamond it is engraved on the tablet of the heart" (Jer 17:1).

[4] This seems to be the simple and quite apposite meaning of what is often a somewhat romanticized text.

Man's heart is often qualified in terms of the inner disposition of his will. The heart of the godly man is firm, trusting in the Lord (Ps 112:7). There is much mention of upright and perfect hearts, pure and clean hearts. "Blessed are the pure in heart", says one of the eight Beatitudes (Mt 5:8). The upright heart can be turned away, seduced. Thus Solomon's wives turned his heart from the Lord (1 Kgs 11:2, 3, 4, 9). The negative picture is of the twisted, vacillating, divided and double heart. The "double" heart is, in fact, a "half" heart. We are not satisfied unless a person does something with his whole heart; then we know that the whole man is behind it. First and foremost this applies to the First and greatest Commandment: "You shall love the Lord your God with all your heart. . ." (Dt 6:5; Mt 22:37; Mk 12:30, 33; Lk 10:27). The heart is particularly susceptible to pride. But the Lord scatters those who are proud in the imagination of their heart—as Mary says in the Magnificat (Lk 1:51). The humble heart is the surest evidence of godliness. Jesus describes himself as "gentle and lowly in heart" (Mt 11:29).

The heart is the locus of everything that is innermost, genuine, precious and essential in man, all that is the opposite of empty superficiality. In a passage concerning women's hair, jewelry and fine clothing, the First Epistle of Peter speaks of the true adorning of "the hidden person of the heart with the imperishable jewel of a gentle and quiet spirit" (1 Pt 3:3f.). As a man is in his heart, so he is in reality. This is shown by the familiar experience so accurately described by the wisdom teachers of the Old Testament. " 'Eat and drink!' he says to you; but his heart is not with you" (Prv 23:7), that is, he is not sincere about it. "Like the glaze covering an earthen vessel are smooth lips with an evil heart" (Prv 26:23). "When [the hater] speaks graciously, believe him not, for there are seven abominations in his heart" (Prv 26:25). The Psalmist too complains of enemies who speak of peace but carry war in their heart (Ps 28:3). "His speech was smoother than butter, yet war was in his heart" (Ps 55:21). In Isaiah, God himself complains that the people honor him only with their lips, while their heart is far from him (Is 29:13; cf. Mt 15:8; Mk 7:6). Things are different with the shattered and repentant Israel of the exile: "Let us lift up our hearts and hands to God in heaven" (Lam 3:41). If the heart is involved, prayer will be genuine. So in the prophet Joel we hear the call: "Rend your hearts and not your garments" (Jl 2:13). At all events the double game cannot be kept going, as Jesus teaches in this proverb: "The good man out of the good treasure of his heart produces good, and the evil man out of his evil treasure produces evil; for out of the abundance of the heart his mouth speaks" (Lk 6:45; cf. Mt 12:34f.). Modern psychology would speak of a "Freudian slip". It is completely impossible to deceive God; for he looks not on the outward appearance, but on the heart (1 Sm 16:7).

A man can only be approached by way of his heart, but everything depends on its openness and receptivity. Lovers' hearts are especially wide-awake and sensitive. The bride in the Song of Songs says, "I sleep, but my heart is awake" (Sg 5:2).[5] In calling for total willingness to learn on the part of his disciple, the wisdom teacher says, "My son, give me your heart!" (Prv 23:26). As long as hearts are separated, they will hardly share the same direction of will. To have a common goal, a community needs to be *one* heart and *one* soul like the initial Jerusalem congregation (Acts 4:32). Paul's heart is wide open to his Corinthians (2 Cor 6:11). They have a place in his heart whether they live or die (2 Cor 7:3). On another occasion he compares them to a letter written on his heart, not with ink but with the Spirit of the living God, not on tablets of stone but on the living flesh of the heart (2 Cor 3:2). Paul also holds his favorite community of the Philippians in his heart (Phil 1:7). God disposes of the human heart. "The king's heart is a stream of water in the hand of the Lord; he turns it wherever he will" (Prv 21:1). It is God who puts intentions into the heart of man (Ezr 7:27; Neh 2:12; 7:5). God gave Solomon the Wise largeness of mind like the sand on the seashore (1 Kgs 4:29). If God enlarges a man's heart —understanding—he runs joyfully in the way of his commandments (Ps 119:32). God touched the hearts of men of valor who joined the newly-elected King Saul (1 Sm 10:26). He opened the heart of Lydia, the seller of purple goods, to the preaching of Paul (Acts 16:14). She is one of those who hold the seed fast in an honest and good heart (Lk 8:15). When the Apostles preach the message of the Crucified, those who hear them are cut to the heart (Acts 2:37). The disciples on the road to Emmaus said, "Did not our hearts burn within us while he talked to us on the road, while he opened to us the Scriptures?" (Lk 24:32).

The heart can close itself to God. Then Scripture speaks of "fat" hearts (Is 6:10; Ps 119:70) or, more often, of the hardening of hearts. The hardened heart can become a stone (Ez 11:19; 36:26) or even diamond [adamant] (Zec 7:12). Hence the Psalmist's cry: "O that today you would hearken to his voice! Harden not your hearts, as at Meribah . . ." (Ps 95:7f.; cf. Heb 3:8, 15; 4:7). God himself hardened the heart of Pharaoh so that he did not let the Israelites go.[6] Jesus gives an urgent warning against letting our hearts be weighed down with dissipation and drunkenness and cares of this life, lest we be unable to wait for the coming of the Son of Man with hearts awake (Lk 21:34).

For God, however, the hardened heart is not invincible. In the time of salvation he will take from the Israelites their hearts of stone and give them a heart of flesh (Ez 11:19; 36:26), but this does not dispense them from getting themselves a new heart and a new spirit (Ez 18:31). God wants to be sure that

---

[5] Though the text is often assumed to refer to a dream experience, this is not certain.

[6] Cf. the Yahwist passages Ex 7:14; 8:11, 28; 9:7, 35 (and the editorial 10:1) and the Elohist passages Ex 4:21; 9:35; 10:20, 27. The Priestly Document (Ex 7:3, 13, 22; 8:15; 8:12; 11:10; 14:4, 8, 17) seems to express not the hardening, but the strengthening of the heart, lest Pharaoh should give up too early in the struggle with Yahweh. This aspect of the strong and courageous heart is also characteristically biblical.

men keep his law, so he writes it in their hearts (Jer 31:33; cf. Heb 8:10; 10:16). For what is written on the tablets of the heart (Prv 3:3; 7:3; cf. Rom 2:15; 2 Cor 3:2f.) or bound upon the heart (Prv 6:21) is constantly present to a man. Love too, as strong as death, impresses itself like a seal on the heart (Sg 8:6). And the Holy Spirit, who changes us inwardly, naturally can only be poured into our hearts (cf. Rom 5:5; 2 Cor 1:22; Gal 4:6).

No wonder, then, that the devil's activity is also directed to the heart. He steals the seed of the Word of God out of the heart (Mt 13:19; Lk 8:12). He puts it into the heart of Judas to betray Jesus (Jn 13:2), and into the heart of Ananias to deceive the Holy Spirit (Acts 5:3). His henchmen, false teachers, deceive the hearts of the simple-minded with fair words (Rom 16:18).

So far we have been speaking of the reason and the will. But in the "heart" expressions we also find the whole gamut of emotions. Here the heart is as courageous as a lion's (2 Sm 17:10); there it melts like water (Jos 7:5) or like wax (Ps 22:15). It leaves a man (Ps 40:12), it sinks (Gn 42:28), it fails (Jer 4:9), trembles with fear like trees of a wood in the wind (Is 7:2), smoulders (Ps 29:4), throbs with pain and distress (Ps 38:11). Under the stress of a war, which he has foreseen in prophecy, Jeremiah cries out: "My anguish, my anguish! I writhe in pain! Oh, the walls of my heart! My heart is beating wildly . . ." (Jer 4:19). When the walls no longer hold, we have the broken heart (Jer 23:9; Ez 6:9; Ps 69:21). God is especially near to those of a broken heart (Ps 34:19; 51:19; Is 61:1; cf. Is 57:15).

Joy and sorrow, above all, are always being ascribed to the heart. "No joy is greater than the heart's joy" (Sir 30:16); it is life to a man (Sir 30:22). "Any wound rather than a wound of the heart!" (Sir 25:13). Even in laughter the heart can be sad (Prv 14:13). "He who sings songs to a heavy heart . . . is like vinegar on a wound" (Prv 25:20). Even people less acquainted with the Bible know that wine makes glad the heart of man (Ps 104:15). "Drunk at the right time and in the right amount, wine makes for a glad heart and a cheerful mind" (Sir 31:28). "Wine and music cheer the heart . . ." (Sir 40:20). The Bible distinguishes clearly between repulsive drunkenness, which causes the heart to speak perverse things (Prv 23:33), and the festive joy in hospitality. "To be of good heart" sometimes has the (positive) meaning of being merry through drinking wine. There is nothing wrong, for instance, in the honest Bethlehemite, Boaz, eating and drinking after a hard day's work and lying down to sleep on the threshing-floor with a merry heart (Ru 3:7). Wine makes the heart glad, and bread strengthens it (Gn 18:5; Jgs 19:5; Ps 104:15). If a man forgets to eat his bread through sorrow, his heart withers (Ps 102:5). What could give the heart more joy and confidence than the experience of salvation? The Psalmist, whose prayer has been heard, encourages others to have trust and calls to them: "May your heart live!" (Ps 22:27; 69:33). When Jesus speaks of going away, sorrow fills the disciples' hearts (Jn 16:6), but he will see them again and their hearts will rejoice (Jn 16:22). Paul's apostolic heart is continually in pain and sadness on account of the unbelief of his fellow Jews (Rom 9:2), and he writes to the Corinthians in distress of heart and with many tears; all the same he urges the believers to sing and make melody to the Lord in their hearts (Col 3:16; Eph 5:19), advice he no doubt applied to himself as well.

One might expect pity and mercy, above all, to be matters of the heart. Surprisingly enough this is not the case. Biblical language prefers to assign to these feelings other terms, meaning approximately "bowels".[7] A typical example is the reaction of the harlot whose child, according to Solomon's wise judgment, was to be cut in two. Her heart was moved to pity for her child. Literally it says "her bowels [rah^{a}mîm] seethed on account of her son" (1 Kgs 3:26).[8] The "tender mercy of our God" (Lk 1:78) is a free rendering of "the bowels [splangchna] of pity of our God". When Paul longs for the Philippians "in the bowels [splangchna] of Christ" (Phil 1:8), we can assume that he is referring in particular to the tender mercy of Christ. Is the biblical "heart" too special to be used for pity and mercy? In a certain sense, yes! The "heart" is the very center of the person, and therefore it is not concerned with emotions directed outwards *as such*. The emphasis on the understanding and the will is also connected with this.

Since Scripture speaks in a human way, God also has a heart, although the relevant occurrences hardly exceed thirty. Perhaps the Bible is reluctant to speak much about God's innermost and most personal area. Far more frequently it speaks of God's face or his mighty hand (arm). In terms of content, the references to God's heart do not yield anything substantially new. But all the same we must mention some good examples. God is grieved to the heart that he has created sinful men (Gn 6:6), and even after the Flood he ponders this question in his heart (Gn 8:21). David is a king after God's own heart (1 Sm 13:14); and in the time of salvation God will give the people shepherds after his own heart (Jer 3:15). God's eyes and heart will be in the Temple in Jerusalem forever (1 Kgs 9:3; 2 Chr 7:16). The thoughts of the divine heart stand for all generations (Ps 33:11). In the latter days people will understand that his anger will not turn back until he has accomplished the intentions of his heart (Jer 23:20; 30:24). Yet he does not afflict and grieve the sons of men "from his heart", that is, deliberately (Lam 3:33). Unwilling to hand Israel over to destruction, he says, "my heart recoils against me" (Hos 11:8).[9]

---

[7] Mainly me'ím (e.g., Is 16:11; 63:15; Jer 31:20; Sg 5:4; Lam 1:20; 2:11) and more frequently rah^{a}mîm Normally rah^{a}mîm is used in metonymy: "tender mercy".

[8] The same expression occurs in Gn 43:30 referring to Joseph's deep emotion at the sight of his brother Benjamin.

[9] Translations such as "my heart turns over" suggest a flood of emotion. But on the basis of usage (cf., Ex 14:5; Ps 105:25; Lam 1:20) the meaning is more likely to be a change of thought and will, a change of mind. I translate the parallel verse "all my *words of consolation* surge up

We have just taken a lesson in the language of the Bible. It is not a fashionable thing to do. For, in spite of all the protests of perceptive people, never before has the biblical language been so widely sacrificed for the sake of the so-called language of our time. We are always hearing the theological catch-phrase that the Bible is of its time and therefore not normative for to-day. If this is meant to apply to matters of faith, then it must apply first and foremost to the way we think, feel and speak—our way of being human. Now of course the Bible is of its time; that is so obvious that it does not need constant stressing. The question is whether, all the same, the Bible contains something of timeless value. What is at stake here is primarily the content of faith, but human values, embodied in the language, are also involved. The in-tensity with which the Bible speaks of the heart should make us think. As if a particular age could decide what kind of thought, feeling and mode of speech to have! What is certain is that our inhibitions about the heart are of *our* time! They arise from a chronically mistaken approach to being human. We do not live in touch with our personal center; we are externalized and alienated. That is why we are not at home with ourselves and try to avoid the heart. Our speech betrays us. Few people realize, at this moment, that in the future the Bible will also have to teach us what it means to be really human.

---

within me". According to Is 57:18 and Zec 1:13, *nihûmîm* means "consolation(s)". *Rah^amîm* is often conjectured on the analogy of Gn 43:30 and 1 Kgs 3:26.

JOSEF HEER

THE SOTERIOLOGICAL SIGNIFICANCE OF THE JOHANNINE IMAGE OF THE PIERCED SAVIOR

The icons of the Eastern Church express high theology in a graphic and visual manner. I suggest we understand the image of the Pierced Savior in St. John's Gospel from such a comparison.

The following is an outline commentary on this Johannine image. In an hour's paper, of course, we cannot concentrate on details. Unfortunately, too, we cannot go through all the alternative interpretations of the text. Consequently I do not claim to be giving *the* correct perspective, but the one I consider to be correct; the listener, the reader, will have to form his own judgment.

First of all let us remind ourselves of the Johannine text and divide it by headings.

The cry of victory of the dying Savior (19:28–30b):

(28) After this Jesus, knowing that all was now finished, said (to fulfill the Scripture), "I thirst." (29) A bowl full of vinegar stood there; so they put a sponge full of the vinegar on hyssop and held it to his mouth. (30) When Jesus had received the vinegar, he said, "It is accomplished!"

He hands over the Spirit (19:30c):

. . . and he bowed his head and gave up his spirit.

Jesus is pierced (19:31–34):

(31) Since it was the Day of Preparation, in order to prevent the bodies from remaining on the cross on the Sabbath (for that Sabbath was a high day), the Jews asked Pilate that their legs might be broken, and that they might be taken away. (32) So the soldiers came and broke the legs of the first, and of the other who had been crucified with him; (33) but when they came to Jesus and saw that he was already dead, they did not break his legs. (34) But one of the soldiers pierced his side with a spear, and at once there came out blood and water.

The solemn testimony (19:35):

He who saw it has borne witness—his testimony is true, and he knows that he tells the truth—that you also may believe.

The first interpretation (19:36):

> For these things took place that the Scripture might be fulfilled, "Not a bone of him shall be broken."

The second interpretation (19:37):

> And again another Scripture says, "They shall look on him whom they have pierced."

This then is our text. Even before we get any closer we are struck by the weight John lays on this scene. The space given to the reasons behind the piercing, the emphasis on the eyewitness (v. 35a,b), the solemn reference to the exalted Lord (v. 35c), the deliberate statement that this very scene is intended to strengthen the readers in their faith (v. 35d), and the use of two Old Testament quotations to interpret the event—all this shows the importance of this passage and suggests that what we have before us is the *climax* of the Fourth Gospel. If this suggestion is valid, however, it will have to be shown how it accords with its content. This I shall do by setting up a number of theses, doing things back to front by beginning with the concluding verse.

1. The Pierced Savior is an image to be contemplated in faith

The Evangelist concludes his account of the piercing of Jesus with the words:

> For these things took place that the Scripture might be fulfilled. . . . They shall look on him whom they have pierced (19:37).

The quotation fulfilled by the piercing of Jesus comes from the Prophet Zechariah, a passage of warning and promise with eschatological implications (12:9–13:1):

> (12:9) And on that day I will seek to destroy all the nations that come against Jerusalem. . . .
>
> (12:10) And I will pour out on the house of David and the inhabitants of Jerusalem a spirit of compassion and supplication, so that, when they look on him whom they have pierced, they shall mourn for him, as one mourns for an only child. . . .
>
> (12:12) The land shall mourn, each family by itself. . . .
>
> (13:1) On that day there shall be a fountain opened for the house of David and the inhabitants of Jerusalem to cleanse them from sin and uncleanness.

Zechariah is feeling his way, in these images, toward speaking of God's *eschatological* action. He speaks of the annihilation of enemies, the outpouring of the *spirit* of compassion and prayer, the sorrowful *beholding* of the One they have pierced, and the opening of a *fountain* which purifies from sin and uncleanness (12:9–13:1). No interpretation in terms of the contemporary historical scene, for example, in relation to King Josiah, does complete justice to the text.

John quotes this passage, saying: now, in the piercing of Jesus, the prophet's presentiment has acquired precision and has been fulfilled; now God *is* acting finally, definitively; now he *is* giving the Spirit; now a fountain *has* been opened; now we *can* look at the Pierced One. . . .

Three remarks on this "beholding of the Pierced One":

1. In John this "looking" goes beyond physical seeing; it means *understanding in faith* what one sees (in contrast to Rv 1:7).

2. In John what is presented to sight, that is, the Pierced One, is a *theological image*. The Fourth Evangelist's meditative approach means that he often heightens his account into an eloquent image. To take just one example, we can see this easily in the three "lifting up" passages. In the first, "And as Moses lifted up the serpent in the wilderness, so must . . ." (3:14), the image of Jesus lifted up is an analogy of the love of God, as the serpent in the wilderness was an image of Yahweh's saving mercy; in the second, "When you have lifted up the Son of Man, then you will know that I am he" (8:28), the image of the lifted-up Savior is meant to reveal his whole significance; and in the third, "and I, when I am lifted up from the earth, will draw all men to myself" (12:32), we are given a visual image of the founding of the community of salvation by the Exalted One.

3. The image of the Pierced Savior presents *more* than the mere historical event. It places before the eyes of believers not only the crucified Lord but also the Risen Lord with all his post-Easter activity. This aspect can be shown to be Johannine both in a general way and through the interpretation of details. We will first discuss the general approach.

In John, Cross and Resurrection generally constitute a unity. They are the *one* "charge" Jesus has received from the Father (10:17f.) and they co-inhere in the *one* "hour" (as Passion, e.g., 7:30; as glorification, e.g., 17:17). John's approach, showing the figure of the earthly Jesus to be constantly irradiated by the glory of the Risen Lord, letting the glorified Christ speak through the words of the earthly Jesus, reaches a climax in his presentation of the *Passion* of Jesus. Here the suffering One is in fact acting in his own power (e.g., 14:31; 18:4), and the entire Passion narrative is shaped according to this principle: "No one takes [my life] from me, but I lay it down of my own accord. I have power to lay it down and I have power to take it up again" (10:18). Thus John passes over Jesus' mortal dread (cf. Mk 14:32ff.); thus the soldiers fall down at the feet of the One they are supposed to be arresting (18:6); thus at his trial before Pilate Jesus' Kingship is emphasized (18:33ff.), and thus the last word of the dying Jesus is not, "My God, my God, why hast thou forsaken me?" (Mk 15:34) but the triumphant, "It is accomplished" (19:30).

Ultimately Passion and glorification are fused in the single concept of "exaltation", which, as we have already indicated, initially means the lifting up on the Cross (8:28a; 3:14b), but which also refers to his being exalted at the

Father's side. The latter is the very basis for his being able to give "life" to believers (3:14b–d), to "draw them to him" (12:32).

The same is true of the image of the Pierced One. As I intend to show in the following theses, it represents both the Crucified, who has completed his work (19:30b) and dies (19:30d), and the Glorified One, who gives the Spirit (19:30d), is at work in the community in baptism and Eucharist (19:34b) and so gives "life". The believer who looks at the Pierced One sees all this.

2. Beholding the image of the Pierced Savior in faith, one sees the attitude of love in which the earthly Jesus completed his work

Jesus dies with the cry of victory "It is accomplished" (τετέλεσται 19:30b) on his lips. The "work" of the earthly Jesus is accomplished (17:4). But at the same time the word indicates two deeper dimensions characteristic of this work:

a. Accomplished is Jesus' loving obedience to the Father

Initially this cry of "It is accomplished" as he dies refers to the fulfilling of Scripture—this is the immediate context (v. 28). But in this Scripture (Ps 69:22; 22:16) Jesus meets with *the Father's will.* So now what is accomplished is also that obedience on the part of Jesus that governs everything he does. Jesus does not come into the world of his own accord but is "sent" (e.g., 17:3); he "must" do whatever the Father chooses (e.g., 3:14); he can only do what he sees the Father doing (5:19), only preach what he has heard from the Father (12:49). The Father's will is so much his element that Jesus can actually say, "My food is to do the will of him who sent me, and to accomplish his work" (4:34).

As a unity of *action* this obedience is rooted in a unity of *love:* "I do as the Father has commanded me, so that the world may know that I love the Father. Rise, let us go hence" (14:31)—and the "going hence" means to the Passion and the Cross. Thus the victorious cry "It is accomplished" includes this love of the Father from which Jesus' obedience arises.

b. Accomplished is Jesus' love for his own

There is, however, a second dimension to this cry. For the "τετέλεσται" refers back to the "εἰς τέλος" of the washing of the feet, which is in turn a sign of Jesus' death on the Cross: the Evangelist comments: "Having loved his own who were in the world, he loved them to the end" (or "to perfection" 13:1).

What is said in the metaphor of the vine and the branches is accomplished on the Cross: "Greater love has no man than this, that a man lay down his life for his friends" (15:13).

So Jesus' dying words reveal the attitude in which he embraces death, an attitude symbolized in the construction of the Cross itself: the vertical post signifies his loving obedience to the Father, the horizontal beam points to his loving self-offering "for" those who are his.

3. Beholding the image of the Pierced Savior in faith,
the believer sees him as the Glorified One who gives the Spirit.

The earthly Jesus promised to send the Spirit (πνεῦμα, παράκλτος) following his "glorification" (7:37ff.), his "going to the Father" (16:7). Now, in his death on the Cross, this glorification is taking place, that is, the unity of obedience and love, which Jesus enjoys with the Father (17:1ff.), is radiantly manifested to believers, and he "goes to the Father" (17:13). It is of a piece with Johannine thought that Jesus should now give the Spirit. John provides a vivid image of this giving of the Spirit when he says that at his death Jesus "bowed his head and gave up his spirit" (literally, "*handed over* his spirit", παρέδωκεν τό πνεῦμα: 19:30c).

Certainly the text speaks initially of Jesus' death, of "giving up" his spirit. But it is highly probable that it also refers to his "handing on" of the Holy Spirit to the community of believers, represented here by the Mother of Jesus and "the disciple whom Jesus loved" (19:25ff.).

1. John's *language* is elaborate and solemn; he says that Jesus "παρέδωκεν τό πνεῦμα", "handed over the spirit", whereas, for example, Mark simply says "εχεπνεῦσεν" (15:37), "he breathed out", he died. It is unlikely that John would have used this unwonted expression without special reason.
2. Elsewhere in John the word "παρέδωκεν" from "παραδίδοναι" always has the sense of handing over, surrendering something or someone to others (e.g., 6:64; 12:4), and this handing over of the Spirit to others — the disciples — was a central promise of the earthly Jesus.
3. In general John likes to hint at hidden connections by using *double meanings*. Thus he uses "temple" in 2:19ff., "water" in 4:7ff., "food" in 4:32ff., "lifted up" in 12:32, and so forth. Thus there is a strong suggestion in favor of seeing a double meaning in "παρέδωκεν τό πνεῦμα".

If these arguments from probability are accepted, we can conclude the following: with his use of double meanings John is vividly portraying Jesus, as he goes to his Father through death and Resurrection, as giving the Holy Spirit to the community of salvation that is present at the Cross in the persons of "the disciple whom Jesus loved" and the "Mother" of Jesus (19:25–27). This also implies that Jesus himself remains with them in the activity of this Spirit. For the Spirit's intention is to facilitate a personal relationship between Jesus, exalted at the Father's side, and the believer. The Spirit's activity will carry out the promise of Jesus: "I will not leave you desolate; I will come to you" (14:18).

4. Beholding the image of the Pierced Savior in faith, the believer discerns in blood and water a reference to the expiatory and life-giving effect of the death of Jesus

John immediately follows the death of Jesus with the piercing and the flow of *blood* and *water* from the pierced *side*. These are both directed against "docetic" (*dokein* = seem) theories that said that Jesus only seemed to have a body and only seemed to undergo suffering and death, whereas in fact he was the impassible and immortal Logos all the time. In opposition to this, John stresses that the Logos has become flesh (1:14) in such a *real* sense—that is, God has come so humanly and genuinely near to us in Jesus—that we see blood and water, the essential constituents of the human body (according to rabbinical teaching), issuing from it. Furthermore, this Jesus died in such a real sense that to doubt it would be as senseless as to say that a person pierced by a spear is only apparently dead. What is at stake in the piercing and the blood and water is the genuine and full humanity of Jesus and the reality of his death.

a. Symbolic meaning of blood and water

But that is not all John wishes to say here. He loves *symbolism*. He likes to let a *background* meaning shine through into the *foreground*. He does this in the prominent "signs" but also in many individual details, such as the "night" into which Judas goes out (13:30), the "competition" between Peter and the Beloved Disciple (e.g., 20:3–10), the "hundred and fifty-three fishes" (21:1ff.) and many more. Symbolism is most concentrated at the Crucifixion of Jesus. The inscription in three languages (19:9f.; for everyone!), the seamless garment (19:23f.: Jesus the High Priest), the Mother of Jesus and the Beloved Disciple at the Cross (19:25ff.: the united community) and the "handing over" of the Spirit, which we have already discussed (19:30c)—all this has always (and no doubt rightly) been understood in the symbolic sense indicated.

Hence we are right to assume a symbolic meaning for the blood and water from the side of the Pierced Jesus.

b. Blood and water in the parallel passage 1 John 5:6

To understand the symbolic meaning of blood and water in 19:34 we need to compare it with the passage in the First Letter of John in which these two concepts occur in a similar context: 1 John 5:5, 6:

(v. 5) Who is it that overcomes the world but he who believes that Jesus is the Son of God?

(v. 6a) This is he who came by water and blood, Jesus Christ,

(v. 6b) not with the water only but with the water and the blood.

(v. 6c) And the Spirit is the witness, because the Spirit is the truth.

Let us try to understand this difficult text by reference to the "coming" of Jesus. The First Letter of John, in opposition to the Gnostics, sees great importance in Jesus' coming "in the flesh" (1 Jn 4:2), that is, as a real man. More specifically, this coming is described as a coming "not only with the water only, but with the water and the blood." What is behind this polemical assertion?

The "coming *in blood*" is often referred to the death on the Cross, the "coming *by water*" to the baptism of Jesus. But in this interpretation the baptism of Jesus would receive more significance than it otherwise gets in the Johannine writings; evidently it cannot be interpreted along the same lines as his death on the Cross. When the *coming* of Jesus is mentioned elsewhere, the subject is not baptism but the *meaning* of his coming. Jesus has come to bring light (12:46) and life (10:10) to the world, to save the world (12:47). But this must take place on the Cross; and it is precisely this soteriological meaning of the death on the Cross that the Gnostics seem to have rejected.

Hence in 1 John 5:6, too, water and blood will be connected with the *significance* of the coming of Jesus (culminating in the Cross). In that case "*water*" will mean what it does elsewhere in the Johannine writings, namely, the *gift* imparted by Jesus, the gift of salvation (cf. Jn 4:10), the gift of the "life-giving" Spirit (Jn 7:37ff.).

However, in the First Letter of John the "*blood*" is usually seen in the context of *expiation* (1:7; 2:2; 4:10), and so here too it will signify the taking away of sin as a result of Jesus' coming (which leads to his death).

Thus 1 John 5:6 does not speak of two saving *events* (Jesus' baptism and death on the Cross) but of the two *meanings* of the one saving event, namely, the expiatory and the "life-giving" meanings of the coming of Jesus with its climax in the Cross. It stresses very strongly that there cannot be the water without the blood; in other words, not without the bloody reality of the expiation wrought in his death on the Cross did Jesus make the gift of "life" available to the believer. Furthermore, man cannot acquire this gift of salvation through "pneumatic" gnosis but only through that faith which "overcomes the world" (v. 5).

c. Blood and water from the side of the Pierced Savior:
  a symbol of expiation and the gift of "life"

Our interpretation of the parallel passage from the First Letter of John can now furnish us with a commentary on the image of the Pierced One. The blood flowing from the side of Jesus means that his death is in expiation; the water means that it gives "life". For, "When the Evangelist speaks in such a solemn and unique way, it is unthinkable that he is referring to anything other than his most central concern at all times: the saving significance of Jesus" (Thüsing).

5. Beholding the Pierced Savior in faith, the believer also sees in blood and water the sacraments of the Eucharist and baptism by means of which the Glorified One is now at work in the community

Initially we may seem to be going too far in assuming a second symbolism for blood and water. But we cannot be accused of "straining the symbolism", since the basis for it is found in the continuation of the passage in the First Letter of John which we have just been considering.

a. The sacramental meaning of 1 John 5:7–8

Let us recall the text with its continuation (1 Jn 5:6–8):

(v. 6b) [He came] not with the water only but with the water and the blood.
(v. 7) And the Spirit is the witness, because the Spirit is the Truth.
(v. 8) There are three witnesses:
(v. 8b) the Spirit, the water and the blood; and these three agree.

Verse 7, which we have already discussed in part, speaks only of the Spirit's bearing witness—and "bearing witness" here means that this Spirit enables believers to understand blood and water as signs of the saving significance of the coming of Jesus (e.g., Jn 16:13). But verse 8 speaks of "three" that also exercise the function of bearing witness. Thus water and blood are seen as present and active in the community, effectively bearing witness along with the Spirit. So a change in the significance of water and blood must have occurred since verse 7, for the expiation and the giving of "life" associated with the earlier death on the Cross cannot now bear independent witness, along with the Spirit, to the saving significance of Jesus' death; rather, they themselves need to have their meaning unlocked by the Spirit (v. 7).

As "witnesses" present in the life of the community, water and blood can hardly be understood here in any other way but as a reference to baptism and Eucharist. Then the meaning is this: the Spirit bears witness by awakening the faith of the community, which is oriented to the saving significance of the death on the Cross (cf. v. 7 in the light of 1 Jn 2:20f., 27). But water and blood, that is, baptism and Eucharist, bear witness in the same community to the same death of Jesus, since both sacraments not only owe their whole existence to this death on the Cross (19:34) but also communicate to the community that "life" that has been made available in principle by it. For baptism is "rebirth" to "life" (cf. Jn 3:5) and Eucharist is the food for this "life" (cf. Jn 6:53–58); "life" itself, in John, is to be understood as summing up the whole salvation that comes from Cross and Resurrection.

At this point, therefore, the First Letter of John draws the connection between the historical event of the death on the Cross and the individual "now" of the believing community, where the Spirit, baptism and Eucharist proclaim and communicate the saving significance of the death of Jesus.

b. The sacramental meaning of John 19:34

If in 1 John 5:6–8b there is a twofold symbolism for blood and water, the same can appply to the scene of the piercing, as the First Letter of John often provides an interpretation of the Johannine Gospel. This is also suggested by the fact that, in this Gospel, "blood" occurs exclusively in a eucharistic sense (6:54–56) and "water" means baptism (including 3:5). Hence very many Fathers and the majority of contemporary exegetes support the sacramental meaning of this passage. Here too, therefore, we see the effect of the Fourth Gospel's community orientation. The Evangelist does not limit himself to describing what is past: that expiation has been achieved and "life" has been given in principle through the Cross of Jesus; he goes on to show how the power and effect of Jesus' death are communicated to the community here and now by the sacraments. But it is the Spirit who makes possible its fundamental condition: faith.

6. Beholding the Pierced Savior in faith, the believer recognizes him as the new Passover Lamb who brings real succor and liberation

Using two Old Testament quotations the Evangelist himself opens up the further meaning of the piercing of Jesus. We have already discussed the second of them, "They shall look on him whom they have pierced" (19:37). Here is the first:

> For these things took place that the Scripture might be fulfilled, "Not a bone of him shall be broken" (19:36).

This comes from the prescriptions concerning the killing of the *Passover Lamb*

(Ex 12:46). Applying it to Jesus, whose bones were not broken (19:32), the Evangelist is indicating a connection between the pierced Jesus and the Passover Lamb. If we take into consideration the fact that, accrording to John—and in contrast to the synoptics—Jesus dies on the afternoon of the Day of Preparation for the Passover Festival (18:28; 19:14), that is, the very hour when the Passover lambs are slaughtered in the Temple, and that right at the beginning of the Fourth Gospel Jesus is called the "Lamb of God" by the Baptist (1:29), we can say that, according to the Fourth Evangelist, the pierced Jesus fulfills everything that was signified by the Old Testament Passover Lamb. He is the true Passover Lamb.

Thus if the blood of the first Passover Lamb preserved the firstborn of the Israelites in Egypt from physical death (Ex 12:12f.), the blood of the second and real Passover Lamb preserves believers from eternal death (cf., e.g., 5:24). The annual celebration of the Passover commemorated Israel's liberation from slavery in Egypt; for John this was a sign of the coming liberation of believers, who were slaves to sin and whom the Son has set free (cf. 8:34ff.). Thus through his death on the Cross Jesus, the Passover Lamb, effects the real liberation from sin (8:24, 32ff.), darkness (8:12), death (8:51) and perishing (3:16); he sets them free *for* "life".

7. Beholding the Pierced Savior, the believer is to grow deeper in faith

In the context of the piercing, the Evangelist immediately mentions his own *pastoral* aim:

> He who saw it has borne witness . . . that you also may believe (19:35).

Here, at the climax of the Gospel, we find something that otherwise is only expressed at the initial conclusion (20:31) but that most profoundly characterizes the whole Gospel, namely, that it is directly addressed to believers. In thus *announcing his aim,* the Evangelist is going beyond the portrayal and interpretation of the piercing and situating himself explicitly within the community for which he is writing. He wants to promote and deepen their *faith.* We shall now go on to indicate three essential aspects of this faith.

a. It is a faith which recognizes love . . .

The "object" of this faith is, of course, the Pierced One, with all the wealth of meaning of this image, as we have seen. But we must again emphasize something we have already heard in the dying Victor's cry: that in the Johannine understanding faith is oriented to the love manifested in Jesus. For example, this can be illustrated by the central "Nicodemus dialogue":

(3:14) And as Moses lifted up the serpent in the wilderness, so must the Son of man be lifted up,

(3:15) that whoever believes in him may have eternal life.

(3:16) For God loved the world so much that he gave his only Son, that whoever believes in him should not perish but have eternal life.

This whole passage—incidentally a distant parallel to the piercing scene—focuses on the boundlessness, the "so much" of the divine love. It is this "world" that the Father loves, that realm of darkness whose sin the Lamb of God is to take away. And since love expresses itself by giving, and the Father loves this world beyond all measure, what he gives is not this or that but what is dearest to him: "His only begotten Son". Moreover, he not only gives him but gives him to be lifted up, that is, initially he surrenders him to death. And love's goal is as great as love itself, for whoever believes in the ambassador of this love may receive "eternal life". People have rightly described this text as the summation of the whole Johannine theology.

b. It is a faith which puts brotherly love into practice . . .

The invitation "that you may believe" has in mind not only a certain intellectual knowledge, not only a meditative beholding; in John, faith means everything that is expected of man in response to God's action in Jesus (cf., e.g., 6:29). Consequently brotherly love is an essential part of this faith; indeed, in John, brotherly love is simply the application of faith to the relationships between believers (1 Jn 4:19–21). The First Letter of John sums it up:

And this is [God's] commandment, that we should believe in the name of his Son Jesus Christ and love one another, just as he has commanded us (1 Jn 3:23).

Faith expressing itself in brotherly love, or the brotherly love that results from faith—this is the governing idea of Johannine ethics. Thus a faith which was limited to the mere meditative beholding of the Pierced One, not resulting in practical acts of brotherly love, would not be faith at all (cf. 1 Jn 4:8ff.).

Brotherly love sees its true self in the image of the Pierced One. At its deepest it is in fact the sacrifice of one's life for another:

By this we know love, that he laid down his life for us; and we ought to lay down our lives for the brethren (1 Jn 3:16).

Its standard is vividly given by the Pierced One:

Even as I have loved you . . . you also love one another (Jn 13:34).

c. It is a faith which is secure in love . . .

"So that you may believe". According to Johannine theology this faith which focuses on the knowledge of love and is realized in acts of brotherly love is meant to become an *abiding* in love. John 15:9 says, "Abide in my love." One starts on this path of "abiding in love" at rebirth (Jn 3:5) and pursues it by striving for a lively faith (Jn 19:35) and overcoming sin (1 Jn 2:1); finally it leads to perfection (1 Jn 3:2). But the believer can travel this path without *fear*; even if his conscience accuses him on account of earlier sins, he can struggle on in spite of it so long as he cultivates brotherly love:

> By this [i.e., true brotherly love] we shall know that we are of the truth, and reassure our hearts before him whenever our hearts condemn us; for God is greater than our hearts, and he knows everything (1 Jn 3:19f.).

There is something of release, of peace, in this attitude of faith. It renders redemption perceivable to some extent (1 Jn 5:10). Man has a great hope of salvation on the basis of his confidence in the unchangeable divine love, which already loved him in advance, which brings him into a relationship (1 Jn 3:1) and holds him even if he falls into sin (1 Jn 1:9). The deeper the believer grows into this love, the more he grows beyond *fear*:

> There is no fear in love, but perfect love casts out fear. For fear has to do with punishment, and he who fears is not perfected in love (1 Jn 4:18).

Freed from the chains of fear, the believer has one aim: to believe and trust in love, to practice brotherly love and to abide in both. And the reflection of such a life is *joy,* here and now:

> As the Father has loved me, so have I loved you; abide in my love. If you keep my commandment, you will abide in my love. . . . These things I have spoken to you, that my *joy* may be in you, and that your joy may be full (Jn 15:9–11).

8. The soteriological significance of the image of the Pierced One

In John's Gospel, therefore, the Pierced One is an image similar to an icon in the Eastern Church. This image illustrates the most important ideas of the Johannine doctrine of redemption. Let us briefly sum up these ideas:

1. In his love, *God* desires the salvation of the world. Therefore he sends Jesus.
2. *In loving obedience* to the Father and in carrying out his mission, Jesus accepts even *death.*
3. For him this death is also the act of his *love for men* (his own).
4. Through his death he achieves *expiation* for the "sin of the world" and in principle makes available to believers the gift of "*life*". This "life" is a different kind of human life, a "*new* life", which can be brought about already

(5:24)—though imperfectly—through the medium of the faith relationship with Jesus Christ and God (17:3) and through brotherly love (15:9–12). It will be brought to perfection (1 Jn 3:2) with the fulfillment of both these relationships beyond the grave (6:54).

5. In order to communicate this "*new* life" to the community of believers, Jesus, the One Pierced on the Cross, the Glorified One, gives the Spirit, the water and the blood. Through the Spirit he reveals the relationship of faith that is both the precondition and the continuing structure of "new life". Through the water of baptism he gives sacramental new birth, and in the blood of the Eucharist he provides nourishment and strengthening for this "new life".

6. In this way Jesus brings the "thirsty" man (7:37) to a new form of existence based on faith in love, realized in brotherly love and marked by confidence and joy.

9. The link with the cult of the Heart of Jesus

The most important biblical passage in support of the cult of the Heart of Jesus is that of the piercing of Jesus. Three reasons from the Fourth Gospel itself speak in favor of it:

1. John speaks of the piercing of the *side* of Jesus, who accepts death in loving obedience to the Father and in "life-giving" love to "his own". Taking the *pierced side* and *love* together, it is legitimate to speak of the Pierced *Heart* of Jesus.

2. In John the "Pierced One" is a vivid *image*, a symbol, and to that extent it corresponds to the significance of the Pierced Heart in the cult of the Heart of Jesus.

3. The Johannine image of the Pierced One sums up the basic concepts of Johannine faith; it is a "*summa fidei Joanneae*". Hence it also corresponds to the picture of the Pierced Heart of Jesus, which in turn is intended to sum up the whole Christian faith under the formal aspect of love, and which is, in short, a "*summa totius religionis*".

All the same it must be admitted that the cult of the Heart of Jesus is in a deep *crisis*. In my view, any renaissance (?) of it would have to involve more than simply putting new life into old forms, especially as we can see in retrospect what a great difference there is between the cult as practiced in medieval religious houses and that of the period after Margaret Mary Alacoque.

In any event, new forms will have to be found, particularly in connection with the idea (essential to the modern cult of the Heart of Jesus) of the *expiation* which a man can perform in the sight of God for the sake of the sins of others. This idea should be traced back to its theological roots, that is, in the utterly fundamental Christian conviction that each person is "for" the other, that he can and ought to share responsibly in the other's destiny. If expiation is traced to this root, it will be found to coincide with "solidarity", especially solidarity with the "underprivileged", and in doing so it will strike a chord in the hearts of many contemporary believers.

Literature:

J. Heer, "Der Durchbohrte: Johanneische Begründung der Herz-Jesu-Verehrung", *Analecta Theologica de Cultu SS. Cordis Jesu,* vol. 1 (Rome: Casa Editrice Herder, 1966).

E. Malatesta, "Blood and Water from the Pierced Side of Christ" (Jn 19:34), *Segni e sacramenti nel Vangelo di Giovanni* (Rome: Editrice Anselmiana, 1976).

F. Porsch, "Pneuma und Wort; ein exegetischer Beitrag zur Pneumatologie des Johannesevangeliums", *Frankfurter Theologische Studien* 16 (Frankfurt, 1974).

W. Thüsing, "Die Erhöhung und Verherrlichung Jesu im Johannesevangelium", *Neutestamentliche Abhandlungen* XXI (Münster, 1959).

FELIX HEINZER

THE SUFFERING HUMANITY OF CHRIST AS THE SOURCE OF SALVATION IN MAXIMUS THE CONFESSOR

Before beginning this essay on Maximus the Confessor I would like to make two observations:

1. In what follows I shall make no explicit mention of the Heart of Jesus, which is the focus of our congress. The connection between what I have to say and our congress topic will become clear, however, if we keep in mind what is signified by it, that is, the human center of him who, in his living and dying as the humanity of God, is empowered to be the Incarnation of God's redeeming love to us men and the source of salvation.

2. According to our program, the very next essay will take us into the Middle Ages. Therefore, lest the bridge from Scripture to medieval theology and piety should have only a single pillar to rest on, I wish, in addition to Maximus, to give space to a number of other representatives of the patristic tradition, at least briefly—particularly as Maximus himself, writing in the seventh century, comes at the end of this tradition and cannot be properly evaluated apart from it.

I. Introduction

Let me introduce my remarks by quoting a document of our own times that has a close relationship to Maximus. This is a passage from article 22 of *Gaudium et spes* entitled "Christ, the new man":

> In reality it is only in the mystery of the Word made flesh that the mystery of man truly becomes clear. . . . He who is the "image of the invisible God" (Col 1:15) is himself the perfect man who has restored in the children of Adam that likeness to God, which had been disfigured ever since the first sin. Human nature, by the very fact that it was assumed, not absorbed, in him, has been raised in us also to a dignity beyond compare. For, by his Incarnation, he, the Son of God, has in a certain way united himself with each man. He worked with human hands, he thought with a human mind. He acted with a human will, and with a human heart he loved. Born of the Virgin Mary, he has truly been made one of us, like to us in all things except sin.[1]

[1] Pastoral Constitution on the Church in the Modern World, *Gaudium et Spes*, art. 22, in *Vatican Council II: The Conciliar and Post Conciliar Documents*, ed. A. Flannery (Dublin, 1975), 922f.

47

In fact this most important text of Vatican II could be described as a summary of the Christology of Maximus the Confessor, a "Christology from above", which at the same time gives the widest scope for what is human in Christ, making his humanity the prototype of our human nature—which is thus seen to be christologically determined.

The relationship of this Christology to that of Maximus is quite explicit in the passage quoted. Twice it refers to the Third Council of Constantinople (680–81), which in a way sanctioned Maximus' fight for the full humanity of Christ. It quotes the sentence applying Chalcedon's "without confusion, without change" to Christ's human will:

> For as his all-holy and immaculate ensouled flesh was not destroyed by being deified, but persisted in its own state and sphere, so also his human will was not destroyed by being deified.[2]

Here the Third Council of Constantinople appropriates Maximus' central achievement, worked out initially at the level of theological dialogue with monoenergism and monothelitism and subsequently sealed with his martyrdom: that, for the sake of our salvation, the full humanity of Christ must be held fast, and in particular his intellectual-spiritual integrity and his human freedom.[3]

When *Gaudium et spes* says that "he acted with a human will" and expressly refers to that sentence from the definition of the Council of 680–81, we can rightly say that we encounter Maximus in the Christology of *Gaudium et spes*, article 22. He is not named, but he is present in substance. We seem to be hearing a vindication of the words he spoke at his trial, "I have no teaching of my own, but what is common to the Catholic Church",[4] in that his "confession" has entered into the anonymous (because universal) confession of the Church, into the κοινὸν δόγμα of the καθολική.

It is the idea of Christ's human nature, Christ's human freedom as the pivot of soteriology: that characterizes Maximus' fundamental insight. Straightaway, however, we have to be more precise. For Maximus, the humanity of Christ loses any soteriological significance if it is looked at in the context of a one-sided and exclusive "Christology from below", that is, torn from its relationship with the Logos. Using the terminology of *Gaudium et spes*

---

[2] DS 556 (quoted in *Gaudium et Spes*, art. 22, nn.22, 23). Cf. the important remarks of F. M. Léthel, *Theologie de l'Agonie du Christ: La Liberté humaine du Fils de Dieu et son importance sotériologique mises en lumière par Saint Maxime le Confesseur*, vol. 52 of *Théologia Historique*, (Paris, 1979), 112n.18. He shows the weakness of the formulation of the Third Council of Constantinople, in terms of *Heilsgeschichte* [salvation history] and soteriology, compared with the creed of the Lateran Synod of 649 (cf., DS 500), substantially inspired by Maximus and even more strongly marked by his Christology.

[3] Cf. in particular J. M. Garrigues, *Maxime le Confesseur: La Charité, avenir divin de l'homme*, vol. 38 of *Théologie Historique* (Paris, 1976), e.g., 33–75: "Les Etapes de la confession".

[4] *Acta* (PG 90, 120C).

we could say that Jesus' human hands, his human spirit, human will, human heart are only significant for the salvation of all men because they are the hands, spirit, will and heart of a Divine Person, the Logos and Son of God himself.

Here we have a principle that has imprinted itself deeply upon the christological reflection of the ancient Church through all her crises, a principle that, however, as we shall see, is by no means always applied in the same manner. In the course of time the question as to the correlation of the human in Christ with the divine Person of the Logos and the resultant theological status of this human nature is answered in quite different ways. What Johannes Betz says in connection with the patristic doctrine of the Eucharist applies to Christology too, especially since, in the view of the Greek Fathers, the Eucharist is the sacramental prolongation and continued working of the Incarnation:

> One could look . . . primarily at the Logos and stress the fact that this Logos becomes tangible in Jesus and in the Eucharist. Or one could look at the way the saving event in Jesus was historically implemented, in which case the bodily person of Jesus and its development and destiny came more to the fore. In principle, of course, the ideal was to comprehend both aspects in one view; if one perspective was stressed, the other was always affirmed implicitly as well.[5]

II. A Survey of Greek Patristics of the First Six Centuries

What follows is a brief survey of the Greek Fathers with regard to these topics. I hope that the inevitable dangers of such an enterprise (oversimplification, overemphasis) will be counterbalanced by the value of illuminating the historical context of doctrine and theology to which Maximus belongs.

Taking up Betz's point, one can say that the Logos idea gains in importance in the second and third centuries. Betz sees in this an influence of the "general intellectual climate of the time", in particular the influence of Hellenism, for which the Logos is the "key to the riddle of the world, the epitome of reality". Christians claim to have, in Jesus, "permanent access" to this very Logos; indeed, they claim "to be able to possess it". I find it remarkable that, in their apologetic dialogue with the Hellenistic worldview, the first Christian theologians used a central concept of this very worldview to interpret the mystery of Christ. What was anticipated in the Logos doctrine of Philo, and what appeared for the first time in Christian terms in the Prologue of John's Gospel, is here developed into a system of its own. Above all, this tendency can be observed in the *Alexandrian theology* of the period

---

[5] J. Betz, *Eucharistie in der Schrift und Patristik,* HDG IV, 4a (Freiburg-Basel-Vienna, 1979), 86.

(Clement, Origen), whereas in the *tradition of Asia Minor* (e.g., Ignatius of Antioch, Polycarp, Melito of Sardis, Justin, Irenaeus, but also Hippolytus of Rome) it is counterbalanced by a stronger emphasis on and a more realistic view of Christ's humanity. Forty years ago Hugo Rahner vividly illustrated this in his study "Flumina de Ventre Christi" on the patristic exegesis of John 7:37f.[6] Here I will summarize his results:

1. For the theologians of Asia Minor, Christ is not so much the Logos (in the sense of Philo and Origen) as the Messiah, the God-Man.
2. Thus he does not appear as the giver of the water of doctrine and knowledge but as the One who, glorified in his genuine human nature, pours out the Spirit, the epitome of all messianic gifts.[7]
3. The water that pours forth from Christ is life-giving not only because it comes from its source in the Father through the Logos but also because it has become life-giving in the blood, that is, in the suffering and death of the God-Man.
4. This means that, in this view, the κοιλία of John 7:38 whence the water springs is not the Philonic, psychological ground of the soul, as it were a mystic inwardness; here it signifies the body of the true man Jesus, and, as Rahner says in conclusion, John 7:38 has the most intimate connection with John 19:34 (cf. note 7).

Thus we can say that, although the Logos is central to the picture of Christ in Asia Minor in the second and third centuries, there is definitely room for a soteriological significance of the human in Christ. Indeed, it serves as a "source", not, however, developed in the intellectual-spiritual sense, but remaining substantially at the somatic level.

In *Origen*, as we have said, the Logos is dominant. Here Christ's humanity is more like the medium whereby divinity can be made visible and communicated to men according to the latter's ability to receive. But in fact, as the believer approaches progressively nearer to the pneumatic reality of the divinity, this mediation retreats more and more into the background, becoming completely transparent and threatening to dissolve into nothing.[8] Yet in spite of this spiritualizing tendency, Origen's Christology is still the doctrine of the Logos *made man*, as we can see in the fact that he was the first to formulate the soteriological argument that eventually, under the heading "*quod non assumptum, non sanatum*", was to play a foundational role.[9] In this connection *Christ's soul* has

---

[6] H. Rahner, *Flumina de Ventre Christi: Die patristische Auslegung von Joh. 7,37.38* (1941), now in H. Rahner, *Symbole der Kirche: Die Ekklesiologie der Väter* (Salzburg, 1964), 174–235, esp. 206–35f.

[7] N.B. the relationship to Jn 19:28ff. (and 1 Jn 5:6ff.). Cf. J. Heer in his paper on the "Pierced Savior".

[8] On these issues, cf. A. Grillmeier, *Christ in Christian Tradition*, rev. ed., vol. 1 (London, 1975), 138–43, to which I am greatly indebted for this summary.

[9] Cf. *Disputatio cum Heracl.* 7,5: "The whole man would not have been saved unless he had taken upon him the whole man" (*Library of Christian Classics*, "*Alexandrian Christianity*"

a central function in his picture of Christ.[10] As the mediating element between *Logos* and *sarx*, it is what makes the christological unity possible.[11]
Then there is the important idea of Jesus' human soul being connected to the
Logos as by a loving devotion to it.[12] Here the connection (and the
christological unity as a whole) is interpreted in terms of acts of the psyche,
not only opening up many possible analogies for our relationship to the
Logos but also running the danger of conceiving the relationship of Christ's
soul to the Logos as only quantitatively different from the relationship which
we are to achieve with the Logos, his "mystical incarnation" in us.

However deficient the theory may be, it is important to realize that a significant development has taken place: for the first time in patristic literature we
have a deliberate theological evaluation of the human, intellectual aspect in
Christ. It is not merely (as so often subsequently) an indicator of the completeness of his human nature, and hence something static: seen in terms of
love, that is, freely offered devotion and loyalty, it is the principle of genuine
human acts and experiences. It must be said, however, that in Origen himself
this initial achievement does not exercise much influence (e.g., with regard to
the Passion of Jesus), nor does it bear much fruit in the immediate future.

This also applies, among others, to a theologian like *Athanasius*, in whose
picture of Christ, the soul of Christ scarcely plays any part as a soteriological
factor.[13] Here the Logos is the central, all-invigorating and all-governing principle of the Person of Christ. Within this horizon Jesus' *acta et passa* are attributed very directly to the Logos, which is conceived not only as their subject
but in a sense as the principle that gives physical life to the body.[14] There is no
room left here for a human soul. The body is appropriated by the all-effecting
Logos as its direct "instrument" (ὄργανον). The resulting problems become
particularly clear when Athanasius attempts to refute the Arian interpretation
of Jesus' suffering on the Mount of Olives.[15] In order to protect the Logos
against any restriction of his transcendence and immutability, Athanasius does
not choose to correct his christological *Logos–sarx* scheme, although it was this
very scheme that gave the Arians the opportunity of making the Logos the soul
of the man Jesus and hence the physical subject of his suffering, reducing it to
the level of a created principle. Instead, he ascribes all weakness to the flesh,

---

[Philadelphia, 1954], 442). For the later development of this principle, cf. A. Grillmeier's article
"*Quod non assumptum, non sanatum*" in LThK 8: 954–56.

[10] Cf. Grillmeier, *Christ in Christian Tradition*, 146–48.

[11] This is most explicit in books 2 and 4 of *Peri Archon* (II, 6, 3–7 and IV, 4, 4f.) [ed. Butter-
worth (London, 1936)].

[12] Cf., e.g., *Peri Archon* II, 6,5.

[13] Cf. Grillmeier, op. cit., 310–28.

[14] Ibid., 312.

[15] *Contra Arianos* III, 54–58 (PG 26, 436B–445C).

which certainly safeguards the divinity of the Logos, yet leads to a problematical restriction with regard to Christ's human nature. Paradoxically, the *sarx* now appears to be the subject of psychological states and acts, in particular of those which evince human weakness and imperfection. On the other hand, his consent to the Father's will is seen as entirely the work of the Logos. As Athanasius puts it, the latter "blends his [divine] will with human weakness".[16] In this view, the human nature of Christ is in danger of being reduced to a mere negative background to the foreground obedience of the Logos. There is scarcely any positive significance left—in the sense of an active collaboration—for the human nature in the act of redemption.

It is true that Athanasian Christology, as a result of its Logocentrism, has an impressive coherence and—particularly in Greek terms—an enormous religious vigor. This is its abiding importance. But its extensive influence on succeeding periods will always be impaired by the one-sidedness we have outlined.

This is the case most blatantly, no doubt, with *Apollinaris of Laodicea*. In his interpretation of the Incarnation, the *Logos* is joined to the human *sarx*, forming a kind of being of body and spirit that Apollinaris likes to call a "heavenly man". Here the anthropological model of the body–soul unity no longer serves as only an analogy but as a precise explanation. Thus the christological unity is conceived basically as a natural unity, in which the Logos is, as it were, the physical vital principle of all states and acts. We must not ignore the fact that Apollinaris's evident attempt to join inseparably (and in a certain sense ontologically) the divine and the human in Christ is clearly a soteriological one. It is a matter of our salvation, and in his view that salvation can only be safeguarded if man is given back his original and unshakeable orientation to God. Thus a νοῦς ταυτοκίνητος must be operative in Christ, as Apollinaris says,[17] that is, a spirit that is constantly and inalienably ordered to one thing, namely, to God and his will. The human spirit, however, due to its obfuscation by sin, is no longer capable of such stability. Hence the Logos himself takes the place of the human spirit in the assumed human nature, in order to achieve this inalienable constancy. The consequences of this view are considerable: not only the integrity of the human in Christ but also the transcendence of the divine are gravely interfered with.

Grillmeier sees in this *Logos–sarx* Christology, together with Arianism, "probably the most serious and dangerous influx of Hellenistic ideas into the tradition's conception of Christ".[18] And even the orthodox forms of this

---

[16] Ibid., III, 57 (PG 26, 441B–C). Grillmeier (313n.50) points out that Marcellus of Ancyra, a contemporary of Athanasius, interprets the Gethsemane scene quite similarly in *De inc. et c. Arian.* 21 (PG 26, 1021B–C). The contrast to Maximus's interpretation of the same scene is considerable: in Athanasius the Logos is the sole agent in the struggle for redemption; as yet, human obedience, human consent to the suffering and death, are not even considered.

[17] *Logoi,* fragm. 153 (ed. Lietzmann 258,22–23).

[18] Grilllmeier, op. cit., 342.

christological perspective—that is, the Christology of Athanasius, and also of the early Cyril—suffer from a certain one-sidedness. Grillmeier again:

> There can be no doubt that the decline in teaching about the soul of Jesus had a detrimental effect on the picture of Christ in the Eastern Church wherever the *Logos-sarx* framework came to occupy a dominant place. It represents . . . a misunderstanding of the whole manhood and human psychology of Jesus. The all-sufficiency of the redeeming act can no longer be given its proper emphasis and, as a result, the place of Christ's manhood in theology and generally in the worship of believers must suffer.[19]

Thus the period after Apollinaris will be marked by attempts to rediscover the humanity of Christ and its theological significance.

This becomes particularly clear in the area of Antiochene theology, followed by the West. Pope Damasus's Letter *"Per Filium"* to Paulinus of Antioch, for instance, puts forward a clear *Logos–anthropos* Christology that was totally in accord with Western theology with its concrete understanding of the humanity of Christ.[20] Thus Hilary of Poitiers had developed an express doctrine of the soul of Christ before the Apollinarian controversy broke out.[21] But in the area of Alexandria itself there is also an interesting example of an approach of this kind in the "Commentary on Zechariah" by *Didymus the Blind*, only discovered in 1941. Here Christ's soul is seen as the principle of his spiritual suffering, temptation and trials, and hence also as the organ of his suffering obedience. This attempt to devote more attention to the human in Christ is particularly significant in that it is integrated into a logocentric picture of Christ familiar to us through Athanasius.[22] Here lies the advantage of Didymus over the Antiochene approach to a soteriological evaluation of the humanity of Christ.

The better approach will be illustrated by one of the most important representatives of Antiochene Christology, *Theodore of Mopsuestia.*

Theodore criticizes the *Logos–sarx* framework, emphasizing the soul of Christ against all attempts to limit it and elevating it to a genuine theological factor.[23] The hegemony of the Logos is, as it were, broken, leaving room for a human psychology and, therefore, for genuinely human action in Christ. In this connection the "Fifth Catechetical Homily" of Theodore is especially revealing. Here, in chapter 9, Theodore attacks the fundamental principle of extreme *Logos–sarx* Christology, that is, the idea that the Logos is the vital, dynamic influence on Christ's flesh:

[19] Ibid.

[20] Cf. J. Liébaert, *Christologie: Von der Apostolischen Zeit bis zum Konzil von Chalcedon* (451), HDG III, Ia, (Freiburg-Balse-Vienna), 86.

[21] Grillmeier, op. cit., 395.

[22] Cf., ibid., 362–63.

[23] Cf. the thorough treatment in Grillmeier, op. cit., 421–39.

The disciples of Arius and Eunomius say that he [Christ] took a body but not a soul; the divine nature, they say, takes the place of the soul. And they lower the divine nature of the one and only Son to the point [of saying] that he declines from his natural grandeur and performs the actions of the soul by enclosing himself in the body and accomplishing everything to make it "subsist". Consequently, if the divinity takes the place of the soul, it [i.e., the body] had neither hunger, nor thirst, nor was it tired, nor did it have need of food; for all this happens to the body because of its weakness.[24]

Here we can see very well how the criticism of Theodore (and of the Antiochenes in general) with regard to the *Logos–sarx* scheme is not only concerned to preserve the full humanity of Christ, as we see at the end of the above quotation, but, as its beginning shows, is equally marked by a concern for the transcendence and divinity of the Logos.

This is how Theodore formulates his own view:

God wished to encourage and lift up man who had fallen—man composed of a body and an immortal and rational soul—so that, "as sin came into the world through one man and death through sin, much more have the grace of God and the righteousness of a single man, Jesus Christ, abounded for many" (Rom 5:12, 15), and "as by a man came death, by a man has come also the resurrection of the dead" (1 Cor 15:21f.).[25]

The emphasis on the continuity of Adam–Christ with regard to the human in Christ shows that Theodore is trying to put this human nature beyond any docetic interpretation: it is fallen man and no other who is to be restored, and the healing activity must start at the very point at which sin took its origin—a thought that is given particular emphasis later in Maximus.[26]

It is plain that the inclination to sin begins in the soul's will, for in Adam too it was the soul that first accepted the challenge of transgression, and not his body. . . . Therefore Christ had to assume not only a body but also a soul; or rather vice versa, first the soul had to be assumed and then the body because of the soul.[27]

Here in Theodore the soul of Christ regains the position that, with the Alexandrians, it was in danger of losing. Grillmeier puts the achievement

---

[24] *Hom. cat. V,9* (ed. Tonneau, 111).

[25] *V,10* (Tonneau, 113–15).

[26] Cf. *Disp. cum Pyrrho*: "For if Adam willingly gave ear (to the tempter), willingly looked and willingly ate, it is clearly the will that was the first casualty in us. But if this is so and if, as they (the Monothelites) say, when the Logos became man he did not take man's will upon himself, I have not escaped from sin and am not redeemed; for what is not assumed is not healed" (PG 91, 325A).

[27] *V,11* (Tonneau, 115–17); on the first part, cf. also *V,13* (119): "Much of this (i.e., the immoralities mentioned in Rom 1:28ff.) is not a question of the powers of the body but of the *will* of the soul."

thus: "The human nature of Christ regains its real physical-human inner life and its capacity for action", so that "the created soul provides the life for the body of Christ and is also the principle of the acts decisive for our redemption."[28] Redemption is achieved by a "man", as the Pauline quotation in verse 10 affirms, and as verse 17 once more clearly stresses:

> Our holy Fathers pointed out these things by saying, "he took flesh and became man", so that we should believe that it was a complete man who was assumed and became the habitation of the divine Logos—he who was perfect in all that pertains to human nature, consisting of a mortal body and a rational soul, since it was "for man and his salvation that he descended from heaven". . . . And he clothed himself with a man like Adam, who was condemned to death following his fall into sin, so that *by one like him* sin in us should be eradicated and death removed.[29]

This seems to anticipate many of the central christological insights of Maximus. At the same time—as we have already indicated—Theodore succeeds only with difficulty in integrating this revaluation of the human into the aspect of the unity of Christ's Person. This is apparent in the text just quoted. When he describes the relationship of the Logos to the assumed humanity in terms of "clothing" and "indwelling", he is using a terminology that as far as the substance of this unity is concerned, does not measure up to the vision of the Alexandrians.[30]

The dogmatic formula of Chalcedon produces a certain synthesis of the two approaches. The anagogical perspective (Christology "from below") is introduced into the Johannine-Nicene picture of Christ—not without influence from Latin Christology—at least in a formal sense.[31] Yet the space made available by the definitions's phrase *"perfectus in humanitate"*, inviting consideration of the human features of Christ, is filled out only very hesitatingly. An inadequate conceptual and logical foundation is partly to blame; in part, too, it is no doubt attributable to the traumatic issue of Nestorius, which continued to trouble Greek theology for a long time.[32] There are beginnings of a development of Christ's full humanity that goes beyond the classical position of Alexandrine Christology (Athanasius): the two Leontii, for instance, also make a substantial contribution toward clarifying

---

[28] Grillmeier, op. cit., 427.

[29] *V, 17* (Tonneau, 123–25).

[30] Cf., e.g., the position of the later Cyril, who thinks in terms of a genuine human psychology of Christ and sees the significance of human obedience in Christ's sacrificial act (cf. Grillmeier, op. cit., 475f).

[31] Cf. Grillmeier's excellent treatment, op. cit., 543–54.

[32] Symptomatic of this is the "Three Chapters" dispute, caused by the condemnation at the Second Council of Constantinople (553) of the person and writings of Theodore of Mopsuestia, the writings of Theodoret against Cyril of Alexandria, and the letter of Ibas of Edessa. In the sixth and at the beginning of the seventh century the spirit of Antioch is practically quenched. Not until Maximus does its basic approach make itself felt again, albeit anonymously.

the formal basis of the christological problem.[33] I would like to quote a short passage from each of these sixth-century theologians.

First, a piece from the second book of the *"Adversus Nestorianos et Eutychianos"* of *Leontius of Byzantium:*

> Just as the Lord surrendered all that is his to the flesh, yet without deserting himself, remaining immutably in that condition that is appropriate to his nature, so his humanity has retained its physical status, with the natural powers and functions of its body, including its universal (not sinful) passibility. Thus it is essentially a perfect human nature and, as such, shares in all the benefits that come from the Logos. Moreover, in possessing the source of benefits, that is, the Logos, his humanity pours these benefits forth, for the sake of the Logos, as out of a springing well.[34]

I have quoted this text because it raises the topic we meet in Justin, Irenaeus and Hippolytus in connection with John 7:38; namely, the vision of the humanity of Christ as the source of salvation. After them the terminology has become more technical and abstract. It seems significant that emphasis is laid on the integrity of the natural powers and functions (the δυνάμεις and ἐνέργειαι) of the flesh. As a result, the humanity of Christ is no longer only a passive instrument of the Logos, but has a positively active role as the source of saving benefits (cf. the active verb πηγάζει at the end of the text quoted). Here, as an interpreter of the Chalcedonian formula, Leontius of Byzantium is in line with Leo's "Tomus ad Flavianum": *"agit enim utraque forma cum alterius communione quod proprium est"*.[35] Like Leo, Leontius holds fast the twofold principle of activity in Christ; its fundamental approach is dyo-energetic.

From *Leontius of Jerusalem* I would like to quote a section of *"Adversus Nestorianos"* (II, 14). This highly technical text is concerned with describing the hypostasis of the incarnate Logos with regard to the specific features (ἰδιώματα) that determine it. In doing so it affirms that, since his Incarnation, the Person of the Logos is no longer characterized only by the inner-Trinitarian attribute of being begotten and distinct from Father and Spirit, but also bears the features of his adopted humanity, features that have consequences for this humanity's relationship to the Father and the Spirit. Here is the central passage:

> The Logos shares a common nature with Father and Spirit, but as for his hypostasis, it is unique in relation to the Father and the Spirit and in relation to all men not born of the Virgin; it is only common to the flesh adopted by the Logos from the Theotokos. Conversely, the flesh that comes from the Virgin shares a common nature with all who come from Adam, as accords with his

---

[33] Cf. my dissertation, *Gottes Sohn als Mensch — Die sohnschaftliche Struktur des Menschseins Christi bei Maximus Confessor* (Fribourg, 1980), esp. the chapter "Die Hypostasenlehre des Corpus Leontii".

[34] PG 86, 1336D–1337A.

[35] "Each 'form' does the acts which belong to it, in communion with the other" (*Library of Christian Classics, "Christology of the Later Fathers"*, [Philadelphia, 1954], 365). Maximus often quotes this formula in his argument against Monothelitism, e.g., in *Opusc.* 15 (PG 91, 168A and 176C–D). Cf. *Opusc.* 2 (PG 91, 49C).

fellowship with us, whereas the hypostasis is unique in relation to us and to Father and Spirit, being common only to the Logos.[36]

The crucial point here is that Christ is distinguished from Father and Son not only *qua* Logos but also, hypostatically, "as man". In other words, there is now room—in principle—for a personal relationship, in the real sense of the word, between the incarnate Son *as man* and the Father. Hence the humanity of Jesus can appear in a new light precisely within the perspective of its intimate unity with the Logos (with which, as our text says, it shares a "common" hypostasis): the Son appears before the Father in his free human nature, a nature that is capable of human obedience and human worship and love.

With this we turn to Maximus.

III. The Soteriological Significance of the Humanity of Christ in Maximus the Confessor

In Maximus the development of the Chalcedonian "perfectus in humanitate" reaches its patristic high-point.

In principle, the dogma of 451 guaranteed the unrestricted activity and freedom of the assumed human nature. Maximus develops this insight not only with regard to this humanity's ontological status, that is, the "completeness" of the Incarnation, but also with regard to its *historical fulfillment* in the action and Passion of Jesus. The instrumental function of Christ's humanity, which we met in the soteriology of Athanasius, is here rendered active and dynamic under the aspect of the will and of freedom and thus of a real personal dimension.

This vision is most evident in *Opusculum 6*. This text deals with the interpretation of the Agony in the Garden, in particular Matthew 26:39 ("My Father, if it be possible, let this cup pass from me; nevertheless, not as I will, but as thou wilt"), a text that plays a central role in the Monothelite controversy.[37]

I will limit myself here to the last part of Maximus's argument, in which he summarizes his position with great clarity:

For our sakes made like unto us, and *as was appropriate for a man* (ἀνθρωπο-πρεπῶς), he said to his God and Father, "Let not my will, but thine, prevail", since he who was by nature God wished to fulfill the Father's will *as a man* also. Thus it could be seen that he willed and effected our salvation *according to the two natures* of which and in which he was. On the one hand, together with the Father and the Spirit he decided upon this salvation; and on the other hand, for the sake of this salvation "he became obedient to the Father unto death, even

---

[36] *Adv. Nest.* II, 14 (PG 86, 1568B–C).
[37] Cf. Lethel, op. cit., 86–99.

the death of the Cross" (Phil 2:8) and so effected the great mystery of our redemption through the flesh.[38]

What are the most important insights in this text? First of all we see that, in contrast to his Monothelite opponents and also to the ancient Fathers, he sees the human at work in Christ not only in the initial rejection of the cup ("Father, if it be possible . . ."), but also in the obedient *acceptance* of suffering: Christ offers his obedience to the Father "as man".

And what of the reasons behind this approach? Space forbids more than a few brief observations. The presuppositions are largely logical in kind, and relate particularly to a more precise differentiation of "nature" and "person" (οὐσία and ὑπόστασις)—a differentiation that was the fruit of a century-long process and to which Maximus contributed substantially.[39] This clarification means that he is able to overcome the basic difficulty that had dogged all previous attempts at an interpretation (including that of Gregory of Nazianzen, which occupies a crucial position in the Monothelite controversy,[40] namely, the mistaken idea that if a thing is other, it must be opposite *eo ipso*; i.e., that to assume any other will in Christ besides the divine will must involve a division of his Person and of the acts emanating from His Person. Maximus shows, however, that a human will in Christ is quite conceivable from the point of view of Chalcedon, indeed, that the latter positively demands it. *Unity in distinctness*—this, for him, is the fundamental structure not only of the Person of Christ but of all emanating acts as well. In *Opusculum* 8, in fact, he formulates this insight as a basic ontological principle that has a wide application far beyond Christology: "Unity among things evidently exists to the extent that their natural difference is safeguarded."[41]

If a twofold willing is compatible with the unity of Christ's Person—is in fact required by it—it follows, for Maximus, that the will is in principle rooted *in the nature*. The text confirms this when it says, "He willed our salvation . . . according to the two natures." This is developed even more clearly in the "Disputation with Pyrrhus", a central christological text of Maximus. Here he distinguishes very carefully between the capacity to will, that is, the will per se (θέλειν), and the way in which this willing takes place (πῶς θέλειν). To will belongs to the nature of man as such; it is part of the definition of man (of his λόγος τῆς φύσεως)—whereas the way in which the will is actually realized is specific to the person and hence ordered to the hypostasis and its individual τρόπος τῆς ὑπάρξεως.[42] He further shows that

---

[38] *Opusc.* 6 (PG 91, 68C–D).

[39] This question is dealt with in detail in my dissertation.

[40] Lethel, op. cit., 29–35, 52f., 71f., 86–99.

[41] *Opusc.* 8 (PG 91, 97A).

[42] *Disp. cum Pyrrho* (PG 91, 292D–293A). Here Maximus takes up a distinction drawn in the Trinitarian theology of the Cappadocians and uses it to good effect in Christology. Cf., the relevant remarks in my dissertation.

the capacity to will is an essential constituent of man as such, citing earlier Fathers in support,[43] by equating θέλησις with freedom, freedom understood as the independent, utterly unconstrained freedom to pursue the Good (αὐτεξούσιος κίνησις), a reflection of the freedom of God himself.[44] This estimate of the will as a constituent of man in the image of God and, hence, of the deepest substance of human nature is no doubt the ultimate reason for Maximus's insistence on Christ's human capacity to will and on his human freedom. In the context of anthropology, or rather, of the theology of grace, this means that "man cannot be made manifest as a son of God in virtue of the deifying effect of grace until he has been born in the Spirit in a prior free decision (κατά προαίρεσιν), since autonomous and independent power (αὐτοκίνητος καὶ ἀδέσποτος δύναμις) dwells in him by nature";[45] indeed, only on this basis, christologically speaking, can the humanity of Christ be truly free and hence human. Two conclusions arise. First, in its soteriological role Christ's humanity is lifted above the level of mere instrumental function to the level of active, dynamic cooperation.[46] Second, Christ's human freedom, manifest in his suffering obedience, is seen as the highest realization of human nature and as its epitome of the image of God.

A further aspect, not directly developed in this text, is that for Maximus the realization of human freedom is in fact synonymous with love, ἀγάπη. Love appears as freedom from oneself, in contrast to φιλαυτία, self-love and self-indulgence,[47] as freedom in relation to created things in order to be free for God,[48] and shows itself most clearly in the love of the neighbor and especially of the enemy.[49] Such love, says Maximus, exhibits "all the divine attributes"; "strictly speaking, it alone is able to show man to be the image of

---

[43] In particular Diadochus of Photice, Cap. Cent. 5 (SC 5, 86): "Freedom (αὐτεξουσιότης) is the willing (θέλησις) of a rational soul ready to move toward its object" (cf. the commentary of E. des Places, the editor: "La vraie liberté, comme celle de Dieu, ne peut vouloir que le bien"). Maximus quotes this definition in 301C.

[44] Disp. cum Pyrrho (304C): "If man has been created in the image of the blessed and supersubstantial Godhead, and if the divine nature is naturally free (αὐτεξούσιος), then man too is free by nature insofar as he is genuinely its image" (cf. the almost word-for-word parallel in 324D). At this point Maximus is very close to Gregory of Nyssa (cf. J. Gaith, La Conception de la liberté chez Grégoire de Nysse [Paris, 1953], esp. 68–81).

[45] Amb. 42 (PG91, 1345D). Cf. Thal. 6 (PG 90, 280D): "The Spirit does not give birth to an unwilling mind (to sonship in the Spirit), but only refashions and deifies a willing mind." The closeness to Gregory of Nyssa is very clear here. Cf. the texts of Gregory cited by Gaith, op. cit., 68–72.

[46] It is characteristic of Maximus that, instead of using the ὄργανον-terminology of Athanasius, he often uses the expression συνεργάτις, which brings the active, cooperating factor more to the fore: cf., e.g., Opusc. 7 (PG 91, 85D) and 8 (101B–D).

[47] Cf. Cent. Char. II, 59 (Ceresa-Gastaldo, 122), Ep. 2 (PG 91, 397B–C), and Thal. 59 (PG 90, 605B and 608A).

[48] Asc. 10 (PG 90, 920B–C), Cent. Char. II, 3 (Ceresa-Gastaldo, 90) and II, 52 (118).

[49] Cf. Char. II, 49 (Ceresa-Gastaldo, 116): "Only the perfect, spiritual love is able to do good to the person who hates." Sim. in Asc. 8 (PG 90, 917B–C).

the Creator."[50] Ultimately, then for Maximus, freedom, the realization of the image of God, and love are one in the life of the Christian, because of their prior unity in the humanity of Christ.

In this view, the assumption of human nature by the Logos means that the original dynamism of this nature is liberated and renewed, once more rendered capable of the Good.[51] Man's original orientation to God (given in creation and hence part of man's nature) is restored in the humanity of Christ, the mode of this humanity being penetrated with and fashioned by the inner-Trinitarian, filial orientation of the Logos to the Father.[52] Here there can be no greater human freedom than this "liberated freedom" of Jesus, because it is the highest realization of what lies in man's innermost being. In other words, the assumption of human nature by the Son of God does not destroy it but leads it to its actual fulfillment; its goal is "this very human nature itself".[53]

It is crucial, however, to understand this human nature as the human nature of the Son of God. Only in relation to the Person of the Son is its soteriological meaning secure. This too is expressed very clearly in *Opusculum* 6, as we have already seen:

> He willed and effected our salvation according to the two natures. . . . On the one hand, together with the Father and the Spirit he decided upon this salvation, and on the other hand, for the sake of this salvation he became obedient to the Father unto death, even the death of the Cross.

He insists "without confusion, without separation" on both aspects here: the inner-Trinitarian plan of redemption, and the fulfillment of this plan in terms of human destiny in the obedience to death; both are the work of one and the same Person. Thus the incarnate Logos becomes the "messenger of the great counsel", as Maximus says, quoting Isaiah 9:6;[54] indeed, he fulfills the

[50] *Cent. Char.* II, 52 and *Ep.* 2 (PG 91, 396C).

[51] Cf. *Ep.* 2 (PG 91, 397B–C), where Maximus says that in his Incarnation the Logos became utterly man and at the same time remained totally God, "in order to destroy the works of the devil, by restoring [man's] powers to his nature, and to renew in man the strength of love, so that we could once again be united with him and with one another".

[52] On this shaping of Christ's humanity by the Person of the Logos cf. *Opusc.* 3 (PG 91, 48A–B) and 7 (80D and 81D), where Maximus says that Christ's human will was always moved and formed (κινούμενον ἀεὶ καὶ τυπούμενον) by his divine will. This fashioning of the human in Christ by the Logos is expressed in a general way in the *Disputatio*, where it is emphasized that this influence does not put an end to human nature as nature but rather maintains it in its λόγος: "In general, everything in Christ that pertains to [human] nature has both its own essential principle (λόγος) and also a supernatural mode (τρόπος), so that both nature and the saving economy are worthy of belief, the one through its essential principle and the other through its mode" (PG 91, 297D–300A).

[53] A. Grillmeier, "Moderne Hermeneutik und altkirchliche Christologie" in *Mit ihm und in ihm: Christologische Forschungen und Perspektiven* (Freiburg-Basle-Vienna, 1975), 489–582, here 545.

[54] *Thal.* 60 (PG 90, 621B).

mystery of this plan in his Incarnation:[55] the obedience that he shows to the Father in his life as man is seen to be the historical continuation and perfection—in fact, the "incarnation"—of the unity of will with the Father (and the Spirit) that he enjoys from eternity as Logos and Son. As Maximus puts it succinctly in *Ambigua* 41: "As man, therefore, the Lord carried out in scrupulous obedience, in deed and in truth, what he had predetermined as God."[56]

In this perspective we may see the suffering obedience that Christ lived out as man as the perfection of that self-emptying that the preexistent Logos took upon himself in his Incarnation. If this kenosis is the act of the divine freedom of the Logos—"He chose it and carried it out deliberately and freely"[57]—his obedience unto death is similarly the fulfillment of this divine freedom in terms of a human destiny. In other words, it Christ's human freedom, manifest in his suffering obedience, we encounter not only human freedom but also the freedom of the Son of God himself, which supports and molds it.

We can summarize the soteriological role of Christ's humanity in the thought of Maximus as follows:

His attention is devoted primarily to the "interior" of this human nature, that is, to the workings of the soul and the psyche. Human freedom, lived out in obedience, is seen to be the source of salvation, supported and molded, to be sure, by the freedom of a Divine Person. The human obedience of Jesus "unto the death of the Cross" (Phil 2:8) becomes the incarnate form of the inner-Trinitarian relationship of Son to Father, and at the same time it is the redemptive perfection of human nature. Thus, for Maximus, Christ's heart—the center of his Person and of his action and Passion—is the locus of interpenetration of divine and human freedoms, which are united "without confusion, without separation" in the filial relationship with the Father in the Spirit.

Our last task is to show that this *perichoresis*[58] of the freedom of God and the freedom of man is revealed concretely, in the existence of Jesus, as divine-human love.

I would like to illustrate this by summarizing several passages from the *Liber Asceticus*, a late work of Maximus[59] written in the form of a dialogue.

---

[55] *Cent. Gnost.* II, 23: "The Father's Great Counsel is the silent and unrecognized mystery of the Incarnation, fulfilled by the only begotten Son when he took flesh. Thus he unveiled it and became the Messenger of the Great Counsel, made before all ages (προαιώνιος)" (PG 90, 1136B).

[56] *Amb.* 41 (PG 91, 1309C-D).

[57] *Ep.* 13 (PG 91, 517B).

[58] On the christological use of this concept cf. *Opusc.* 4 (PG 91, 60B-C), *Opusc.* 7 (PG 91, 88A), *Pyrrh.* (PG 91, 337C and 345D), *Amb.* 5 (PG 91, 1053B), *Amb.* 42 (1320B) and *Acta* (PG 90, 157D).

[59] On the question of dating cf. I. H. Dalmais, "La Doctrine ascétique de S. Maxime le Confesseur" in *Irénikon* 26 (1653): 17–39, esp. 32. The style of this work is unmistakably different from that of the *Opuscula* or the *Disputatio*. Dogmatic argument no longer occupies the foreground, but spiritual experience and meditation upon it. Yet the basic theological insights of the dogmatic and polemical works are the supporting, though invisible, structure of the whole. This fact reveals a striking characteristic of Maximus: for him there is an unshakeable connection between Christology and Christ-spirituality, theological reflection and theological experience.

An old monk is initiating a young novice into the spiritual life; after he has given a terse account of Christ's saving work, the conversation turns to what man must do to appropriate the salvation that the Lord has achieved. What are the commandments that are to be kept with a view to this salvation? How can they be kept, since they are so many and various? The teacher's reply to these questions is epigrammatic: "If a man imitates the Lord and follows in his footsteps, he will be able to keep the commandments."[60]

The decisive concept here is that of μίμησις. To follow and imitate Christ, however, is not easy. The novice persists in his questioning; he needs a λόγος σύντομος,[61] a concise summary to help him. Thus the sage replies:

> The Commandments are indeed many, my brother, and yet they are all summed up in the one: "You shall love the Lord your God with all your mind and with all your strength, and your neighbor as yourself" (Mk 12:30f.). Therefore he who struggles (ἀγωνιζόμενος) to keep this commandment will keep them all.[62]

Thus the twofold commandment of ἀγάπη is the compendium of Christian existence. However, in his present condition, darkened by sin, man is not of himself capable of this love. Christ must first open the way.[63] So ἀγάπη is Christ's very own gift; only he can give it, having put it into practice along the path of his own life as man.[64] This leads to a consideration of Christ's praxis:

> Our Lord Jesus Christ, who was by nature God and deigned to become man for love of us, was born of a woman under the law as the Apostle says (Gal 4:4), in order *as man* to keep the commandment and thus lift the ancient curse.[65]

"Commandment" here means the twofold commandment of love, as is apparent from the next sentence:

> Now since the Lord knew that the whole law and the prophets are contained in these two commandments of the law: "You shall love the Lord your God with all your heart and your neighbor as yourself", he was at pains to observe the same from beginning to end, as a man should (ἀνθρωποπρεπῶς).[66]

Christ's whole praxis ("from beginning to end"), his path as man, is concentrated on a single point: the struggle against Satan to vindicate love. A struggle that, on behalf of all of us, he endured in a human way (ἀνθρωποπρεπῶς — we have already met this expression in *Opusculum* 6).

---

[60] *Asc.* 3 (PG 90, 913B).

[61] *Asc.* 6 (916B).

[62] Ibid. (916B–C). Cf. also the prologue to the "Quaestiones Thalassii", where love is described as σύντομος πρὸς σωτηρίαν λόγος (PG 90, 260C–D).

[63] *Asc.* 8 (917B–C). Cf. also *Ep.* 2 (PG 91, 404C): "By his suffering Christ has given us an example of the utterly glorious path of love and has freed it from obstacles for everyone."

[64] In doing so he has become our "forerunner" (πρόδρομος): *Cent. Gnost.* II, 25 (PG 90, 1136B–C). Cf. also *Amb.* 42 (PG 91, 1333B–C) and *Ep.* 2 (PG 91, 404C, cf. n.63 above).

[65] *Asc.* 10 (920B).

[66] Ibid.

The initial focus of this struggle is the Temptation in the Wilderness.[67] The description of the scene is jejune but vivid, including the psychology of it, especially if we bear in mind all that Maximus has written (in the "Centuries on Charity" for instance), on the dire battles a man has to go through in his struggle to acquire and maintain his love for God. Here our author is putting Christ forth as our example in the battle for love;[68] an example that can only be of full significance if Christ endured his struggle in a truly human manner, with a vulnerable human sensibility. For Maximus, man's three basic temptations at issue here are the roots that yield that baneful power he calls φιλαυτία: the self-indulgence that tears a man away from God and causes him to fall back upon himself—which is therefore the exact opposite of ἀγάπη.[69] So Maximus sees the ἀγάπη-φιλαυτία polarity as the decisive "either/or" of human existence in this world—and this also applies to the human existence of Jesus, which thus acquires a positively dramatic quality. It becomes even more concrete in the second focal point of his earthly existence, in the Passion, which Maximus interprets as the ultimate proof of faithfulness to the commandment of love—here concerning the love of neighbor:

> As for those deceived [by the devil]—those who could have resisted but who listened to the whisperings of the deceiver through a lack of vigilance—he admonished, rebuked and corrected them, nor did he cease from doing good to them. He was long-suffering when accused, patient in his pains, and showed them all the works of love. The deceiver himself, however, he fought with all the power of his love for those who had been deceived—a paradoxical battle!—showing love instead of hate and thus by his goodness slaying the father of evil. By enduring all the evil from their quarter, or rather, on their behalf, fighting to the death in a human manner (ἀνθρωποπρεπῶς) for the sake of the commandment of love, he won complete victory over the devil and received the victor's laurels, the Resurrection, for us all.[70]

Keeping faith, to death, with the commandment of love—this then Maximus sees as the content and the ultimate motivation of Christ's earthly journey as man. It is summed up in the next quotation: "The Lord's aim (σκοπός) was to be obedient to the Father as man for us, keeping the commandment of love unto death."[71]

So the circle is complete: Jesus' human, suffering obedience to the Father—the subject of our first quotation from Maximus—is seen to be at its deepest

[67] Ibid. (920B–C).

[68] Cf. the ἀγωνιζόμενος in *Asc.* 6 (n.62 above).

[69] On the roots of φιλαυτία, cf. *Cent. Char.* II, 59 (Ceresa-Gastaldo, 122) and III, 56 (170). On the relationship of ἀγάπη and φιλαυτία, cf. *Ep.* 2 (PG 91, 397C), *Cent. Char.* II, 59 (cf. n.68 above) and *Thal.* 59 (PG 605B and 608A). This polarity already occurs in Diadochus of Photice, *Cap. Cent.* 12 (SC 5, 90) and 14 (91): ἑαυτὸν φιλεῖν-τὸν θεὸν ἀγαπᾶν.

[70] *Asc.* 12 (921A–B).

[71] *Asc.* 13 (921B).

a martyrdom for the sake of love. And when we said that Christ's human freedom was rooted in the divine freedom of the Logos, supported and molded by it, the same thing applies to his love: it is the σκοπός of the path the incarnate Son of God takes, just as the ultimate reason for his Incarnation was nothing other than love. Thus the human realization of ἀγάπη is the continuation of that movement of love that caused the Logos to empty himself and assume our nature[72] — the historical, incarnational shape of the eternal love that God bears for us men.

Maximus presents us with a picture of Christ. At its center is love, a love that originates in God's eternity and, by emptying itself, enters history, reaching its perfection in the free, human obedience of Jesus, even unto the death of the Cross.

In his explanation of the Sacred Liturgy, using a boldness that seems to anticipate Pascal, Maximus affirms that the Heart, which was enabled to give visible expression to this redemptive love, at once divine and human, remains *permanently* open to all the human suffering of this eon, as a sign of God's unshakeable solidarity with us:

> For our sakes God has made himself poor and, in fellow suffering, has taken upon himself the pains of every man; thus, in his loving kindness to us, in a mysterious manner he suffers continually until the consummation of the age, according to the measure of suffering which each man bears.[73]

I will conclude my remarks with a reference to the encyclical *Haurietis aquas* of Pius XII, where it speaks of the three ways in which the Heart of Jesus symbolizes the love with which the Redeemer "unceasingly loves the eternal Father and all men":

> The Heart of the Incarnate Word . . . is a symbol of that divine love by which he communes with the Father and the Holy Spirit, but which is only manifest to us in him as the Word made flesh through a perishable and fragile human body. . . . Moreover, it symbolizes this most ardent charity, which, infused into his spirit, crowns the human will of Christ.[74]

I hope I have been able to show that the real patristic basis for the above statement — especially its third and concluding element — is located in the Christology and soteriology of Maximus the Confessor.

[72] On love as the "motivum incarnationis" cf. *Ep.* 2 (PG 91, 404B).

[73] *Myst.* 24 (PG 91, 713B).

[74] "Incarnati Verbi Cor . . . symbolus nempe est divini illius amoris, quem cum Patre et Spirito Sancto communicat, sed qui tamen in ipso tantum, utpote in Verbo, quod caro factum est, per caducum et fragile humanum corpus nobis manifestatur . . . symbolus praeterea est incensissimae illius caritatis, quae, eius in animum infusa, humanam ditat Christi voluntatem": *Hauretis aquas*, AAS 48 (1956): 327–28 (DS 3924).

LEO ELDERS, S.V.D.

THE INNER LIFE OF JESUS IN THE THEOLOGY
AND DEVOTION OF SAINT THOMAS AQUINAS

This paper does not attempt to summarize research into a theological doctrine of St. Thomas in its historical context but simply to assemble the
materials that seem to provide a theological basis for the main elements of the
Devotion to the Heart of Jesus.

It is to be observed at the outset that the Christology of St. Thomas is not
subordinated to any philosophical views or categories of thought; it is subject
only to the Word of God. What supports his theological structure are the
biblical quotations in the *sed contra* arguments and in the *corpus* of the individual articles. A careful and reflective reading of the relevant texts makes it
clear that the Christology of St. Thomas is truly the fruit of meditation in the
area of biblical theology, inspired by prayer and devotion. At the same time,
it is by no means an uncritical theology but a *quasi explicatio* of the Church's
doctrine of faith; it was based on the whole of the tradition available to him
and it took into account penetrating counterarguments.

Central to his teaching on the inner life of Jesus is Thomas's conviction
that Christ's fullness of grace and knowledge is a consequence of the personal
unity of his human nature and the Word of God, which he found indicated in
John 1:14: "We have beheld his glory, glory as of the only Son from the
Father, full of grace and truth."[1] The grace of this union is thus the ground
and origin of the graces that Jesus enjoys and of his inner life: just as the sun
fills the air with light, so the presence of God causes grace in Jesus. Consequently, too, when dealing with the question of the endowment of Christ's
soul, Thomas deals first with the fullness of Christ's grace and then with his
knowledge. Fundamental to the solution of these questions are the biblical
texts of the *sed contra* arguments,[2] especially Isaiah 11:2: "The Spirit of the
Lord shall rest upon him". Thomas adds that the soul of Jesus, in accordance
with its rank and disposition, was most intimately bound to God, and

---

[1] Cf. III, 7, 9 arg. *sed contra*; III, 7. 13. English translations of quotations of the *Summa
theologiae* are taken from the Dominican Edition (Eyre & Spottiswoode).

[2] On the significance of the *sed contra* argument, see my essay "Structure et fonction de l'argument Sed contra dans la Somme théologique de saint Thomas", in *Divus Thomas* 80 (1977):
235–60.

therefore it must have been elevated by grace.[3] By this grace the virtues were infused into all the powers of the soul, to perfect the various faculties.[4] Christ possessed virtue to perfection. The spark of evil desire (*fomes peccati*) was totally absent in his case. He had no inner temptations as a result of this desire, but he was acquainted with the desire ordered by reason, that is, for food, drink, sleep and the like.[5]

Through this fullness of grace Christ was entirely oriented to God internally: he was entirely sanctified yet, through grace he was at the same time preeminently man; that is, the possibilities and the deeper yearnings of the human heart were found in him to the highest degree. And this fullness did not exclude the possibility of growth and further development; it could manifest itself in greater and greater works of wisdom, love and virtue, in harmony with Jesus' natural development and progress in age and experience.[6]

In treating Jesus' fullness of grace, Thomas devotes particular attention to the presence of the gifts of the Holy Spirit. To give just one example: Thomas emphasizes that Jesus also had the gift of the fear of God in the sense of a deeper reverence for God's towering greatness.[7] Here we already have a contribution toward the theological basis of one of the chief elements of the devotion to the Sacred Heart.

As previously mentioned, in this theology of Christ's internal endowment by grace, Jesus remains truly man—in fact he comes nearer to us as a result and becomes our model. Now the Savior's fullness of grace is ordered to communicate with men. If the Sacred Heart of Jesus is also venerated as the source and treasure house of all graces,[8] it is important to note that, on the basis of the Scripture passage "He has made him the head over all things for the Church" (Eph 1:22), Thomas discusses the question of the grace of Christ as Head of the Church, after the question of the personal grace of Christ insofar as he is man. He stresses that, since the Church is the mystical Body, the power and movement of the individual members must proceed from the Head.[9] "The entire humanity of Christ, body and soul, acts upon men, on their bodies as well as on their souls—although it acts primarily on their souls and only secondarily on their bodies."[10]

In connection with the texts "He is the Savior of all men, especially of those who believe" (1 Tm 4:10) and "He is the expiation for our sins,

---

[3] III, 7, 1
[4] III, 7, 2.
[5] III, 15, 2.
[6] III, 7, 12.
[7] III, 7, 6.
[8] Pius XII, *Haurietis aquas* (*Discorsi e radiomessagi* XVIII, 833).
[9] III, 8, 1.
[10] III, 8, 2.

and not for ours only but also for the sins of the whole world" (1 Jn 2:2), Thomas takes up again that beautiful doctrine of the Fathers according to which the Church must be thought of as a mystical reality: if the Church is seen as a reality of grace (*quantum ad esse gratiae*), its members must also include those who are potentially so; some of them will become living members in their own lifetime, while others will not attain this. But when the latter depart from the world without having attained grace, they cease to be potential members of Christ since they are no longer able to become one with him.[11] These remarks form the basis for Thomas's discussion of Christ's knowledge, which is the precondition for the ardent love and mercy of the Sacred Heart of Jesus.

At this point we come up against a thoroughly contemporary set of problems: since about 1935 theology has engaged in intensive research into the question of the consciousness of Jesus.[12] Particularly under discussion have been the precise meaning and consequences of the doctrine formulated at the Council of Chalcedon, the "unconfused" and "inseparable" divine and human natures in Christ. In the meantime, however, the focus of research has changed: the critical method in biblical studies has had its effect.

Radical solutions were proposed with regard to the historicity of the Gospels, the New Testament Christologies and the preexistence of Christ, which seem to reject the Church's received teaching. On the question of the knowledge of Jesus, E. Gutwenger doubts whether it is necessary to assume an infused knowledge in Christ,[13] and J. Riedlinger tries to reduce Jesus' knowledge of his Father to a historical vision of God.[14]

However, the doctrine of St. Thomas on the three kinds of knowledge in Christ (the vision of God, infused knowledge and acquired knowledge) has a basis in the patristic tradition and does most justice to the various scriptural texts. In this context Thomas likes to refer to Jesus' conversation with Nicodemus (Jn 3:11; cf. Jn 5:19; 8:38), where the Savior claims the most intimate knowledge of God. Thomas goes on to assert that if Jesus had not had the vision of God, he could only have had knowledge of his own "I", as man, in the darkness of faith. Furthermore, he says, it was appropriate for the One who was the cause of our salvation to himself have reached the goal whither he would lead us.[15]

Thomas solves the problems that arise from the assumption of the vision of

[11] III, 8, 3.

[12] Cf. P. Galtier, *L'Unité du Christ: Etre, Personne, Conscience* (Paris, 1959); P. Parente, *L'Io di Cristo* (Brescia, 1951).

[13] E. Gutwenger, "The Problem of Christ's Knowledge" in *Concilium* 1/2 (Jan. 1966): 48f.

[14] H. Riedlinger, *Quaestiones Disputatae* 32 (Freiburg, 1966): 158

[15] III, 9, 2. Cf. Heb 2:10.

God in Christ by teaching that Jesus was both Beholder and Pilgrim. The apex of Jesus' mind (*apex mentis*) was bathed in the light of the Divine Being, without the help of created imagination.[16] Thus Thomas regarded Christ's fullness of knowledge and vision of God as the necessary consequences of the *unio hypostatica*. But he also knew that, as far as we are concerned, it is an impenetrable mystery how this vision of God can coexist in the *apex mentis* with a normally developing human knowledge and experience.

In Christ "are hid all the treasures of wisdom and knowledge" (Col 2:3). Thus his human nature, united with the Word of God, must have no imperfection.[17] In this way Thomas substantiates the necessity of so-called infused knowledge, whereby Jesus knew creatures in their own nature through images when he wished to do so. So he recognized angels,[18] for instance, and the individual events of the past and the future.[19]

Since in his human reality Jesus had also to possess a perfection that consists of the free acquisition of experience and knowledge, and to keep his mental life in step with his physical development, he also had acquired knowledge. In the *Summa theologiae* Thomas says that he has changed his opinion from that expressed in the *Commentary on the Sentences* (where he made Jesus' experiential knowledge dependent on his infused knowledge),[20] evidently because he had come to see that the inner life of Jesus also had to be brought to perfection in its orientation to sensuous images.[21]

It should be mentioned at this point that Thomas believed Jesus' infused knowledge was never employed in its full compass, but only insofar as circumstances required it.[22]

In his teaching on the knowledge of Christ, Thomas has put forward a magnificent synthesis: it does justice to the many utterances of Holy Scripture, and it explains the rich development of Jesus' love and mind, which is presupposed in devotion to the Sacred Heart. But Thomas links the glory of the inner life of Jesus, "glory as of the only Son from the Father, full of grace and truth",[23] with Christ's humiliation, which he describes prosaically in terms of the weaknesses of body and soul that Christ accepted along with human nature. Before turning to the Savior's love, we must first see how Thomas handles the mystery of Christ's weakness.[24]

[16] III, 9, 3 ad 3.
[17] III, 9, 3.
[18] III, 11, 2 *sed contra.*
[19] III, 12, 1 ad 3.
[20] III, 9, 4.
[21] III, 9, 4 ad 2.
[22] III, 11, 5 ad 2.
[23] Questions 7–12; and on the related issue of Christ's power, Qu. 13.
[24] Questions 14–15.

At the very beginning of Question 14 we become aware of this immense tension: if Christ's soul was endowed with every perfection of grace and knowledge, surely his body too must have been perfect in every respect.[25] The answer to this difficulty lies hidden in the mystery of faith: the Son of God came into the world in order to atone for the sin of humankind and thus took upon himself the death, hunger, thirst and physical infirmities that are the punishment for sin. In our place and in our flesh Christ has borne these trials, as Isaiah prophesied: "Surely he has borne our griefs and carried our sorrows" (53:4). Thomas adds that in this way the Savior has also strengthened faith in the reality of his human nature and has given an example of his patience.[26] Thus he leads us to the very core of Jesus' inner life: although Jesus' fullness of grace and greatness of soul, in themselves, would have called for an intact human nature, such as that possessed by the first man prior to the fall, Christ took these infirmities upon himself freely, out of love, and in obedience to the will of his Father.[27] All the same, his body was not subject to those weaknesses that men bring upon themselves as a result of particular causes or moral trespass.[28]

As to whether Jesus was acquainted with weakness in his soul, it must be emphasized that he could not be touched by anything that would conflict with his holiness or his knowledge,[29] but that in other ways he experienced all the feelings common to men. He felt bodily pain and sorrow of soul and emotions such as grief and fear—albeit differently from us. In his case his emotions were never attached to what was forbidden; they came into play only under the free control of reason and remained completely governed by it.[30]

According to God's design, the full vision of God in Jesus was restricted to his spirit, with the result that pain was not excluded from the sensuous faculty of the soul. Thus Jesus could feel grief and experience misfortune inwardly and outwardly, in himself and in others. He also felt fear in the presence of impending evil.[31]

In Question 46, which is devoted to the suffering of Christ, St. Thomas bases his discussion on the words of Lamentations 1:12: "Look and see if there is any sorrow like my sorrow which was brought upon me". Thomas stresses that, in both physical injury and inner pain, Jesus' sufferings were the most grievous possible in any human life. He adduces four reasons:

[25] III, 14, 1.
[26] III, 14, 1.
[27] III, 14, 3.
[28] III, 14, 4.
[29] III, 15, 1–3.
[30] III, 15, 4.
[31] III, 15, 7.

1. Christ's pain on the Cross was sharpened by its extent and kind and by the burden of all the sins of men for whom he was carrying out satisfaction.
2. The sensitivity of his body and soul.
3. Jesus did not seek to mitigate the intensity of his pains by mental activity.
4. He freely took upon himself the suffering and pain in order to redeem men from sin.[32]

There is a fine application of this teaching in the *Commentary on St. John's Gospel*, in which Thomas explains the words "Now is my soul troubled" (Jn 12:27), showing how this troubling of the soul, although freely willed by Jesus (*ex imperio rationis*), was yet fully human and "natural" in the proper sense, because the soul delights to be joined to the body and naturally fears separation from it. Of Jesus he says that "*ad passionem appropinquans omnia humanitus agit*".[33]

Now let us turn to the theme of Christ's love. Straightaway we notice that Thomas devotes no special question to it. But if we gather together what he writes in various places about Christ's will, we discover a striking wealth of reflections and probing examinations. First we come to Question 18, which discusses the effect of the hypostatic union on the will of Christ. (It is assumed that readers have read the theological background [opposition to the Monothelite heresy] and the Thomist doctrine that a person's being and activity belong to him and depend on his nature[34] — nature being the direct physical matrix of the faculty that is realized by the various acts.) Since Christ possesses a human nature, he also possesses the faculty of will and hence, of necessity, an orientation to happiness.[35] But, in its acts, the human will remains dependent on the divine will of the eternal Word, and the human will can only operate through the subsistence of the divine Word in the human nature (*agere est suppositi*), so that it was always moved in obedience (*ad nutum*) to the divine Word.[36]

Thomas makes a further distinction between the sensuous will (called will insofar as it is, by nature, subordinate to the spiritual will) and the spiritual will. The latter possesses a basic striving toward the Good (*voluntas ut natura*) and wills the means whereby the Good may be achieved (*voluntas ut ratio*).[37] This latter distinction is the basis for Christ's freedom, with respect to his choice of the path he will take to achieve the good. But in accord with his utterly superior knowledge, Jesus experiences no hesitation when he comes to choose.[38]

---

[32] III, 46, 6.
[33] *Super Io. Evang.*, c. 12, lectio 5, N. 1651–52.
[34] III, 19, 1 ad 4.
[35] III, 18, 1 ad 3.
[36] III, 18, 1 ad 4.
[37] III, 18, 3.
[38] III, 18, 4 ad 1.

Thomas found it necessary to make these technical distinctions in order to do justice to the facts of the inner life of Jesus as they have come down to us in the New Testament. Christ's rational will (*voluntas ut ratio*) freely conformed to the will of the Father, and, in obedience and love, also willed what was repugnant to his sensuous will (*voluntas ut natura*), such as the suffering and death involved in his redemption of mankind. It is to be noted that Thomas traces this conformity of Christ's will with that of the Father back to the *amor amicitiae*,[39] that is, freely willed love.

Thomas continues and further stresses Christ's harmonious unity: in him, sensuous desire is no more opposed to his rational will than is his natural will.[40] In fact, the unity of Christ's human nature was such that the rich and varied multiplicity of levels, organs and faculties in Christ was permeated and fashioned by his will, resulting in his nature's unique poise and unity. In a way that is inaccessible to us "mere humans", the rational will of Christ ordered the whole gamut of movement in his body and his senses. This means that Christ's human nature was animated by his love.[41]

Later, in Question 34, which concerns the perfection of the Child Jesus in the womb, Thomas will go on to say that Jesus was already consecrated to God from the first moment of his existence and autonomously aligned himself toward God.[42] This implies, in turn, that his whole life and all the motions of his soul were guided and animated by love and were thus meritorious. So not only Jesus' whole inner life but also every single external movement were like a dialogue of love with God. The most profound quality of free personal autonomy consists in giving oneself to God. And this is what Jesus did preeminently.

In his first act of will he affirmed the Father's will by consenting to give his life for the salvation of men.[43] Hence Christ's inner attitude can also be called obedience, an obedience that sprang from love and was sustained by love. Thomas traces back Jesus' consent to the surrender of his own life to a revelation or inspiration from the Father.[44]

In his commentaries on Holy Scripture in particular, Thomas sang the praises of the redeeming love of Christ. Here are quoted merely a few examples:

> For whatever occurred in the mystery of human redemption and Christ's Incarnation was the work of love. He was born out of charity. . . . That he died also

[39] III, 18, 5 ad 2.

[40] III, 19, 2.

[41] III, 19, 2. Thomas refers to III, 18, 5, where he speaks of the *amor amicitiae* as a fundamental element of Christ's rational will.

[42] III, 34, 2.

[43] *Super epist. ad Hebr.*, c. 10, lectio 1. N. 490.

[44] *Super Io. evang.*, c. 14, lectio 18, N. 1967: ". . . secundum quod Pater movet eum ad mortem suscipiendam . . . inquantum animae eius inspiravit necessarium esse saluti humanae ut Christus in natura humana moreretur."

sprang from charity. . . . It follows that to know Christ's love is to know all the mysteries of Christ's Incarnation and our redemption. These have poured out from the immense charity of God; a charity exceeding every created intelligence and the [combined] knowledge of all of them because it cannot be grasped in thought.[45] [Furthermore,] "no one could know how much Christ has loved us";[46] "Christ did not seek what pleased him" (Rom 15:3).

Consequently we too must not seek what pleases us, that is, we must not follow our own will.[47]

The love of Christ has also become for us the law of the New Covenant, and the reason is threefold: first, because it is through love that the New Covenant is distinguished from the Old; second, because Christ said explicitly that his disciples will be recognized by their love (Jn 13:35); and finally, because Christ himself has fulfilled love perfectly and given us an example of how to fulfill it. For it is out of love that he took our sins upon himself.[48]

Jesus' love for his Father is also friendship with men, in which he is so much one heart and one soul with us that he reveals to us what he has heard from his Father.[49] The crucified Savior's "I thirst" is a sign of his ardent desire for the salvation of all men.[50]

In harmony with the whole tradition Thomas sees this loving self-offering to save all men[51] as unique in history, as an act of mercy and righteousness, and hence of satisfaction and atonement. But he has uncovered a deep connection between these two aspects, something which is the key to a better understanding of the inner life of Jesus. Christ came into the world in order to break the rule of the devil; not by a show of power, however, but by suffering at the hands of the devil and those who belong to him. Thus he overcame the devil through righteousness and love, and the disobedient Adam through obedience.[52] The great evil of sin and guilt is expiated through the fullness of love. So righteousness springs from mercy, just as creation is primarily a work of love. As God's mercy is over all his works as the prime motive of his creating and saving activities, including righteousness which it transforms,[53] so it was with Jesus. Sin is a perverse "turning to creatures", falsifying man's orientation to God. By his obedience and love Jesus has

---

[45] *Super epist. ad Eph.*, c. 3., lectio 5, N. 178 [*Commentary on Saint Paul's Epistle to the Ephesians* (Albany, N.Y., 1966), 144].

[46] Ibid., N. 180 [146].

[47] *Super epist. ad Rom.*, c. 15, lectio 1, N. 1146.

[48] *Super epist. ad Gal.*, c. 6, lectio 1, N. 348 [*Commentary on Saint Paul's Epistle to the Galatians* (Albany, N.Y., 1966), 190].

[49] *Super Io. evang.*, c. 15, lectio 3, N. 2016.

[50] Ibid., lectio 5, N. 2447.

[51] *Super epist. ad Rom.*, c. 5, lectio 2, N. 396.

[52] III, 41, 1 ad 2.

[53] I, 21, 4.

reestablished the *conversio ad Deum* and has offered to God something greater than the mere counterpart of the insults offered to God by men. In this way, righteousness is swallowed up in love, and satisfaction becomes mercy.[54]

Even in his public life Jesus showed that the fullness of mercy outshone righteousness—the rejection of sin—as in the case of the woman taken in adultery: "Neither do I condemn you; go, and do not sin again" (Jn 8:11), revealing, says Thomas in his commentary, how kind is the Lord and righteous in his truth.[55]

Christ's mercy is evident now too, writes Thomas in his exposition of Hebrews 4:15 ("For we have not a high priest who is unable to sympathize with our weaknesses"): since Jesus knows our misery by experience, he is immediately available to help us.[56]

The theme of the inner life of Jesus embraces his life of prayer as well. In fact, the New Testament emphasizes that the Savior prayed and cultivated the various forms of prayer such as worship, thanksgiving and petition. With regard to the higher forms of prayer, Thomas stresses that Jesus' human spirit did not need to rise to God since he was always united to God; aware of God as someone above him, he always enjoyed the vision of him.[57] His inner "abiding" with the Father was an uninterrupted song of worship and jubilant thanks. Then in Question 21 Thomas discusses Christ's prayer of petition. Whereas in many of his commentaries on Scripture, as was traditional, he explained the prayer of Jesus by referring to the need to give an example of prayer, in the *Summa theologiae* he goes beyond this and links the theological explanation of the petition of Jesus with his remarks on the doctrine of two wills in Christ. Thus he writes:

> Prayer is a way of unfolding to God our desires so that he may fulfill them. Now if Christ had only one will, the divine, there would be no question of his praying.[58] In fact there are two wills in Christ, one divine, the other human; and the human will by itself is incapable of effecting its desires; for this it needs divine help. It follows from this that Christ as man and as possessing a human will needs to pray.[59]

Thomas's remarks in the second article are important for the connection of our theme (Jesus' life of prayer) with devotion to the Heart of Jesus. The question is, Did the Savior pray with emotion (*secundum sensualitatem*)? The answer draws a distiction: one cannot pray with emotion if this implies that prayer is an effect of the emotion. Prayer must in fact rise above the realm of

[54] III, 48, 2.
[55] *Super Io. evang.* c. 8, lectio 1, N. 1139.
[56] *Super epist. ad Hebr.*, c. 4, lectio 3, N. 235.
[57] III, 21, 1 ad 3.
[58] III, 21, 1.
[59] Ibid.

the senses, for it is an act of the reason. On the other hand, one can pray with emotion if by this is meant that the prayer puts into words the emotion of longing and the longing of the simple will (*voluntas simplex, quae consideratur ut natura*).[60] Thus Christ prayed in Gethsemane. Furthermore the spirit (*cor*) may overflow on to the flesh, to the extent that the sensuous desire follows the movement of the spiritual, as Psalm 84:3 says in the Person of Christ: "My heart and my flesh sing for joy to the living God."

In his prayer the Savior thanked his Father for the gifts already contained in his human nature, acknowledging his father as their origin. Similarly Christ besought him in prayer for whatever his human nature lacked, for example, the glorification of his body.[61] "The very glory that Christ sought for himself in prayer was relevant to the salvation of others, 'He rose again for our justification' (Rom 4:25). Consequently even the prayer that he uttered in his own name was in some degree for the benefit of others."[62]

In the last article of this question on the prayer of Christ, basing himself on Hebrews 5:7 ("In the days of his flesh, Jesus offered up prayers and supplications, with loud cries and tears, to him who was able to save him from death"), Thomas observes that Christ willed with his rational will only those things that he knew to be the will of God. Thus every unqualified will on the part of Christ, including his human will, was fulfilled, because it accorded with God.[63]

Thomas deals with the topic of Christ's atoning self-surrender in Question 22 on the priesthood of Christ, and also in Question 48 on the effects of the Savior's sufferings. Since the priest's specific Office is that of a mediator, bringing the prayers of the people before God and in some degree making satisfaction for their sins, we must attribute this to Jesus in the highest degree and call him Priest.[64] For Thomas, on the authority of the Epistle to the Hebrews, "the propitiatory Office of the priesthood is central" because he sees man in his concrete situation, that is, as a sinner.[65] By freely surrendering himself to death for us, Christ has blotted out our sins, won grace, and guaranteed complete fulfillment in heaven. Thus Christ as man was simultaneously sin-offering, peace-offering and burnt-offering.[66]

Not only has he won the grace whereby our hearts are turned back to God; he has also taken upon himself the punishment of sin. "Christ made full reparation for us for 'He has borne our infirmities and carried our

---

[60] No doubt this also refers to the desire of the simple will (*voluntas simplex, quae consideratur ut natura*). Cf. III, 21, 3.

[61] III, 21, 3.

[62] III, 21, 3 ad 3.

[63] III, 21, 4.

[64] III, 22, 1.

[65] Cf. A. Hoffmann in the German edition of the *Summa*, vol. 26, 495.

[66] III, 22, 2.

sorrows.' "[67] "Now the purpose of Christ's sacrifice was not any temporal benefit; it consists rather in those eternal gifts that we lay hold on through his death; for Christ is 'a high priest of the good things to come' (Heb 9:11)". That is also why the priesthood of Christ is said to be eternal.[68] Just as the High Priest of the Old Law entered the Holy of Holies once a year, "Christ has entered into the Holy of Holies, that is, into heaven, furnishing a way of entry for us by the power of his own blood that is shed for us here on earth."[69] "While it is true that the Passion and death of Christ are never to be repeated, nevertheless the efficacy of his sacrifice remains for ever, 'By one oblation he hath perfected for ever them that are sanctified' (Heb 10:14)."[70]

Thomas devotes special attention to the basis, extent and intensity of Jesus' sufferings in satisfaction for our sins. "The liberation of man through the Passion of Christ was consonant with both his mercy and his justice. With justice, because by his Passion Christ made satisfaction for the sin of the human race, and man was freed through the justice of Christ. With mercy, because since man was by himself unable to satisfy for the sin of all human nature, . . . God gave him his Son to do so. . . ."[71]

God's design for our redemption was highly appropriate, because in it we see how much God loves us and are challenged to love him in return. It has also given us an example of obedience, humility and justice and has shown us the necessity of keeping away from sin.[72]

Christ submitted to all forms of suffering in order to show us the greatness of his love and the vast compass and ramifications of sin.[73] The pain experienced by Christ on account of the sins of others exceeded the pain of every penitent man, since his pain proceeded from a greater wisdom and love, which increases the pain involved. It was also greater because he was suffering simultaneously for the sins of all, according to Isaiah 53:4: "Surely he has borne our grief."[74] Christ suffered these pains with his entire soul, because the soul is so wedded to the body that it is entirely present in every part of the body, and thus the pains penetrated (*perveniebant*) into all faculties of the soul.[75]

So we come to the theme of the death of Jesus as an atoning sacrifice. Thomas points out that, properly speaking, a sacrifice is an act of reverence due to God in reconciliation. He quotes St. Augustine's famous definition ("a true sacrifice is every work performed for the purpose of being united to God

[67] III, 22, 3.
[68] III, 22, 5.
[69] Ibid.
[70] III, 22, 5 ad 2.
[71] III, 46, 1 ad 3.
[72] III, 46, 3.
[73] III, 46, 5 ad 3.
[74] III, 46, 6 ad 4.
[75] III, 46, 7.

in holy fellowship",[76] but sharpens it in terms of atonement. In Jesus' freely willed self-offering as an atoning sacrifice, Thomas sees the paradigm of all sacrifice whatsoever. Together with Augustine, however, he indicates that Chirst's sacrifice has the greatest possible power of union through love; in offering himself, Christ was identical with that which he offered, with God to whom he offered, and with us for whom he offered, making us one in him.[77]

The unifying effect of Jesus' love surely could not be better described. Thomas repeatedly says that it is because of Jesus' love that his sacrifice of his own life, his own flesh, was so pleasing to God.[78] "Christ, suffering in a loving and obedient spirit, offered more to God than was demanded in recompense for all the sins of mankind, because first, the love that led him to suffer was a great love; second, the life he laid down in atonement was of great dignity, since it was the life of God and of man; and third, his suffering was all-embracing and his pain so great. . . ."[79] Thus Christ's suffering is a superabundant atonement for our sins and the sins of the whole world (1 Jn 2:2).

In this connection Thomas points out that we and Christ form one mystical Person (quasi una persona mystica).[80] This implies, first, that Christ's atonement is regarded by the Father as if he has not performed it alone, but together with us.[81] But it follows that we must actively share in Christ's atoning sacrifice. Hence in his commentary on Colossians 1:24 (". . . in my flesh I complete what is lacking in Christ's afflictions for the sake of his body . . ."), Thomas refers to this same teaching that Christ and his Church form a single mystical Person.[82] In fact he tries to explicate this relation of Head and members by using his doctrine of the unity of the human being: the Mystical Body of Christ is the fullness (plenitudo) and completion of Christ in somewhat the same way that our natural body constitutes a certain fullness of the soul (quaedam plenitudo animae). In the absence of this completion of body and members, the soul could not fully (plene) develop its powers.[83] This shows how important it is to share in Christ's atonement in the way the Devotion to the Heart of Jesus, for instance, seeks to do.

---

[76] De civitate dei, X, 6.

[77] III, 48, 3.

[78] III, 48, 3 ad 1; ad 3.

[79] III, 48, 2.

[80] III, 48, 2 ad 1; De veritate, 29, 7.

[81] III, 69, 2.

[82] Super epist. ad Col., c. 1, lectio 6, N. 61.

[83] Super epist. ad Eph., c. 1, lectio 8, N. 71 [Commentary on Saint Paul's Epistle to the Ephesians (see n.45 above), 81f.]. In the Catena aurea, Super evang. Lucae, 15, textus 1, Thomas adds a few lines from Gregory the Great (on Lk 15:6 "Rejoice with me, for I have found my sheep which was lost"): "quia videlicet eius est gaudium vita nostra, et cum nos ad caelum reducimur, solemnitatem laetitiae illius implemus."

In passing we should note the significance of the *quasi una persona* for the theology of grace: the fullness of grace in Christ, our Head, becomes a well-spring of grace for us.[84] Thomas uses the image of a stream of life flowing forth from Christ, which, provided we put no obstacle in the way, actually pours a spiritual sense and the virtues into us,[85] so that Christ is even said to be our life, since he is the beginning and the cause of our supernatural life and all our acts.[86]

This efficient causality of Christ belongs to his Person in his human nature, and particularly to his sufferings that issue from love and possess a spiritual power through his union with the Godhead.[87] It also adds to the meaning of his Resurrection, which, by divine power, acts as an efficient cause at all times and places.[88] And this is the power that is at work in the sacraments.

Furthermore, the life and work of Jesus is also an exemplary cause for us. Thomas discusses Christ's exemplary causality in Question 40 of his Christology (whether Christ had to live among men and have dealings with them), giving an affirmative answer: Jesus' actions were intended to teach us.[89] This applies particularly to Jesus' actions insofar as they express an inner attitude, as exemplified in the temptations, in his prayer and in his obedience to the Father's will. In his treatise *De perfectione vitae spiritualis*[90] Thomas cites the example of the obedience of Jesus, who came down from heaven not to do his will but the will of him who sent him. Thus, says Thomas, Jesus founded religious life, for since he set the pattern by subordinating his human will to the divine will, we too can subordinate our will entirely to God and to those of our fellow men who are set above us as God's servants.

He says the same with regard to evangelical poverty in the little work *Contra retrahentes homines a religionis ingressu*.[91] In his treatment of the Christian virtues Thomas repeatedly justifies our calls for a certain attitude, founding his basic *sed contra* argument on the example of Jesus.[92] Important too are observations on the words of Jesus, "I have given you an example, that you also should do as I have done to you" (Jn 13:15); in human affairs actions speak louder than words. For a man chooses and does what seems good to him, and what this "good" is, is revealed far more clearly by his actually choosing it, than by talking about choosing it. The example of one human being would scarcely be sufficient for the whole human race to follow, and so the example of the Son of God was given us, infallible and adequate to all life situations.

---

[84] III, 8; *Super Io. evang.*, c. I, lectio 8, N. 190.
[85] *Super epist. ad Eph.*, c. I, lectio 8, N. 69.
[86] *Super epist. ad Phil.*, c. I, lectio 3, N. 32.
[87] III, 19, I; 48, 6; 48, 6 ad 2.
[88] III, 56, I.
[89] III, 56, I ad 3.
[90] C. 10, N. 603.
[91] C. 15.
[92] II–II, 76, 2; 83, 5; 101, 2.

This is also the case because he is the Father's masterpiece (*ars Patris*): as he was the prototype of creation, he is to be likewise the prototype of justification.[93]

Now we must address the question of devotion to Christ, and in particular worshipful devotion to his inner life. Thomas treats the subject of the adoration due to Christ in the context of what is appropriate for Christ in terms of being and development. In common with Thomas we must distinguish between adoration in the strict sense (*latria*), shown only to God, and veneration (*dulia* or *hyperdulia*), which may be shown to creatures. A further important distinction is that between the person thus honored and the reasons for the veneration (e.g., knowledge or virtue).

Veneration, properly speaking, is accorded to the entire person, even if one only takes the person's hand or kisses his foot, for instance. These parts of the body are not honored in themselves; in them the whole is honored. Now since in Christ there is only a single Person, there can only be one worship. However, if we look at the reason for it, we can speak of a pluriform worship (*plures adorationes*). Keeping this distinction in mind, we can speak on the one hand of the adoration of Christ, which is directed to him as the incarnate Word of God, and on the other of a veneration of his sacred humanity, possessing as it does all the gifts of grace. In this latter case we no longer speak of worship in the strict sense. In itself, veneration of the sacred humanity, or of one of its preeminent effects or perfections, is in fact *hyperdulia*, highest veneration. So we can contemplate and venerate specifically Christ's human love and his Sacred Heart. But the direction of the veneration will then also move toward the loving Person of Jesus; thus this highest form of veneration will pass over into adoration.[94]

This also applies to the veneration of images of Jesus. No veneration is due to images as material things, but if, in being drawn to the representation of Christ we are carried further to him who is depicted there, the veneration or adoration due in this case is the same as that addressed to Christ.[95] In this context Thomas mentions the veneration and worship of the Cross of Christ.[96] (We may note parenthetically that, according to Thomas, it is fitting that Christ's Wounds should eternally remain in his glorified body: they are thus a sign of his merciful love.)

At this point the question arises, to what extent does Thomas see the heart as the symbol of the inner life (or of a part of it). A full discussion of this topic would exceed the scope of this paper. Here we can merely note that Thomas often uses the word *cor* in a technical philosophical sense, to mean the vital

[93] *Super Io. evang.*, c. 13, lectio 3, N. 1781.
[94] III, 25, 2.
[95] III, 25, 3.
[96] III, 25, 4.

principle of animal life and of movement.[97] To that extent the heart is not seen as the principle of cognitive life.[98] But where Thomas adopts biblical usage, he equates *cor* with *spiritus*.[99] He also thinks of the heart as the organ of the passions, in the sense that the motions and affections of the sensitive part of the soul are joined with a powerful motion (*commotio*) of the body, and in particular of the heart.[100] In this way love produces a *dilatatio cordis*. Grief has the greatest effect.[101] Thus for Thomas the heart is not an exclusive symbol for love. Yet there is an analogy between the love of Jesus and his physical heart: just as the heart is the principle of bodily movement, so love is the central moving force behind all affections and psychic activities. All that we do is done on the basis of some love or other,[102] and this was true preeminently in the case of Jesus.

Let us return to the subject of devotion to and veneration of Jesus. According to Thomas we venerate Christ not only by our adoration, praise, thanksgiving and petitionary prayer: all our moral life is meant to be an expression of the virtue of *religio*. Like the Savior himself, the Christian who dedicates himself to God in love and obedience performs an act of *religio*.

We can see how Thomas himself venerated the Son of God in his human nature by looking at his prayers and poems, such as the *Lauda Sion*. Here Thomas addresses the Person of Christ; the human nature of Jesus is the way of approach to God. He sees the saving events as a manifestation of God's merciful love and righteousness, and he never loses sight of the fulfillment of the redemption in the homeland of heaven. Sentimentality in the contemplation and veneration of the life of Jesus is entirely foreign to him — at the same time Thomas devotes great attention to his merciful kindness. In Thomas, veneration of the sacred humanity of Jesus does not focus so much on individual parts of Jesus' body; rather it addresses the virtues and the love of Jesus, which he sees as an expression of the mystery of God.

[97] III, 90, 3 ad 3; I, 20, 1 ad 1; In IV Sent., d. 14, q. 1, ad 2.

[98] III, 90, 3 ad 3: ". . . *sed caput est principium sensuum et motus*".

[99] Cf. *Super epist. I ad Thess.*, c. 5, lectio 1, N. 120; *Super Io. evang.*, c. 14, lectio 1, N. 1850: "*cor, id est spiritus.*"

[100] *Q.d. de veritate*, 22, 2.

[101] *Super Io. evang.*, c. 13, lectio 4, N. 1796.

[102] I-II, 28, 6: "*Omne agens, quodcumque sit, agit quamcumque actionem ex aliquo amore.*"

KEY ISSUES IN MEDIEVAL SACRED HEART PIETY

Sixty years ago K. Richstätter[1] and A. Hammon[2] wrote pioneering works on the history of Devotion to the Heart of Jesus. Toward the end of the Second World War, Hugo Rahner[3] developed new ideas and outlined a new history of the Devotion, but so far his work has not been further developed. E. Agostini[4] clarified matters by distinguishing four stages in the development of the Devotion. The substantial collection of essays entitled *Cor Salvatoris*[5] fills in a number of gaps in the history. Stimulated, no doubt, by Pius XII's encyclical *Haurietis aquas*,[6] there appeared in 1959 the comprehensive two-volume work *Cor Jesu*.[7] In its second volume, eminent writers portray the devotion to the Heart of Jesus in the Church's great and ancient religious orders (although the Carthusians were omitted).

Karl Rahner's interpretations of the object of the cult of the Heart of Jesus have not always met with approval.[8] His views were seen in the context of the whole discussion in the doctoral thesis of Michael J. Walsh.[9] For years, however, little work has been done in the historical area. In the meantime

---

[1] *Die Herz-Jesu-Verehrung des deutschen Mittelalters*, 2nd ed. (Munich-Regensburg, 1924) [the abridged English edition: *Illustrious Friends of the Sacred Heart* (London 1930)].

[2] Histoire de la dévotion au Sacré-Coeur, 5 vols. (Paris, 1923–39); cf. also J. Saenz de Tejada, *Bibliografía de la devoción al corazón de Jésus* (Bilbao, 1952). Valuable supplementary material, especially with regard to those writers who mediated the Fathers to the Middle Ages, is to be found in C. G. Kanters, *Le Coeur de Jésus dans la littérature chrétienne des douze premiers siècles* (Bruges-Avignon, 1930).

[3] "Grundzüge einer Geschichte der Herz-Jesu-Verehrung" in ZAM 18 (1943): 61–83.

[4] *Il Cuore di Gesù: Storia, teologia, practiche, promesse* (Bologna, 1960).

[5] J. Stierli, ed., *Heart of the Savior: A Symposium on Devotion to the Sacred Heart* (Herder, 1957). H. Schwendimann's contribution appeared separately: *Herz-Jesu-Verehrung heute* (Regensburg, 1974).

[6] AAS 48 (1956): 309–53.

[7] A. Bea et al., ed., *Cor Jesu*, 2 vols. (Rome, 1959). The following also refer to the encyclical: J. Leclercq, "Les Sources liturgiques de la dévotion au Sacré-Coeur" in VS 104 (1961): 377–93; J. Calveras, "Objeto completo de la devoción al Corazón de Jesús" in EE 37 (1962): 443–56; L. Fernandez de la Fuente, "El P. Ordeñana, S.J., en la controversia en torno al objeto de culto al Corazón de Jesús" in MCom 306 (1972): 293–328; P. Jobert, "Fondements de la théologie du Sacré-Coeur" in RThom 76 (1976): 591–98.

[8] As well as those already mentioned, cf. A. Morgenroth, "Devotion to the Sacred Heart", *Review for Religious* 24 (St. Louis, 1965): 418–28; G. de Becker, "La Théologie actuelle du Sacré-Coeur" in Div 13 (1968): 173–90.

[9] *The Heart of Christ in the Writings of Karl Rahner: An Investigation of Its Christological Foundation as an Example of the Relationship between Theology and Spirituality*, AnGr 209 (Rome, 1977).

research has produced editions of the works of many authors, in particular the pseudepigrapha, which are often an important source in the history of spirituality. So a new presentation of the history of devotion to the Heart of Jesus, utilizing these results, is long overdue.

The most this paper can do is to indicate a few relationships that are often too easily ignored and to uncover the key issues in medieval devotion to the Heart of Jesus, which was a determining factor in the spirituality of the early Jesuits.[10] In fact, this was how the Jesuit Order came to be one of the chief propagators and protagonists of the cult of the Heart of Jesus in modern times and to plant the Devotion in the New World.[11]

First, in order to dispel the stubbornly held prejudice that represents medieval piety as something extreme, we shall look at the early Fathers (I), whose approach was taken up in the early Middle Ages and then developed throughout the period (II). Then we shall draw our observations together by reference to concrete models of devotion to the Heart of the Savior (III).

I. Prelude

"Heart" signifies the deepest and innermost part of a man, the core of his personality. To venerate a person's heart is to venerate the person in terms of his most original, interior and creative center.[12] As a result of the hypostatic union, the organic Heart of Jesus represents the whole Person of the incarnate Word of the Father and manifests the love of God and of the Redeemer. This revelation of divine love reaches its climax in the opening of the heart of Jesus: the Pierced heart proclaims the Redeemer's death and the opening proclaims the access to life. It remains a powerful image, drawing us into the union of love, of the transition from death to life.[13] It has an objective role in redemption, displaying the source of all the messianic treasures of salvation.[14] So much for fundamental historical observations. H. Rahner[15] pleads for a distinction, in the history of devotion to the Heart of Jesus, between the knowledge and the cult of the Heart of Jesus; between theological knowledge and the knowledge

[10] On Ludolph of Saxony (d. 1378) and St. Alphonsus Rodriguez (d. 1617) cf. M. Barth, *Die Herz-Jesu-Verehrung im Elsass von 12. Jahrhundert bis auf die Gegenwart* (Freiburg, 1928), 143. On Johannes Justus Lanspergius of Landsberg (d. 1539) and St. Peter Canisius, cf. M. Boutrais, *Der Karthäuser Landsberger, ein Vorläufer der sel. Maria Margaretha Alacoque im 16. Jahrhundert und die Andacht zum göttlichen Herzen Jesu*, trans. B. Hermes (Mainz, 1880); H. Rossmann, "Lanspergius" in DSp 9: 230–38, esp. 236, and see nn.87–93 below.

[11] F. Mateos, "Principios del culto al Corazón de Jesús en America", in RF 164 (1961): 205–16.

[12] Cf. K. Rahner, "Some Theses on the Theology of the Devotion" in J. Stierli, *Heart of the Saviour*, 138.

[13] G. de Becker, "La Théologie", 176–79.

[14] J. Stierli, "Devotion to the Sacred Heart from the End of Patristic Times to St. Margaret Mary" in *Heart of the Saviour*, 60.

[15] "Grundzüge", 64; on what follows, ibid., 76.

that comes from personal love; between private and public devotion (i.e., ecclesial devotion, such as is found preeminently in Mass and Office). Whether such a separation can be maintained in the affective theology of the Fathers and the monastic theologians is something we shall have to consider, for as Rahner himself admits it is difficult to discover much about private prayer in the earliest Christian times because of meager source material. There is little that would bear on the contemplation of the Lord's wounded side, a practice that has been a feature of the Church's life since its inception. Moreover, Rahner rightly repeats the ancient maxim that private devotion always precedes official cult. Thus where we come across an official pronouncement in a document of the early Church, it will be highly significant. It is noteworthy that the texts cited are largely from the area of the Liturgy.

Reflection and meditation on the Wounds and the open side of the Lord often focus on biblical texts, in particular, of course, John 19:33, but also Isaiah 53:5: "But he was wounded for our transgressions, . . . and with his stripes we are healed."

The Song of Solomon 2:14 ("O my dove, in the clefts of the rock. . . .") is linked to 1 Corinthians 10:4: ". . . all drank the same supernatural drink. For they drank from the supernatural Rock which followed them, and the Rock was Christ." The Vulgate of Songs 4:9 has: "You have wounded my heart, my sister, my bride, you have wounded my heart." And Ambrose[16] refers Songs 1:4 ("The king has brought me into his chamber") directly to Christ's Passion: it refers to "the time of the Passion, of the pierced side, of the shedding of his blood. . . ."[17]

Nowadays Origen (d. 254) is generally held to be the founder of medieval spirituality. His meditations on Songs 4:9 point the way to the veneration of the Lord's Wounds: "How wonderful, how rapturous, to receive a wound at the hand of love!"[18] In a very concrete sacramental sense Origen sees the benefits of redemption and the cleansing from sins welling from the Redeemer's side: "Every purification from sin, including the purification sought through penance, needs the help of him from whose side 'water' and 'blood' (Jn 19:54) flowed."[19]

The figure of John the Evangelist plays an important part in the development of devotion to the Heart of Jesus. At the Last Supper he lay close to the breast of Jesus (Jn 13:25), and Origen comments: "This signifies that John rested in Jesus' innermost heart (in principali cordis Jesu) and in the inner meaning of his teaching."[20] H. Rahner[21] is inclined to see here a not entirely

---

[16] For further technical details on these writers, cf. W. Baier, *Untersuchungen zu den Passionsbetrachtungen in der "Vita Christi" des Ludolf von Sachsen — Ein quellenkritischer Beitrag zu Leben und Werk Ludolfs und zur Geschichte der Passionstheologie*, 3 vols., Analecta Cartusiana 44/1-3. (Salzburg, 1977).

[17] *In Ps* 118 I/1, 16; CSEL 62:16.

[18] *In Cant. Cant.* hom 2, 8: GCS 33:53.

[19] *Lev.* hom 8, 10: GCS 28:411.

[20] *Com. Cant Cant.* 1: GCS 33:93.

[21] "Grundzüge", 68.

harmless spiritualizing tendency, a reluctance to speak of the true physical nature of the wounded side of the man Jesus. But unless we are prepared to assume that Origen's homilies betray a different view from that in his theoretical theological writings, we must regard H. Rahner's conclusion as groundless. The preceding quotation shows this, as does the research of F. Bertrand,[22] who has discovered in Origen a concrete life-of-Jesus spirituality, which is not surpassed in originality even by the Cistercians and Franciscans of the Middle Ages. According to this spirituality, every experience of union must be rooted in discipleship of Jesus.

The same theme is found in Ephrem the Syrian (d. 373). In this representative of a decidedly graphic theology of the Passion, too, we find several topics that will become familiar in medieval piety. To the Mary who stands beneath the Cross, Ephrem says:

> Christ was not ungrateful for your love; the son of your womb gave and entrusted you—to the son of his bosom. You caressed him as a child upon your breast—he too, on his breast, has experienced caresses. On the Cross he restored to you all that you had given him, all he owed to you for bringing him up. . . . From your breast he drank visible milk—John drank invisible mysteries at his breast. With confidence the Christ-Child approached your breast—in confidence the disciple approached his breast and rested there. Since you miss his voice, he has given you his harp to console you. . . . He left you, Mary, and yet he has not left you; for in that disciple he came back in order to be with you.[23]

Here, resting on Christ's breast leads to a deep and intimate friendship with Jesus, best described in the language of mystical union.

Paulinus of Nola (d. 431) apparently links John 7:3f. with John 13:25: the John who "lay on the Lord's breast" was "transported by the Holy Spirit".[24]

From about 586 we have the first realistic and fully formed portrayal of the crucifixion in the form of a harmony of the Gospels: the *Rabbula Gospels*.[25] This compilation, though from a Syrian source actually originates in the private prayer life of a monk of the Zagbar monastery in Mesopotamia.

John Chrysostom (d. 407) was substantially influenced by Syrian monasticism. He preaches a very practical Passion spirituality: since baptism we can say that "We are all one, for we issue together from the side of Christ."[26] The opening of the side of the Crucified proclaims that redemption is accomplished

---

[22] *Mystique de Jésus chez Origène*, Théologie 23 (Paris, 1951).

[23] *Des Heiligen Ephraem des Syrers Hymnen de virginitate* 25, 2. 3. 5: GSCO 224: 78f.

[24] *Ep.* 21, 4: CSEL 29: 151.

[25] C. Ceccheli, G. Furlani, M. Salmi, *The Rabbula Gospels* (Olten-Lausanne, 1959). On interpretation cf. J. Leclercq, "Les Sources", 383; P. Hinz, *Deus Homo: Das Christusbild von den Ursprüngen bis zur Gegenwart*, vol 1: *Das erste Jahrtausend* (Berlin, 1973), 96.

[26] *In Epist. ad Col.* 2 n.6, 4: PG 62: 341.

and announces the beginning of salvation in the Church: "We must receive the Church's sacraments with such dedication as if they came from the very side of Christ. For in fact access to the sacraments is through Christ's wounded side."[27] Ludolph of Saxony (d. 1378)[28] and Jordan of Quedlinburg OESA (d. 1370/80)[29] quote this passage before that from the commentary of St. Augustine (d. 430) on St. John's Gospel, which speaks in almost identical terms: from the open side of Christ "flow the Church's sacraments, without which one cannot enter true life".[30]

In prayer we leave behind the level of mere knowledge and theoretical understanding. It is scarcely possible to separate the cult of the wounded side from that of the Heart of Jesus. Around A.D. 215 Hippolytus of Rome had given this as a reason for praying at the ninth hour: "At that hour Christ's side was pierced and he poured forth water and blood."[31]

For the most part, the Ethiopic Church of the end of the fifth century clung to Monophysitism. But S. Salaville[32] defends it against the accusation of K. Adam and J. A. Jungmann which stated that, in its anti-Arianism, it had disdained the humanity of Christ. A book of prayers refers, for the sixth hour, to the nailing of Christ in these terms: "At the sixth hour say thrice: Alleluia to the Father, Alleluia to the Son, Alleluia to the Holy Spirit, for it was at this hour that they crucified the Lord and water and blood poured forth from his pierced side."[33] In another prayer Christ is called the "friend of men". At the ninth hour there is further reference to the wounded side: "At this hour the Lord, the life of believers, was pierced, and from his side flowed water and blood."[34] The Ethiopic litanies were for private use and unfortunately are only preserved in manuscripts of the eighteenth century. But although we cannot reach any certainty about their actual age, they are to be treated as original Ethiopic material.[35] There we find in the Litany to Christ: "O Thou whose side they pierced with a lance for our sakes, hear us, our God and our Redeemer, O Christ. O Thou whose blood was shed for us, hear us. . . ."[36] And in a Litany of Mary we read: "O Mary, my Queen, I

---

[27] *Hom. Io.* 85, 3: PG: 59, 463.

[28] *Vita Christi* II, 64 (Paris, 1865), 675b.

[29] *Meditationes de passione Christi*, art. 63 (Strasbourg, 1483).

[30] *Tr. Io. Ev.* 120, 2: CChr. 36: 661; cf. also S. Tromp, *De nativitate Ecclesiae ex corde Christi* (Rome, 1933).

[31] *Hippolyte de Rome: La Tradition apostolique d'après les anciennes versions*, 2nd ed. (Paris, 1968); also appears as SC 11: 128.

[32] *Studia orientalia liturgico-theologica* (Rome, 1940), 177, n.1.

[33] Ibid., 177.

[34] Ibid., 180.

[35] E. Hammerschmidt, *Äthiopische liturgische Texte der Bodleian Library in Oxford* (Berlin, 1960), 11–15.

[36] Now reproduced in R. Scherschel, *Der Rosenkranz—das Jesusgebet des Westerns* (Freiburg, 1979), 168. Cf. also: S. Grébaut, "Litanies de Jésus-Christ" in *Aethiopica* 3 (1935): 13–19, esp. 18.

take refuge in the piercing of the side of your Beloved Son. O Mary, my Queen, I take refuge in the pouring of blood and water from the side of your Beloved Son."[37]

II. Development

1. In the Context of Other Forms of Christ-centered Purity

If we locate the beginnings of medieval thought in late antiquity, as H. Rahner does,[38] we can speak of an organic transition from the initial devotion to the Heart of Jesus to a developed stage exhibiting a distinctive Heart-of-Jesus language.[39] The patristic elements were taken up and enriched with new ideas, in particular with a personal and affective quality. Probably the development spread from Syria, by way of Spain, southern France and Ireland, and thence back to the Continent. It was the Syrian popes who introduced the phrase "You pierced your Savior's side with a lance" into the Good Friday Liturgy. They are in the tradition of Melito of Sardis, whose "reproaches", in the first recorded Easter sermon (ca. 175), state: "You made ready for him sharp nails, false tongues, chains and scourging, vinegar, gall and the sword. . . ."[40]

Now two theologians of the Carolingian period are cited. St. Bede the Venerable (d. 765) attributes Songs 4:9 to Christ, who "by speaking of his wounded Heart expresses the great love he bears for the Church".[41] Haymon of Auxerre (ca. 850) adopts this interpretation almost literally and goes on to say: "Through Thy love Thou hast caused me to be wounded on the Cross."[42]

The Benedictine John of Fécamp (ca. 990–1078) is one of the most important initiators of a concrete Passion spirituality that concerns Christ's human feelings, involving a loving and almost inflamed veneration of his Wounds and, germinally, of his Heart. The *Liber Meditationum*[43] and the *Manuale*[44] are essentially his works. In the twelfth century they were favorite spiritual reading in the Benedictine and Carthusian monasteries, comparable to the

[37] R. Scherschel, *Rosenkranz*, 170.

[38] "Grundzüge", 72.

[39] J. Stierli, *Heart of the Saviour*, 75; F. Schwendimann, *Herz-Jesu-Verehrung*, 17.

[40] Meliton v. Sardes, *Vom Passa: Die älteste christliche Osterpredigt*, trans. J. Blank (Freiburg, 1963), 122n. 78f. [Melito of Sardis, "Homily on the Passion", ed. C. Bonner; *Studies and Documents* XII, ed. K. & S. Lake (1940)]

[41] *In Cant. Cant.* exp. 4: PL 91: 1139.

[42] *En. in Cant. Cant.* 4: PL 117: 320.

[43] PL 40: 901–42; c. 1–9, 12–25, 27–33, 35–37 are undoubtedly by John of Fécamp.

[44] PL 40: 951–68; c. 4–12 are undoubtedly by him.

later *Imitation of Christ*. In the "school" of John of Fécamp his spirituality was further developed and his works were completed and imitated. Thus he prays to the Crucified:

> White shines the naked breast, red the bloody side, the heart pants, exhausted. . . . Where is thy kindness, thy love? Where is pity?[45] I pray thee, by the saving Wounds thou didst suffer on the Cross for our salvation, whence that precious blood flowed by which we have been redeemed, wound this sinful soul for whom thou hast deigned to die. Wound it with the fiery, sharp arrow of thy overflowing love . . . , so that my soul may be able to say to thee: "I am wounded by thy love".[46]

The following excerpts from a long prayer show how, indirectly, through the Benedictine's yearning for a loving heart after the pattern of Christ's, he called into being a spirituality of the Heart of Jesus:

> Give me a contrite heart, a pure heart . . . , a gentle heart . . . , an honest heart, a devoted heart, a chaste heart . . . and a simple heart that thinks no ill of the brethren, a heart that shares in the suffering and distress of others and rejoices in their goodness and virtues. . . .[47]

A somewhat later colleague, also from Normandy, is Goscelin of St. Bertin, OSB (d. 1090). He too recommends his readers to contemplate in faith the Wounds in the feet, the hands, and the side of Christ, "which redeem our senses so that we can live with him in his love with thanksgiving".[48]

Very clearly aware of human sinfulness and the vulnerability of salvation, John of Fécamp is all the more grateful for redemption: "The nails and the spear tell me that I am really reconciled to Christ if I love him. Longinus opened Christ's love to me with his spear; I enter and rest there in safety."[49]

No doubt influenced by Augustine,[50] either John of Fécamp[51] or an

---

[45] John of Fécamp [Pseudo = Anselm], *Or.* 2: PL 158: 861.

[46] *Liber Med.* 37: PL 40: 935; a better edition in *Confessio theologica* 3, 32 in J. Leclercq/J.-P. Bonnes, *Un Maître de la vie spirituelle au XIᵉ siècle* (Paris, 1946), 180f. (Particularly applied to the Wound in Christ's side by Ludolph of Saxony, *Vita Christi* II, 64 (Paris, 1865), 675b; see n. 110 below.)

[47] *Conf. theol.* 1, 7: ibid., 133; full discussion in GuL 54 (1981): 316f. It is highly reminiscent of a prayer to the Heart of Jesus by Dionysius Ryckel, Denis the Carthusian (d. 1471): J. Stierli, *Heart of the Saviour*, 90.

[48] C. H. Talbot, "The *Liber confortatorius* of Goscelin of St. Bertin", in AnMo 3 (1955): 1–117 (also in StAns 37), 110.

[49] *Man.* 24: PL 40: 961. Fairly certainly by John of Fécamp or someone of his school.

[50] *De. s. virg.* 54, 55: CSEL 41: 300: "*Internis luminibus inspicite vulnera pendentis, cicatrices resurgentis, sanguinem morientis. . . .*" An unknown 12th-century writer (Ps. Augustine, *Serm. ad fr. in eremo* 32: PL 40: 1293) adds: ". . . *caput inclinatum ad vocandum et parcendum, cor apertum ad diligendum, brachia extensa ad amplexandum. . . .*"

[51] *Man.* c. 23: PL 40: 961: "Extendit brachia sua in Cruce et expandit manus suas paratus in amplexus peccatorum. Inter brachia Salvatoris mei et vivere volo et mori cupio."

unknown author of the school of Anselm of Canterbury (d. 1109)[52] produced a "Meditation on the Crucified" devoted entirely to Christ's self-abnegating love, which invites all to come to him. Its aim is to transport the meditating soul into the yawning abyss of divine love—its focus is the Pierced Heart. The most widespread version is that attributed to Bernard, known to Ludolph and others before him:

> Who, beholding the disposition of Christ's body, is not transported to hope and confident petition? See, his head is bent to kiss, his arms are outstretched to embrace, his hands are pierced to give, his side is open to love, his feet are nailed to stay with us, his body has become pliable to be given to us.[53]

Bonaventure was very fond of this passage.[54] It is still to be found in the sixteenth century in G. J. Cisneros.[55]

But let us return to the eleventh century. Robert of Tombelaine, OSB (d. 1090), the continuator of Gregory the Great's *Commentary on the Song of Songs*, endeavors to refer Songs 2:14 to the Wound in the Lord's side, the memory of which brings healing.[56] Later, Bernard of Clairvaux will do the same.[57] Peter Damian, OSB (d. 1072) meditates upon John on Jesus' breast "in which are concealed all the treasures of wisdom and knowledge", which are richly poured out upon our poverty.[58] We find the same thing in Pseudo-Anselm (twelfth century): "How sweet he is in his opened side: for each opening shows us the riches of his kindness, that is, his Heart's love for us."[59] Subsequently Gottfried von Admont (d. 1165) speaks in much the same terms: John lay on the Lord's breast, drinking heavenly wisdom from the Heart within.[60]

Bernard of Clairvaux (d. 1153) is the dominant spiritual figure of the twelfth century, the one who gave new expression to the rich religious inheritance. His Heart-of-Jesus spirituality is found entirely in his *Sermons on the Song of Songs.*

---

[52] Ps.-Anselm, *Med.* X: PL 158: 761: "Dulcis Jesus in inclinatione capitis et morte, dulcis in extensione brachiorum, dulcis in apertione lateris, dulcis in confixione pedum clavo uno." *Med.* X. was not adopted into the critical edition of F. S. Schmitt. A. Hammon, *Histoire* II, 90 n.2, rightly attributes it to Anselm or a twelfth-century author, as does E. Agostini, *Il Cuore*, 29.

[53] *Vita Christi* II, 64 (Paris, 1865) 677b. Cf. my study (n.16 above), 223, 245.

[54] *Soliloquium* I, 39: BAC 28: 184; *De perf. vitae ad sorores* 6, 19: BAC 20: 372; also in the work *Vitis mystica* (not by Bonaventure), 24, 3: BAC 9: 507.

[55] *Obras compl.*, ed. C. Baraut, 2 vols. (Montserrat, 1965), 15.

[56] Ps.-Gregory, *Exp. in Cant. Cant.* 2, 15: PL 79: 499.

[57] *Serm. super Cant. Cant.* 61, 3: ed. Cist 2, 149; n.2 omits the reference to Robert of Tombelaine. [*On the Song of Songs* vol. 3 (Kalamazoo, Michigan-London-Oxford, 1976), 142].

[58] *Sermo* 43: PL 144: 853.

[59] *Med.* X: PL 158: 761; see n.52 above.

[60] *Hom.* 12: PL 174: 671.

As a supreme gesture of love he surrendered himself to death and from his own side produced the price of satisfaction that would placate his Father. . . . Utterly generous [redemption], for not a mere drop but a wave of blood flowed unchecked from the five Wounds of his body.[61]

So we see the continuing influence of the veneration of the holy blood and Wounds of the Lord. Sermon 61 is concerned with Songs 2:13f. and will thus be influenced by the traditional Heart-of-Jesus associations. First he speaks generally of Christ's Wounds, which, as symbols of his redeeming love, give Bernard a sense of security and peace, forgiveness and confidence. But the greatest revelation of love is the wounded heart:

But as for me, whatever is lacking in my own resources I appropriate for myself from the Heart of the Lord, which overflows with mercy. And there is no lack of clefts by which they are poured out. . . . "The iron pierced his soul" (Ps 104:18) and his Heart has drawn near so that he is no longer one who cannot sympathize with my weakness (Heb 4:15). The secret of his Heart is laid open through the clefts of his body; that mighty mystery of love is laid open, laid open too the tender mercies of our God, in which the morning sun from on high has risen upon us (Lk 1:78).[62]

Naturally, Bernard's veneration of Christ's wounded side has had an influence on his friend Aelred of Rievaulx OCist (d. 1167)[63] and others of his imitators and disciples, such as the German Pseudo-Anselm, Ekbert von Schönau, OSB (d. 1184), whose *Stimulus dilectionis* Bonaventure reworked in his *Lignum Vitae* numbers 18–31. The issue of the present reality of the saving events is evident in Ekbert's plea that the Father in eternity will not "turn his eyes from his Son's Wounds, and thus keep in mind how great a satisfaction for sins he has received from him."[64]

When Bonaventure beholds the Pierced Savior, he brings together all the biblical and patristic ideas—the Church is formed from the side of Jesus, the sacraments receive their power thence as sources of salvation, and all life is from the Lord's side:

Christ's beloved, arise and be like "the dove in the clefts of the rock. . ." (Sg 2:14). There press your lips to the source, and "with joy you will draw water from the wells of the Savior" (Is 12:3). For here is the "source which wells up from the place of bliss, dividing into four streams" (cf. Gn 2:10), pouring itself into the hearts of the godly, watering the whole earth and making it fruitful.[65]

---

[61] *Serm. s. Cant. Cant,* 22, 7: ed. Cist. 1, 333 [*On the Song of Songs* II: 19].

[62] Ibid., 61, 3–4: ed. Cist. 2, 150f. [*On the Song of Songs* III, 143].

[63] E.g., *De institutione inclusarum* 31: CChrCM 1: 671

[64] Ps.-Anselm, *Med.* IX: PL 158: 748–61. See also PL 189: 953–66; new ed. in F. W. E. Roth, *Die Visionen der hl. Elisabeth und die Schriften der Äbte Ekbert und Emecho von Schönau* (Brünn, 1884), 300; cf. Origen, *Io. Com.* 2, 8: GCS 10: 62.

[65] *Lignum vitae* n. 30: BAC 9: 304; cf. n. 17 above; taken over from *Vita Christi* II, 64 (Paris, 1865), 676b; see n.26 above.

To some extent the influential Franciscan mystic Jacopone da Todi (end of the thirteenth century) popularized the learned tradition in his *Stimulus amoris*:[66] "Happy the spear and nails privileged thus to make the opening! Had I been that spear, I would never have wanted to remove from Christ's side."[67] "He opened his side in the excess of love, in order to give you his Heart."[68]

Bernard's *Sermons on the Song of Songs* were not restricted to commentary and hence to the learned world—and the same applies to many of the texts quoted. So at an early stage he contributed to the literature of the life of Jesus and of the Passion and thus gained a wide influence. His sermons are used extensively for their theological profundity by an unknown Tuscan Franciscan in the epilogue to his *Meditationes vitae Christi*.[69] Written toward the end of the thirteenth century, it is the most widespread and most translated of all the works of Franciscan spirituality. Ludolph of Saxony, "the Carthusian", who wanted to create a *Summa evangelica*, first gathered together all the texts from the tradition of spirituality. With these in hand he interpreted the scriptural texts and presented a work in the form of a harmony of the Gospels. In this way, like rays of light through a prism, he brought to a single focus all that had been said in the past and in his own time on the subject of devotion to the Heart of Jesus, as we have pointed out several times, and fashioned from it his wide-ranging reflections on the piercing (in *Vita Christi*, part II, chap. 64). He regarded Bernard as the prime authority for the Heart-of-Jesus spirituality, which is of course one with veneration of the holy Wounds. A passage quoted by K. Richstätter[70] and J. Stierli[71] was taken over from Jordan of Saxony, OESA, or from an unknown source common to both,[72] and from Mechthild of Hackeborn.[73] Bearing in mind the Carthusians' generally admitted traditionalism and reserve toward innovations, Ludolph would not have adopted and transmitted this form of piety unless it had seemed to him to be tried, tested and theologically substantiated. In his caution regarding visions, which borders on repugnance, he divests Mechthild's passages of their visionary context, selects the masculine elements

[66] Quaracchi (1905; 2nd ed. 1949).
[67] *Stim.* 14: ed. Quaracchi, 74.
[68] Ibid., 74f.
[69] *Bonaventurae Op. Om.*, ed. Peltier, 12 vols., 509–630.
[70] *Illustrious Friends*, 177ff.
[71] *Heart of the Saviour*, 89.
[72] See nn.16,29 above. My views have not been changed by subsequent challenges, since many of my arguments have been simply ignored, e.g., by J. M. Willeumier-Schalij, "Is Michael de Massa de Auteur van de latijnse Grondtekst van het zgn. Pseudo-Bonaventura-Ludolphinaanse Leven van Jezus?" in *Nederlands Archief voor Kerkgeschiedenis* 60/1 (1980): 1-10, esp. 7; cf. EuA 57 (1981): 424f.
[73] See nn.78ff. below.

and values their ascetical-theological content only if these passages are not already found in earlier (as yet unknown) works on which Mechthild may have depended. Much from these latter works may have influenced Mechthild's visions via the Dominicans, who lived and worked in Helfta. So we can maintain that the first Carthusian[74] to work out the ascetical significance, for the inner life, of devotion to the Heart of the Redeemer was more receptive than creative; nevertheless, Ludolph greatly influenced its development in this period and in the time to come—for he was among the most read authors of the *devotio moderna*. The Carthusian Order, especially in Germany, was in any case already committed to the apostolate of the Heart of our Lord.

2. Growing Autonomy of the Devotion

In the twelfth century, out of the blue, in the Premonstratensian Abbey of Steinfeld in the Archdiocese of Cologne, we come across mature language and devotion to the Heart of Jesus in the form of the hymn *Summi Regis Cor Aveto*.[75] This hymn is ascribed for good reasons to St. Hermann Joseph von Steinfeld (d. 1241) but certainly belongs to the twelfth century. Whereas the first stanza addresses the Heart of the great King, the second shows how he has become such a king, why he is dear to us; it reveals the origin and goal of our whole perspective, namely, the life and Passion of the Lord:

Summi regis cor aveto!	Hail, great Heart of my great King!
Te saluto corde laeto,	Heart's delight thy praise to sing.
Te complecti me delectat;	Sweetest solace thy embrace,
Et hoc meum cor affectat,	To speak with thee face to face,
Ut ad te loquar animes.	Is my longing, Lord.
Quo amore vincebare,	With what love that Heart was torn,
Quo dolore torquebare,	What the sorrow it has borne,
Cum te totum exhaurires,	All its wealth of life to drain,
Ut te nobis impartires,	All its blood on me to rain,
Et me a morte tolleres!	Me to lift from death.

Love is impelled toward the Beloved and is filled with contrition for all that keeps them apart. To rest in his love means to actively share his life:

Da cor cordi sociare,	Let my heart to thee be bound,
Tecum Jesu vulnerari,	With thee, Jesus, feel thy Wound;
Nam cor cordi simulatur,	For then heart is like to heart
Si cor meum perforatur	When it feels the self-same smart
Sagittis improperii.	Of ignominy.

[74] Thus K. Richstätter, *Illustrious Friends*, 177ff; cf. also J. Stierli, *Heart of the Saviour*, 88–91.

[75] K. Richstätter, *Illustrious Friends*, 41ff. (cf. AHMA 50: 537). [Latin and English text here from *Devotions for Holy Communion*, ed. A. Goodier, S.J. (London, 1910).]

Hic repauset; hic moretur;	Here its fast abiding be
Ecce jam post te movetur;	Closely following after thee,
Te ardenter vult sitire,	Longing with thee aye to stay,
Jesu, noli contraire,	Jesu, do not it gainsay,
Ut bene de te sentiat.	For it loves thee well.

We can see how rooted the author is in the contemporary Life-of-Jesus and Name-of-Jesus spirituality by comparing this with another hymn to Jesus. It is based on the Song of Songs and in many ways recalls the impassioned speech of the great Cistercians. Mystical union here consists in becoming one with the Lord's will:

> Call me after thee, Beloved,
> Take my senses prisoner;
> Make me sick with love and passion,
> Thy sweet footsteps following;
>   Give thy hand and bid me "Come!"
> Let my heart be mine no longer,
> Thou its life, and it thine own;
> Two hearts joined in one embrace:
> One in will and one in senses,
>   Perfectly at rest in God.[76]

We can get beyond the "sweetness" of these texts, which offends our modern ears if, like E. Jungclaussen,[77] we see it as a cipher "for that inner experience of God that transcends every human horizon of experience and cannot really be put into words".

C. Vagaggini[78] considers that at the end of the thirteenth century a thousand-year milestone was reached in devotion to the Heart of Jesus with the Cistercian nuns of Helfta, near Eisleben. It was there that the Devotion came directly and fully into the light as never before. After two hundred years it was taken up again in similar proportions. In Helfta, Vagaggini says, it was built into the Liturgy and the Life-of-Jesus and Passion spirituality without putting undue emphasis (as often occurs nowadays) on Jesus the man, prior to his Resurrection. Here too no official cult existed in isolation from consolation, satisfaction and an intimate relationship with the Eucharist.

At this point, however, we encounter the limits of communication and imitation. We have seen a devotion to the Heart of Jesus develop that drew deeply on Scripture and was handed on to like-minded people in the context

---

[76] Ibid. (AHMA 50: 542ff.); cf. also J. Stierli, *Heart of the Saviour*, 66.

[77] *Die Fülle erfahren: Tage der Stille mit Franz von Assisi* (Freiburg, 1978), 26f.

[78] "La Dévotion au Sacré-Coeur chez Sainte Mechthilde et Sainte Gertrud" in A. Bea, *Cor Jesu* II: 31–48; cf. C. Vagaggini, *Il senso teologico della liturgia: Saggio di liturgia teologica generale*, 4th ed. (Rome, 1965), 696–752.

of prayer, so that they too could use it in their praying and living and to experience something similar. But in the case of Mechthild of Hackeborn
(d. 1299) the Devotion is almost totally enclosed in an overflowing wealth of
visions. Inevitably, this restricts its appeal. Furthermore, at almost every
apparition, which occurs each time within the liturgical framework of the
monastic Office, Mechthild is given a particular grace. Thus her writings are
entitled *The Book of Special Grace*.[79] For this reason C. Vagaggini,[80] otherwise
so full of praise for these nuns, is inclined to see this devotion to the Heart of
Jesus as extreme. If we are to retain and enrich the Church with the univer-
sally valid elements contained within these extreme phenomena (which, unfortunately, often afflict the Devotion in modern times), we must always try
to apply critical discrimination and separate what is a matter of personal,
feminine sensibility and elements purely conditioned by the time, from what
is central, and to see the latter in the context of the Church's tradition of
faith, so that it can be fruitful in a more general way in Christian living.
With Mechthild this is difficult, because apart from Origen it is not clear
what strands of tradition are operative in her visions. At any rate it is
astonishing that such an exuberant form of devotion to the Heart of Jesus
should appear so suddenly in Helfta.

In the Life-of-Jesus spirituality all Christ's actions are seen to arise from his
love, which is meant to lead us to a loving response in return. This is evident
in Mechthild's devotion to the Heart of Jesus, where it is precisely Christ's
love that is expressed under the image of the Heart. For instance in the "Mirror" vision she sees the Lord in a garment covered with mirrors, with a particularly radiant one at his breast, seemingly the source of the others'
brightness. "In this she understood that Christ's members, in all that they do,
are like a mirror to us, and all his works proceed from his Heart out of
love. . . . Christ's Heart is to us a mirror of ardent love, in which we can see
how cold our hearts are toward God and our neighbor. Christ's mouth is the
mirror of gracious speech, praising and thanking . . ." (*Lib.* 3, 15). Or: "At that
hour the Lord's Heart in his breast was like a vessel with three spouts, which
signify the three conditions of the divine Heart that he experienced on earth,
and his will was that all should dispose their hearts according to these three
conditions. First, Christ's heart was full of reverence and love toward his
Father; second, it was full of pity and mercy toward all men; third, it was full
of humility and self-abasement with regard to himself" (*Lib.* 4, 1).

---

[79] *Der hl. Mechtildis Buch besonderer Gnade: Leben und Offenbarungen der hl. Mechtildis und der
Schwester Mechtildis* (Regensburg, 1880); *S. Mechtildis virginis O.S.B. Liber specialis gratiae: Revela-
tiones Gertrudianae ac Mechtildianae*, ed. Solesmensium O.S.B., 2 vols. (Poitiers - Paris, 1877), 1–422;
Mechthild von Hackeborn, *Das Buch vom strömenden Lob*, trans. H. U. von Balthasar, Sigillum 4
(Einsiedeln, 1955).

[80] "La Dévotion", 33.

The entire humanity of Christ has entered into God's mind, and thus is present here, eschatologically effecting our salvation. Therefore we must not be too quick to separate the earthly Jesus from the glorified Jesus. Of his tears Christ says: "they have a secret place in my Heart; like someone who has a very precious treasure and keeps it in a special, hidden place. . . . They are kept secure in the mystery of my Heart" (*Lib.* 1, 21).

In an almost Johannine way the Cross is projected into the glorification:

> The soul arose and saw the Lord sitting on his throne, saying, with outstretched hands: "Thus I was on the Cross with outstretched hands unto death; so now I continue to stretch out my hands before my Father on behalf of men, as a sign that I am truly willing to embrace each and every one who comes to me. If anyone desires this and is ready, for love of me, to suffer any adversity, it shall be a token to him that he has come to my embrace. But let anyone who desires my kiss take care that he loves my will in truth and in all things, and that my will is his greatest delight" (*Lib.* 1, 35).

In this vision we are reminded of the image of the Passion of the preceding Middle Ages.[81] Much, too, reminds us of the veneration of the Holy Wounds in this period, culminating in the devotion to Jesus' Heart's Wound: "From the Wound of his most sweet Heart there poured forth for us the life-giving water and the intoxicating wine, that is, the blood of Christ, and the inexhaustible treasure of all good things" (*Lib.* 1, 18).

Devotion to the Heart of Jesus is Trinitarian and Incarnational:

> Then she saw a light shining from the Heart of God, which came and nestled beside the soul's heart in the form of a little child. She greeted the child with the words, "Hail, Thou reflection of the eternal glory", etc. Then she carried the child round to all present and gave him to each one, yet at the same time she herself clasped him to her heart (*Lib.* 1, 5).

From the divine Heart salvation pours into the Church, his vineyard:

> He opened the gate of his Heart, the treasure house of the blessed Godhead, and she entered as into a vineyard. There she saw from dawn to dusk a river of living water, and around the river twelve trees carrying twelve fruits which are the virtues St. Paul speaks of in his Epistle: love, joy, peace and so forth (Gal 5:22). This water is called the River of Love. . . . And the Lord said: "This my vineyard is the Catholic Church, in which I have labored with much toil for thirty-three years. Come and work with me in my vineyard" (*Lib.* 2, 2).

The Church is not a cul-de-sac. No one who comes into contact with this love will be allowed to rest in a complacent quietism. In Christ's love, which is given to all, he involves all in loving response and responsibility: "And she saw a cord extending from the Lord's Heart into her soul, and by this cord

---

[81] See nn. 50–55.

she led all around her to God. The cord signified the love which God had richly poured into this soul, and by which she drew everyone to God through her good example and her teaching" (*Lib.* I, 10).

We cannot fail to mention, however, that very often the exclusive theme of the narrative is what takes place between the visionary and the Lord's Heart, and often the latter is addressed in a rather abstract way. J. Stierli[82] considers that in Gertrude the Great (d. 1301) the Lord's Heart is again seen more in terms of the mystery of the Passion. In comparing Mechthild with Gertrude, it would be more correct to say that Gertrude, also a Helfta sister, does not see everything in visions, but presents many things in the form of teaching. Otherwise there is little difference between the two.

At Terce the Lord Jesus appeared to Gertrude "with both hands turned toward her, pointing to his Heart, which is full of every sweetness" (*Leg. div.* IV/38, 1).[83] In addition we find passionate prayers to the Redeemer's Heart: "O Heart running with sweetness! O Heart overflowing with kindness! O Heart streaming with love! O Heart exuding delight! O Heart full of mercy!" (*Ex.* 7).[84] Now Origen's interpretation of Songs 4:9—still detectible here under the surface—is fully applied to the love from the Heart of the Lord: "By Thy wounded Heart, dearest Lord, pierce my heart with the arrows of Thy love so deeply that it can no longer understand anything earthly, but must be controlled by the operations of Thy Godhead alone" (*Leg. div.* II/5, 1).[85]

The writings of the Helfta nuns experienced a renaissance at the beginning of the sixteenth century through the efforts of the Carthusians of St. Barbara in Cologne. These, like the whole order of silent monks at the end of the Middle Ages, were very open to Church reforms and scholarly research, which was expressed in much work on editions of texts. The famous Prior of the Charterhouse, Peter Blovenna (d. 1536), undertook to print the works of Denis the Carthusian, a devotee of the Heart of Jesus.[86]

Johannes Justus von Landsberg (d. 1539)[87] commended the veneration of Christ's Holy Wounds and suffering,[88] edited the works of Gertrude of Helfta and was himself a devotee of the Heart of Jesus.[89] He wrote to a pupil: "The Heart of the Lord Jesus is open to you. May you enter with great dedication. Venerate it assiduously by asking through it what should be asked,

---

[82] *Heart of the Saviour*, 76

[83] Gertrude d'Helfta, *Le Héraut*, SC 225, book IV (Paris, 1978), 312; cf. *Leg. div.* IV/2, 5: SC 225:30.

[84] Gertrude d'Helfta, *Exercices*, SC 127 (Paris, 1967) 286.

[85] Gertrude d'Helfta, *Le Héraut*, SC 139 and 248, books I and II (Paris, 1968).

[86] J. Stierli, *Heart of the Saviour*, 91.

[87] See n.10 above.

[88] *J. J. Lanspergii Cart. Op. Om.*, 5 vols. (Montreuil-sur-Mer, 1888–90); esp. vol. 4, 64f., 238ff., 409–14.

[89] DSp 9: 233f.

and offer your exercises to God through it, for it is the storehouse (*apotheca*) of and the entrance to all spiritual gifts. Through this Heart we approach God and he himself draws new to us."[90] In many ways he reminds us of Mechthild of Hackeborn, as for instance when, in beholding the Lord's Heart, he often sees that of Mary too. The following is from his "Prayers to the Heart of Jesus": "Ah kindest Jesus, enclose my heart in thine so that thou alone shalt live there and possess it, so that, through the nobility of thine Heart, my heart shall be ennobled and glorified."[91] This Carthusian, born in Landsberg in Bavaria and active in Cologne, was fortunate in finding receptive pupils to carry on his love for the Heart of the Redeemer, in the shape of Peter Canisius (d. 1597) and Peter Faber (d. 1546).[92] The fact that Peter Canisius was acquainted with the rich treasures of Mechthild of Hackeborn's prayers to the Heart of Jesus, copying some of them into a pocketbook and using them continually, even on his very deathbed,[93] is due in no small way to the consistent practice of devotion to the Heart of Jesus in the Cologne Charterhouse. "Devotion to the Sacred Heart is a Carthusian devotion", so writes A. Hammon[94] concerning these sixteenth-century Carthusians who transmitted their exercises of piety in a living form but, it should be noted, did not invent them. Only in this sense is Hammon's statement true.

III. Models of Devotion to the Sacred Heart

1. During the larger part of the period we have been surveying, people contemplated the Pierced Jesus, from whose side the gifts of his redemption poured into the Church;[95] they yearned to experience his love in order to become open to God and their neighbor, *although there was no official cult*. In this sense devotion to the Heart of Jesus was actively cultivated on a broad social spectrum, particularly as the Middle Ages drew to a close. We live in a century familiar with official Church documents on the theology of Our Lord's Heart, acquainted with the practice of consecration to the Heart of Jesus. In spite of this, we have retained little of the vitality evident in the most recent past. It may be possible, as E. M. Heufelder does,[96] to discern in the renewal movements inspired by the spirit of the Pierced Savior a new

[90] *J. J. Lanspergii Ep. 26: Op. Om.* 4, 138b.

[91] Ibid., 62, 63f., 139.

[92] DSp 9: 237.

[93] J. Stierli, *Heart of the Saviour,* 74.

[94] *Histoire* II, 270f.

[95] Cf. the treatment by J. Ratzinger, *Introduction to Christianity* (London, 1969; New York, 1979), 179f.

[96] *Christus in euch: Betrachtungen über Jesus Christus und das christliche Leben* (Regensberg, 1976), 42f.

blossoming of the original meaning of veneration of the Lord's Wound of love. In historical perspective these may indeed be legitimate forms, in which people are deliberately trying to live in the spirit of Jesus, to give and experience his love, to "live with Jesus at the center", to "live to Jesus", to "exchange hearts" with him, to mention but a few of the formulas used. It is no accident that Charles de Foucauld,[97] with his symbol of the Pierced Heart (*Jesus Caritas*), is so popular with these movements today. The conclusion drawn here is this: the current crisis in devotion to the Heart of Jesus will not pass unless and until the artificial polarities can be overcome in the triangle composed of the Bible as the living Word of God, the Liturgy and life itself.

2. Medieval devotion to the Heart of Jesus is often accused of being too introverted, dependent on feeling, irresponsible and individualistic. Even H. Rondet[98] feels justified in pronouncing judgment on the Devotion as practiced at Helfta, saying that it fails to insist on the renewal that man owes to the Lord, that it is only concerned with "God and me". These accusations are as common as they are false when applied to the chief representatives of Heart-of-Jesus spirituality. This has already become clear to some extent from the passages we have quoted. Now we shall fill out the picture in terms of fundamental Christian attitudes.

Jesus says to Mechthild of Hackeborn in a vision: "Nothing delights me as much as the human heart, which, alas, so rarely attends to me. I have such a superabundant wealth of all things, except man's heart, which is so often stolen from me" (*Lib.* 4, 54). And in another vision: "So long as the sinner sins, he keeps me stretched on the Cross. But as soon as he turns to me through penance, he sets me free" (*Lib.* 4, 56).[99] This is almost pure Origen: "My Savior still grieves. He cannot be glad while I remain in guilt."[100] "The man who acts ill releases Barabbas in his body and binds Christ. But he who acts well sets Christ free."[101] Of course Origen knows that, because of his divinity, Christ cannot grieve; but in his humanity, in his Church, he can grieve, because his work of redemption is not yet finished and the mysteries of his life and suffering need to take shape in ever new ways in those who are his. For him, without forfeiting the historical distance, the saving event is present at all times: "He who sins after having received illumination and God's other favors crucifies the Son of God through his own sins to which he

[97] Cf. J.-F. Six, *Charles de Foucauld: Der geistliche Werdegang* (Munich, 1978); C. Lubich, *Im Menschen Christus erkennen* (Munich, 1979).

[98] "Le Péché et la réparation dans le culte du Sacré-Coeur" in A. Bea, *Cor Jesu* I: 683–720, esp. 704; against this see nn.45ff. above and the excerpts from Mechthild, *Lib.* I, 35; 2, 2.

[99] In Ludolph also, *Vita Christi* II, 65 (Paris, 1865), 679a; also appears as Jordan, *Med.* art. 64. Both contain interpolations emphasizing the application to the sinner.

[100] *In Lev.* hom. 7, 2: GCS 29: 374.

[101] *Com. Ser.* 121: GCS 11/2: 256. Also taken over from Ludolph, *Vita Christi* II, 62 Paris, 1865), 636b, and II, 59, 615a; Jordan, *Med.* art. 6; Mechthild, *Lib.* 5, 17.

has returned."[102] "Thus the Gospel includes every act done for Jesus, and every trespass too." Here, as often in his commentaries on the Gospels, he is very direct: those who receive the Word of God but produce no fruit "bear thorns and damnably crown Jesus with them".[103] It was Paulinus of Nola (d. 431) who built Origen's ideas into western monastic spirituality: Christ is "the man who for our sakes is still covered with suffering . . . who endures the world for us and in us, in order by enduring it to conquer it, perfecting strength in weakness. He suffers disgrace in you; it is him the world hates in you."[104] Here spirituality is removed from the sphere of mere ethical obligation. Representative atonement acquires a personal, christological aspect.

This aspect is often missing in discussions about "consoling the Lord", which formerly played a significant part in the "Holy Hour" on the eve of the First Friday. K. Rahner[105] tries to approach it from the real presence, now, of the Lord who suffered and was pierced. C. Vagaggini[106] does not deal with it at all.

3. The idea can be deepened by being linked to another, namely, suffering with the suffering Lord. There is nothing sentimental about this; it involves the praying person and his entire environment. Unfortunately it has been almost totally stripped of its original meaning. "Learn therefore who is this Sufferer, and who it is that suffers with him, and why the Lord is present on earth, so that, when we have clothed ourselves with the Sufferer, he may speed us to the heights of heaven" — so Melito of Sardis[107] introduces every genuine contemplation of the Passion, particularly that which sees the Redeemer as the one who allowed himself to be pierced in pity for us. Contemplating the Pierced Heart, which manifests the love of God and suffers with the manifold sufferings of men, John of Fécamp cries, "Where is Thy love? Where is pity?"[108] To love the Pierced Savior, whose Heart is open to all, involves suffering with him, and he suffers, even today, in those who are his.

4. Every failure to love, to respond to Christ's Wound of love, is thereby judged. The approach to God is barred. From Christ's side the Church continually receives its being, in the sacraments that are central to it, as the gift of his love. All love offered to the opened Heart of Jesus will therefore always have ecclesiological dimensions, just as many of our texts from meditations on the Passion are closely linked with passages referring to the birth of the

---

[102] *Jo. Com.* 20, 12: GCS 10: 342.

[103] *Jo. Com.* 1, 11: GCS 10: 16f.

[104] *Ep.* 38, 3: CSEL 29/1, 326f.

[105] "Some Theses" (see n.12 above). Cf. also G. de Becker, "La Théologie", 184: the Passion cannot be restricted to the past; full treatment in my study (n.16) 481ff.; see n.64 above.

[106] "La Dévotion", 47.

[107] *Vom Passa* n.46 (see n.40 above).

[108] See n.45 above. Ludolph also mentions love and pity together in *Vita Christi* II, 64 (Paris, 1865), 676a; cf. also n.44 above.

Church from the side of the New Adam. "Christ's Heart was wounded for our sakes with the Wound of love. Therefore we can only return to his Heart by a love that takes the same path, entering through the opening in his side and there uniting all our love with his divine love."[109]

Love for the Heart of Jesus avoids all moralizing and unfruitful rigorism. "If we have died with Christ, that is, to the world and sin, we must also be pierced, together with him, by the spear, that is love."[110] This love can almost "polarize" all moral action and all discipleship of him who, in love and obedience to the Father, has submitted to the limitations of human life: "For a man's desires must be based on and ordered to God out of love for Christ: . . . He must harmonize his entire will with the divine will for the sake of love's Wound which he received on the Cross for men, when the spear of unconquerable love pierced his sweet Heart."[111] Our living and suffering, thus united with the life and suffering of Christ, becomes fruitful for others and for ourselves.[112]

"For it was from the side of Christ as he slept the sleep of death upon the Cross that there came forth 'the wondrous sacrament of the whole Church' "[113] — thus teaches the Second Vatican Council on the Church's life in the Liturgy. A knowledge of the medieval spirituality of the Heart of Jesus, as it was reawakened, cultivated and deepened during a period of internal Church reforms, could help us to see how today's Church should keep faith with its origin or endeavor to regain it.

[109] Ibid.; also appears in Jordan, *Med.* art. 63.

[110] Ludolph op. cit., 675b; also appears in Jordan, ibid. Both writers go on with a lengthy quotation from John of Fécamp. See n.46 above.

[111] Ludolph, *Vita Christi* II, 64, 676a; based on Mechthild, *Lib.* 1, 18.

[112] Mechthild, *Lib.* 2, 36; some central passages are taken over by Ludolph, *Vita Christi* II, 59, 606b; also appears in Jordan, *Med.* art 1.

[113] "The Constitution on the Sacred Liturgy" no. 5, in *Vatican Council II: The Conciliar and Post Conciliar Documents*, ed. A. Flannery, O.P., (Dublin, 1975), 3.

Addendum:

During the printing of the German edition the following work was published: R. Vekemans, ed., *Cor Christi: Historia, Teologia, Espiritualidad y Pastoral* (Bogotá-Estella, 1980).

Anton Mattes

DEVOTION TO THE HEART OF JESUS
IN MODERN TIMES: THE INFLUENCE OF
SAINT MARGARET MARY ALACOQUE

I. Francis de Sales (1567–1622) and the Primacy of Love

Theology and spirituality, reflection and prayer, depend on one another. To alienate and separate one from the other is to endanger the substance of faith and its lived expression. This is no less true in the case of devotion to the Heart of Jesus. Let us pose a hypothetical question (which cannot be answered because we human beings have no access to the ultimate thoughts and dispositions of God's providence): Why was the great revelation of the Sacred Heart of Jesus given to Margaret Mary Alacoque, one of the Visitation nuns, the Order founded by Francis de Sales?

It can be clearly shown that, in his main theological opus, the *Treatise on the Love of God*, the Bishop of Geneva was especially concerned to portray the mystery of love, and that the most profound revelation of this divine love, the revelation that comes closest to man, took place in the Heart of Our Lord, opened on the Cross "to give us life". But K. Richstätter is critical of this approach: "It is true that St. Francis de Sales founded the Order of the Visitation in which Margaret Mary took the veil. It is also true that the Bishop of Geneva speaks of the Heart of the Redeemer in his writings. All the same his influence on modern devotion to the Heart of Jesus has been considerably exaggerated."[1] I do not share this view. In Francis de Sales we find all the essential dogmatic dimensions of the Devotion present in surprising clarity (however much the language and form may reflect its time): the Trinitarian aspect — the christological locus of the "whole Christ"; the soteriological aspect — the spiritual focus of adoration. To all this is added the pastoral aspect of following after Jesus: the "imitation" of the attitudes and virtues of lowliness and meekness, commended by the Lord as the "fundamental disposition of his Heart".

---

[1] K. Richstätter, *Die Herz-Jesu-Verehrung des deutschen Mittelalters* (Munich, 1924), 372. [Cf. abridged trans.: *Illustrious Friends of the Sacred Heart* (London-St. Louis, 1930).]

At all times Christianity needs, in addition to creative theological theory and research, the encounter with the great models down the centuries. It cannot do without the saints, for they are the "living gospel"; a language addressed to all times, in order to render visible the divine work of salvation. Faith catches fire from the believer. So we are not afraid, in this connection, to point to a churchman who is not only personally one of the great examples of the Christian virtues, but who, over and above this, taught and showed people how to live their faith authentically.

Jacques Leclercq has strikingly formulated the distinction between Salesian and Ignatian spirituality: "The Jesuit and those trained by Jesuits are men of will. They perform the Good because they wish to, because they know it to be rational and their will is subordinated to their reason. By contrast, St. Francis de Sales addresses the heart. According to him it is love that guides men. . . ."[2] Let us leave aside the question whether this distinction is or is not a crude one: it is a fact that for Francis de Sales love is the epitome of all theology. To him and his own *theologia cordis* can be applied his own modest expression of amazement: "O my God, how different is the language of the great lovers of ancient times, of an Ignatius, a Cyprian, a Chrysostom, an Augustine and a Bernard! How different is their language from that of theologians who love God less."[3]

Thus Francis de Sales is part of the western tradition of the *philosophia* and *theologia cordis*,[4] recalling people to the primacy of love, the powerful witness of life, the creative influence of theology on prayer, to a love that is both affective and effective. Theological thought can only breathe within the atmosphere of dialogue with God. That is why his *Treatise on the Love of God* is difficult, particularly for those who do not have a deep prayer life.[5] How appropriate, then, is Hans Urs von Balthasar's ironic analysis: "At some point there came a change from 'kneeling theology' to 'sitting theology'. Thus the dichotomy was internalized. 'Academic' theology becomes estranged from prayer and does not know how to speak of holy things, whereas 'devotional' theology increasingly lacks content and often becomes merely unctuous."[6] The aim of the Bishop of Geneva, then, was a "prayed dogmatics", a *theologia mystica et spiritualis.*

In his life and work Francis de Sales offers us a whole worldview of love.

And in doing so he touches the most intimate relationships between God and the human soul, the mysterious ways of what, for lack of a better expression,

[2] J. Leclercq, *François de Sales* (Paris, 1948), 89f.
[3] German edition [Deutsche Ausgabe] of the works of Francis de Sales, vol. 3 (Eichstätt, 1959), 273. (Cited hereafter as DA Francis de Sales.)
[4] R. Guardini, *Christliches Bewusstsein* (Munich, 1956), 185.
[5] DA Francis de Sales 3: 271.
[6] H.U. von Balthasar, *Verbum caro* (Einsiedeln, 1960), 224.

we call "grace"; in a word, he touches God in the highest regions of our soul. Surely, then, he also touches the very heart of Christianity, indeed, of any religion worthy of the name. Surely this is the most sublime and exciting subject presented to man! He discusses this central theme not merely externally, like a scholar who puts his observations together into a book, but from inside, as a connoisseur of souls. . . . He endeavors to draw up a psychology of the supernatural in nature. No one before him has done so with such clarity.[7]

If spirituality is "the subjective side of dogmatics", the process of development that takes place between God's grace (the persuasive call, offer and promise of the God of love, addressed to man) and man's creaturely existence (his hearing, awareness of involvement and response), then the inductive way of experience in faith is also a part of theological thought. Here we recall the well-known dictum of Karl Rahner:

> If he is to exist at all, tomorrow's man of faith will have to be a mystic, a person who has experienced something. For tomorrow's spirituality will no longer be supported by unanimous and publicly accepted conviction and custom independent of and prior to personal experience and decision; our inherited religious education can no longer be anything more than a very secondary polish put on for the sake of the religious establishment.[8]

Rahner goes on to call for a "mystagogy" in the experience of God and of faith. This is what Francis de Sales endeavored to do. If we are to understand this Saint, we need to remember what he wrote to his friend St. Jane Frances de Chantal, with such unique discretion: "I confess my opinion that no man loves more fervently, more tenderly—frankly that no one is more in love—than I. But it has pleased God to give me such a heart."[9]

With regard to the purpose of the founding of his Order he says: "I have always felt the spirit of the Visitation to be a spirit of profound humility toward God and gentleness toward our neighbor. The less corporal severity, the more kindness of heart there needs to be. . . . The spirit of meekness is so much *the* spirit of the Visitation that anyone who wanted to introduce more fasting and discipline, and so forth, than we have prescribed, would immediately destroy the Order."[10] Just as clearly, in a letter to Madame de Chantal, he urges her to try to anchor the sisters' discipleship in the center of God's love, in the Lord's Heart:

> Tonight God inspired me with the following idea, and . . . if you are in agreement, my dear Mother, we shall take as our device a single Heart, pierced by

---

[7] J. Calvet, *La Littérature religieuse de François de Sales à Fénelon* (Paris, 1956), 57.

[8] K. Rahner, "Alte und neue Frömmigkeit" in *Theologische Akademie* 4 (Frankfurt, 1967): 20.

[9] DA Francis de Sales 5: 364.

[10] DA Francis de Sales 2: 191.

two arrows and encircled with a crown of thorns. This poor Heart, engraved with the sacred names of Jesus and Mary and surmounted by a cross, shall be our sign. My Daughter, at our next meeting I will tell you of a thousand little ideas I have had in this connection; in very truth, our little Congregation is the work of the Hearts of Jesus and Mary. By opening his Sacred Heart in death the Savior has given us life.[11]

Many ideas from his sermons show how, as Bishop, Francis de Sales promoted devotion to the Heart of Jesus. Here is an exmple from the year 1617:

Our Lord wished his side to be opened. First, so that people should see the dispositions of his Heart: his thoughts of love and his heartfelt mercy toward us, his well-beloved children and creatures, made in his *image and likeness*. . . . Second, so that we might come to him in all confidence, retreat into his side and hide in his Heart; in order to rest there, seeing that with incomparable kindness and love he has opened it to receive us, if we give ourselves to him and abandon ourselves entirely and without qualification to his kindness and providence.[12]

Long before the events of Paray-le-Monial, a Sister of the Visitation had written: "Our holy Founder has established an Order in the Church to glorify the Heart of Jesus, worthy of adoration, in the two preeminent virtues that form the basis of the rules and constitutions of the Visitation."[13] For Francis de Sales the basis for a genuinely Christian spirit was the admonition: "Learn from me, for I am gentle and lowly in heart" (Mt 11:29). There is hardly any word that occurs as often, in Francis's writing, as "gentleness". For him, it embodies the true spirit of Christ, and it has no limits. It was *the* characteristic Christian spirit for the Bishop of Geneva. "O love above all love of the Heart of Jesus, where is the heart which could ever praise you with adequate self-surrender? . . . Mount Calvary—the opened Heart is the Mount of Lovers . . . the academy of love."[14]

Let us give the last word to the Saint himself, the "Doctor of Divine Love" as Paul VI called him: "Man is the perfection of the universe, spirit is the perfection of man, love the perfection of spirit, and divine love is the perfection of the merely natural. Therefore divine love is the goal, the perfection and the crown of the universe."[15] This panoramic vision is at the heart of Salesian theology and spirituality, and we are convinced that it can be the valid answer to twentieth-century man's wearied, and often anonymous and lonely, search for *meaning*. In the Heart of Jesus Christ the love of God has been revealed to us. This is what the Bishop of Geneva wanted to say by his

[11] DA Francis de Sales 5: 225.
[12] DA Francis de Sales 9: 245f.
[13] E J. Lajeunie, *Franz von Sales* (Eichstätt, 1975), 613.
[14] DA Francis de Sales 4: 315f.
[15] DA Francis de Sales 4: 168.

life and his teaching, and he succeeded to an astonishing extent. "A man who was in the highest degree the image of the Son of God living on earth" — only a saint could speak thus of another saint. These words are those of Vincent de Paul, who said this, in the canonization process in Paris, about the lofty virtues of Francis de Sales:

> Msgr. de Sales was filled with the burning desire to be an image of the Son of God. To my knowledge he came so close to this that I was often amazed at how a simple creature in all his human weakness could have achieved such a high degree of perfection. . . . The power of his faith was equally evident in his public discourses and in intimate conversation. . . . Whenever subsequently I recalled his words to mind, I was filled with a great sense of wonder and recognized in him a man who was in the highest degree the image of the Son of God living on earth.[16]

"The God of Francis de Sales is truly the God of the human heart."

II. Margaret Mary Alacoque (1647–1690) and the Vocation of Paray-le-Monial

The life of this Saint, a Sister of the Order of the Visitation, was animated by a particular message and vocation. We know about her revelations of Jesus and his Sacred Heart, but her task was to make devotion to the Heart of Jesus, including the Lord's specific requirements, the common property of the whole Church. It is for this that, until death, she worked, prayed, suffered and made reparation.

These are the most important visions that included a request:

First vision: "My divine Heart burns with love for men. . . ." On December 27, 1673, Christ showed his Sacred Heart to Margaret Mary for the first time. Like the Beloved Disciple, whose Feast Day it was, he let the Sister's head rest for a long time on his breast. Then he revealed to her the ineffable mysteries of his Sacred Heart.

> He said to me, "My divine Heart is so impassioned with love for men, and for you in particular, that being unable any longer to contain within itself the flames of its burning charity, it must spread them abroad by your means and manifest itself to others in order to enrich them with the precious treasures that I reveal to you, and that contain graces of sanctification and salvation necessary to withdraw them from the abyss of perdition. I have chosen you, unworthy and ignorant as you are, for the accomplishment of this great design, in order that it may better appear that all is done by me."[17]

[16] P. A. Raviet, *Franz von Sales* (Heidelberg, 1963), 8.

[17] *Leben und Werke der hl. Margareta Maria Alacoque*, 2nd ed. (Heidelberg, 1926), 55. [G. Tickell, S.J., *The Life of Blessed Margaret Mary* (London, 1874), 137–38.]

Christ did not tell her yet what she had to do. But the experience entered her so deeply that her behavior in the community appeared peculiar.

Second vision: the picture of the Heart of Jesus as the source of blessing. Somewhat later (we have no precise dates here) Margaret Mary Alacoque received her second vision, with more definite instructions: "The divine Heart was represented to me as on a throne of fire and flames, shedding rays on every side, brighter than the sun and transparent as crystal. The Wound which he received upon the Cross appeared there visibly; a crown of thorns encircled the divine Heart, and it was surmounted by a cross."[18]

Christ repeated his intention, as in the first vision, and Margaret Mary adds: "he gave me to understand afterwards that it was the great desire he had to be perfectly loved by men that had made him form the design of disclosing to them his Heart."[19]

He intended that his Heart should be venerated in its physical form. A picture should be made, and exhibited or worn on the breast, to be a source of blessing. Veneration of his Heart was the final effort in these last centuries, on the part of his love, to wrest men from the dominion of Satan.[20]

Third vision: reparation for others by means of frequent reception of Communion, especially on the First Friday of each month, and the practice of the "Holy Hour".

The third vision with a mandate occurred the same year. This revelation took place before the exposed Blessed Sacrament. Jesus revealed himself in glory with his five Wounds shining like five suns. He opened his breast, which was like a furnace, and showed his Heart as the living source of all the flames.[21]

Then he revealed to her the limitless extent of his love for men, from whom, however, he received nothing but ingratitude and neglect. Each First Friday of the month Margaret Mary was to receive Holy Communion, and during each night from Thursday to Friday Christ would let her share in his mortal grief on the Mount of Olives. This grief would cause her to experience a kind of death-struggle, harder to bear than death itself. In addition she should get up between eleven o'clock and midnight and lie for an hour with her face to the ground, praying with Christ "in order to calm the divine anger and plead for mercy upon sinners".[22] Subsequently this exercise became widespread under the name of the "Holy Hour".

After this revelation Margaret Mary was at the end of her strength. She was discovered huddled in a corner of the convent and it was thought she had fainted.

[18] *Leben und Werke*, 55. [*The Life of Blessed Margaret Mary*, 153–54.]
[19] H. Waach, *Margareta Maria Alacoque, Skizze eines Lebens* (Eichstätt, 1962), 72. [*The Life of Blessed Margaret Mary*, 154.]
[20] F. Schwendimann, *Herz-Jesu-Verehrung heute* (Regensburg, 1974), 33.
[21] K. Richstätter, op. cit., 369. [*Illustrious Friends*, 244ff.]
[22] H. Waach, op. cit., 73.

Fourth vision: Christ asks for a special Feast to honor his Heart.

This fourth vision took place on the Octave of Corpus Christi, 1675. Like the third, it happened before the Blessed Sacrament.

Christ showed her his Sacred Heart and said:

> Behold this Heart which has loved men so much that it has spared nothing but has utterly consumed and exhausted itself in order to show them its love. And for reward I receive from most of them nothing but ingratitude, through the irreverence and blasphemy, the coldness and contempt, which they show toward me in this Sacrament of love. But it hurts me still more that hearts consecrated to me should treat me so. Therefore I require of thee that on the First Friday after the Octave of Corpus Christi, a special Feast shall be instituted in honour of my Sacred Heart. On this day men shall receive Holy Communion and offer to it a reparation of honour, by a solemn act of sorrow as reparation for all the insults which are offered to it in its presence on the Altars. I promise thee that my heart shall expand and pour forth the fullness of its divine love upon all those who themselves show it this honour or procure it from others.[23]

To this period belong two more important revelations. In 1689[24] Margaret Mary received a message for King Louis XIV, that he was to consecrate himself and his country to the Heart of Jesus, but it was not acted upon. Not until two bloody revolutions had taken place did France build a basilica on Montmartre in Paris, as an abiding symbol of its consecration to the Heart of Jesus. Margaret Mary was also shown in a vision that her Order of the Visitation and the Jesuits were called "to be especially active in propagating devotion to the Heart of Jesus in the Church".[25]

Margaret Mary also received promises which were to be granted to all those who honored the Heart of Jesus. The Lord said to her: "I promise you, in the immense mercy of my Heart, that everyone who receives Holy Communion on nine consecutive First Fridays will be granted the grace of a good death."[26]

The nineteen years she spent in the Visitation Convent at Paray-le-Monial were an uninterrupted succession of physical and spiritual trials. It was Christ's particular wish that she should be a victim soul. She had to offer herself in a unique way as an atoning sacrifice, making satisfaction for the low level of love that existed in her community at that time. In her following of the crucified Jesus, Margaret Mary wanted to be made like him; this is what instilled into her that great love of suffering that so amazes us.

This concrete devotion to the Heart of Jesus spread throughout the world because of Margaret Mary Alacoque, after much opposition and contradiction

23 K. Richstätter, op. cit., 370f. [Illustrious Friends, 246].

24 H. Waach, op. cit., 188.

25 F. Schwendimann, op. cit., 38.

26 H. Waach, op. cit., 187.

in the Church. The "Messenger" of Paray-le-Monial was beatified by Pope
Pius IX on September 18, 1864, and canonized by Pope Benedict XV on May
13, 1920.

III. The Church's Reaction and Reception: Liturgical Development and Form of Devotion to the Heart of Jesus

Initially the message of Paray-le-Monial met with skepticism, opposition and
rejection — for years — in the very convent of the Visitation itself. The Saint's
way of the Cross was hard, but she bore all her humiliations as a sharing in
the Lord's atonement. Rome too was being cautious and to some extent
disapproving. Shortly after Margaret Mary's death, Fr. Croiset[27] published
the first significant book on the Heart of Jesus, referring particularly to the
visions of the Saint. The book was reprinted several times and won friends,
but enemies too. Thus in 1704 it was put on the Index ". . . on account of
the novelty of this devotion and certain formal defects in its propagation".[28]
It remained forbidden right into the nineteenth century, only being released
in 1887. In 1696 another Jesuit, Joseph de Gallifet,[29] submitted to the Roman
censor a work on the "Veneration of the Most Sacred Heart of Jesus", but initially this too was granted no *imprimatur*. Not until 1741, three years after his
death, was the book published, with insignificant alterations. After the death
of Margaret Mary, devotion to the Heart of Jesus spread throughout the entire Catholic world by leaps and bounds, and Sacred Heart confraternities
multiplied. But although the Heart-of-Jesus movement proliferated more and
more among Christians, and more and more petitions were drawn up calling
for worldwide recognition of the Feast of the Heart of Jesus with its own
Mass and Office, Rome maintained its aloof and waiting stance. There were
many opponents not only in Jansenist, Gallican and Enlightenment circles but
also in the Church itself, so that "the start of this new devotion was also the
beginning of its persecution. . . . And strange to say, even the term 'devotion
to the Heart of Jesus' so roused the anger and indignation of many, that it
could not be used publicly without giving offense."[30]

Rome's long resistance to implementating the mission of Paray-le-Monial
cannot be seen as a rejection of devotion to the Heart of Jesus, for the latter is
older than Paray. It would also contradict Rome's willing promotion of the
Sacred Heart sodalities by allowing them to celebrate the Feast of the Heart of

---

[27] F. Schwendimann, op. cit., 38.

[28] H. Waach, op. cit., 204.

[29] K. Richstätter, op. cit., 373.

[30] F. Hattler, *Über die Andacht zum hochheiligen Herzen unseres Herrn und Gottes Jesu Christi* (Inns-
bruck, 1884), 69.

Jesus as a confraternity Feast, and by the granting of indulgences and other privileges. Rome's resistance was only to the concrete form of the Devotion demanded in St. Margaret Mary Alacoque's visions, the supernatural character of which Rome was not yet certain. Thus in 1697, at the request of the Order of the Visitation, Rome was asked to permit a priest to celebrate a special Mass in honor of the Most Sacred Heart of Jesus in all Visitation convents on the Friday after the Octave of Corpus Christi. The special Mass was refused, but the Mass of the Five Wounds was allowed to be celebrated on the desired day. In 1707 a further request by the Visitation Order was again turned down. Then in 1727, as a result of the publication, in Latin, of Gallifet's book (1726) and at the request of the Visitation Order and of several bishops and kings, a second round of negotiations took place in Rome. But the result was that the petitioners were requested not to make any further petitions. Basically three reasons were given:

1. It was a new Feast, and there were insufficient grounds for its introduction.
2. First of all there would have to be a judicial examination concerning Sister Margaret Mary Alacoque, who was responsible for the whole issue.
3. Gallifet's view, according to which the heart was the seat of love and all the emotions, was highly disputed, since modern philosophy attributed these activities to the brain.

However, a year later another petition was presented, signed by the kings of Poland and Spain, the Visitation Order, 117 archbishops and bishops and 349 confraternities. But again the resultant negotiations brought no positive result. Petition followed petition. In fact it was no longer a question of the official introduction of the Feast of the Heart of Jesus, since for a long time now this had been celebrated not only by the Sacred Heart confraternities but also, with Rome's knowledge, in many dioceses; now it was a matter of extending the ecclesial celebration of the Feast by providing it with a special Mass and Office. Some bishops had already introduced both of these in their dioceses. This was done without reference to Rome, but Rome knew about it and did nothing. Then in 1765 it happened: the Polish Bishops drew up a memorandum and presented it as a petition for the introduction of a special Heart-of-Jesus Mass and Office. This time the negotiations produced the long-awaited result. The Congregation for Sacred Rites promulgated a decree rescinding the refusal of the 1729 petition and establishing a consultative board to work on the official approval of a Mass and Office. Two months later Office and Mass were approved, yet only for the Bishops of Poland and the Roman Archconfraternity, which had associated itself with the Polish Bishops' petition. After the success of 1765 devotion to the Heart of Jesus was like a river which, having once broken its banks, spreads out over the whole plain. The "headlines" period was over. Almost one-hundred years went by before the next great Heart-of-Jesus event. In 1865 Pius IX extended the celebration of the Feast of the Heart of Jesus to the whole Church. The French Bishops had requested this, saying that in any case there was hardly a diocese that did *not* celebrate the Feast of the Heart of Jesus. In 1864 Margaret Mary Alacoque was beatified, which, indirectly, was also a vindication and an encouragement of devotion to the Heart of Jesus. In 1899 Leo XIII made the Feast a first-class Feast and permitted the Mass of the Sacred Heart to be celebrated every First Friday as a solemn votive Mass. In the same year the Litany of the Heart of Jesus was also approved for the whole Church. Finally, in his encyclical *Annum sacrum* of May 25, 1899, Leo XIII announced that he would consecrate not only the Church but the whole human race to the Most Sacred Heart of Jesus, which he did on June 11, 1899.

With the canonization of Margaret Mary Alacoque in 1920 by Benedict XV, devotion to the Heart of Jesus received a new confirmation. In 1928 the encyclical *Miserentissimus Redemptor* of Pius XI appeared, laying special emphasis on the aspect of reparation. The last significant utterance of the magisterium on devotion to the Heart of Jesus is to be found in the encyclical *Haurietis aquas* of Pius XII. This addressed an already perceptible decline in the Devotion and was an attempt to provide a new stimulus to it. John XXIII considered devotion to the Sacred Heart as one of the three devotions on which the genuine Christian life is built.[31] Paul VI commended devotion to the Heart of Jesus above all "as the most effective means of promoting the reform of life and the defeat of atheism, which are the aims of the Council".[32]

1. Official Sacred Heart Texts

a. The Sacred Heart Masses

Here we shall take a closer look at three of the fourteen Masses of the Sacred Heart that have arisen in the course of time.

The Mass *"Miserebitur"* was approved in 1765 by Clement XXIII for the Diocese of Poland and the Archconfraternity of Rome, following the success of the Polish memorandum. In content this Mass concentrates on the merciful disposition of Jesus. The word *"misereri"* occurs three times in the Introit itself. The reading from Isaiah 12 is a hymn in praise of God's mercy. In the Gospel we have the Pierced Heart as a symbol of mercy (Jn 19:31–35). The aspect of Jesus' disposition is continued in the Offertory, Secret and in the Postcommunion, which speaks of Jesus being *"mitis et humilis corde"* (gentle

[31] F. Schwendimann, op. cit., 19.
[32] F. Schwendimann, op. cit., 23.

and humble of heart) and says that we should learn from him to "disdain the vain pomp of the world". There is a complete absence in these texts of the element of reparation; it is Jesus' disposition that is central.

The Mass "*Egredimini*" was approved for Portugal by Pius VI in 1778; in 1856 Pius IX adopted it for the whole Church, and Leo XIII also took this Mass when he accorded the Feast of the Sacred Heart the highest liturgical status. Here again the theme is the disposition of Jesus, but there is also an accompanying feeling of joy. Thus the Introit: "*dies desponsationis, dies laetitiae cordis*" (a day of betrothal, a day of heart's joy). The Oration speaks of us being "made like him" and "clothed with virtues and inflamed with love". The Gospel is taken from Jesus' farewell addresses: "Abide in my love . . . that my joy may be in you, and that your joy may be full." In the Offertory, too, and even in the Preface (the Christmas Preface), we find this mark of joy. Joy, thankful love — these are the dominant themes — again there is no mention of reparation or atonement.

The Mass "*Cogitationes*" was approved by Pius XI in 1929 for the whole Church. Here all is permeated by a deep seriousness and the atmosphere is entirely one of atonement. In the Introit we meet the words "*mors*" (death) and "*fames*" (hunger), "which can only be overcome by the thoughts of the Heart of God". The Oration then takes up the theme of sin and atonement. Although the reading speaks of "being rooted in the love of Christ", in the Gradual we encounter the "*delinquentes*" (those who err). The Gospel is the same passage from St. John as in the Mass "*Miserebitur*", but here it does not end with the Evangelist's testimony but with an emphasis on sacrifice in the two verses John 19:36–37. The Offertory again speaks of sin and atonement. The Sacred Heart Preface of this Mass is new, speaking less of Jesus' dispositions than of "the objective mystery of the Pierced Heart, open even to sinners".[33] This comparison clearly shows how variously the Feast of the Heart of Jesus has been celebrated throughout history.

b. The Litany of the Sacred Heart

As early as 1691 Fr. Croiset had made a collection of twenty-three invocations to the Sacred Heart for private use. Of these the Sacred Heart Confraternity of Marseilles adopted seventeen into its Litany of twenty-seven invocations. This Litany was used in 1721 by the local archbishop in a rogation procession on the occasion of an outbreak of plague, but not until 1898 was it approved by the Congregation for Rites, with a small alteration. The invocations were increased to thirty-three, said to be a recalling of Our Lord's thirty-three

---

[33] R. Gutzwiller, "Notes on Some Official Texts of the Church's Devotion to the Sacred Heart" in J. Stierli, ed., *Heart of the Saviour* (Herder, 1957), 159–60.

years. The following year the Litany was approved for the whole Church. It is composed of three groups of invocations:

1. Those that address the relationship of the Heart of Jesus to the triune God: the Heart of the Son to the Father, the relationship to the Spirit who formed it in the womb of Mary, and to the Son, substantially united to it.
2. Those that consider the Heart of Jesus considered in itself, as the "furnace of love", the "abyss of all virtues", "in which the entire fullness of the Godhead dwells".
3. Those that dwell on the relation of the Heart of Jesus to men, characterized above all by the atonement aspect: "atonement for our sins", "bruised for our sins".

As a whole, the Litany of the Sacred Heart manifests "an unmistakably biblical character", for no less than nineteen invocations are biblical quotations "and several others contain allusions to scriptural phrases".[34]

c. Prayers of consecration

Of course there are a great many ecclesial prayers of consecration, but I will restrict myself to the texts cited by R. Gutzwiller.[35] The first prayer of consecration, which goes back to St. Margaret Mary Alacoque, begins like this: "I surrender and consecrate to the Most Sacred Heart of My Lord Jesus Christ my self, my life, my actions, my troubles, my sufferings, my love, my work, so that everything I am and everything I possess shall serve only to honor and love his Most Sacred Heart. . . ." According to Gutzwiller the magnificent "interiority" and the "intensity of love" that speak through this prayer are at the same time its weakness, evidence of its strongly subjective, individualistic character. Similarly in the first prayer of consecration published by Pius XI in connection with his encyclical *Quas primas* (1925) there is no sign of atonement. However, in contrast to Margaret Mary's prayer, this one "breathes the spirit of Catholic universality" in the way it addresses itself to the great community of all human beings. Thus it speaks of God's sovereignty over all people—heathens, Jews, Muslims, those in error and schism; the Lord is asked to grant prosperity, peace and freedom to his Church and quiet and good order to all nations. The second consecration prayer of Pius XI appeared in connection with his encyclical *Miserentissimus Redemptor* and, like this document, it is entirely built around the theme of atonement. By means of devotion, atonement is to be offered to Jesus Christ's neglected and despised love. What kind of atonement? "We offer to thee the satisfaction which, on the Cross, thou once didst offer to the Father." It is not a new atonement:

---

[34] R. Gutzwiller, op. cit., 166–67.
[35] Ibid., 167–71.

what Christ receives from us now is the very same that he performed, for our sake, to the Father.

> We possess then three formulas for public devotions that complete one another to some extent and progress from the consideration of individual needs and aspirations to those of the community and from Christ's reign of love in the community to his work of reparation for it. Only the future can tell whether the present formula is the definitive one, or whether the living growth of the Liturgy and of the worship of God will produce still further acts of consecration, which will take into account contemporary attitudes and the religious sensibility of succeeding generations.[36]

2. Veneration of the Sacred Heart and Indulgences

Long before devotion to the Sacred Heart received official recognition by the approval of the Feast of the Sacred Heart with its proper Mass and Office, Rome had been actively promoting devotion to the Heart of Jesus in the private sphere. An indication of this are the countless indulgences granted by Rome, initially to the Sacred Heart confraternities. And even at the time when Rome was making clear its opposition to a proper Mass and Office, it was also facilitating devotion to the Sacred Heart by granting indulgences. Even after the significant breakthrough of 1765, indulgences continued to be given, and not only for invocations and aspirations in honor of the Heart of Jesus but also for praying the Sacred Heart Litany, for certain hymns, for the contemplation of a picture of the Sacred Heart, for participation in Sacred Heart Devotions, for prayers of consecration and reparation, for wearing the badge of the Sacred Heart, and so forth.

IV. Modern Crisis and Reappraisal Desiderata and Prospects

For decades now, devotion to the Sacred Heart has been in a serious crisis and decline. What are the reasons for this? We can approach this in two ways: first, inductively, by assessing the existing forms and evaluating them in the context of the modern experience of existence and of faith; second by a theological diagnosis, examining how deeply devotion to the Heart of Jesus is rooted in fundamental biblical and dogmatic truths of the Christian faith. Both ways are necessary and must be performed simultaneously. Paul Nordhues says: "We all know that devotion to the Sacred Heart—without quarreling with its meaning and content—has suffered both from weaknesses of devotional language and also from certain forms of personal piety and pictorial representation."

[36] Ibid., 168–69.

But he goes on to say that "the lost or disappearing appeal of devotion to the Heart of Jesus" is connected not only with a "decline in the value of its language and concepts, false sentimentality and anemic artistic efforts"; it is also influenced "by the increasingly intensive christological debate in recent decades, a debate that was not always carried on at a deep enough level and did not always come to grips with the whole Christ".[37] Furthermore, the more rationalist approach of the younger generation, its reserve in matters of religious feeling and its greater preoccupation with work and life-style, means that, in general, it presents a less favorable environment for the growth of Christians and ecclesial life. At the same time Nordhues thinks that this same generation's restless search for "someone with a heart", someone who understands and helps, is a development that offers new opportunities for devotion to the Heart of Jesus, "albeit not initially under the aspect of atonement but rather with regard to service, dedication, and the heart as the center of the loving person".

On the question of the justification for a Devotion, F. Schwendimann notes that its practical results are not the only criterion. There is something else: "Once it becomes clear that Christ has given this form of devotion for our time, the question of its justification loses its meaning. In such a case it is automatically justified, even if, for whatever reasons, people do not know how to adapt it to modern conditions."[38] According to Schwendimann, the fact that the Popes have energetically promoted devotion to the Heart of Jesus right down to the present time shows that it still has special relevance today. Christ has given men the devotion to his Heart as a particular medicine for their love grown cold (cf. the visions of St. Margaret Mary Alacoque): consequently both form and content of the Devotion must be directed to the goal of representing the love of Jesus as well as possible, so as to stir men to love in return. For Schwendimann the central issue in adaptation is not primarily the linguistic and stylistic alteration of texts, however necessary this may be, but the awakening of a desire in people to concern themselves with the Heart of Jesus. He is surely right here, for none of the officially presented forms of liturgical devotion to the Sacred Heart can take effect unless man is awake and open to this mystery in his basic approach, his awareness and his practice of the faith. What good are the most splendid texts if man cannot respond to them? This kind of interior openness for devotion to the Heart of Jesus could yield many new ideas for refashioning the Devotion. Schwendimann sets up three requirements to be observed in any adaptation:[39]

1. Devotion to the Sacred Heart cannot dispense with the message of St. Margaret Mary Alacoque; it cannot try to be a merely biblical veneration

[37] P. Nordhues, "Am grössten aber ist die Liebe: Gedanken zur Verlebendigung der Herz-Jesu-Verehrung" in *Anzeiger für die katholische Geistlichkeit* 6 (Freiburg, 1979): 200–201.
[38] P. Schwendimann, op. cit., 9.
[39] P. Schwendimann, op. cit., 133f.

of the Heart of Jesus, recognizing, as it were, the "relevance and appropriateness" of the Devotion without being able to affirm it as a particular help given by Christ for our times.

2. Devotion to the Sacred Heart cannot dispense with the physical Heart of Jesus as a symbol of his love.

3. Devotion to the Sacred Heart cannot be cultivated solely through the celebration of Mass. In addition it needs a permanent place both within the Liturgy and outside it. This means that Christian spirituality must make room for the so-called private and subjective devotion to the Heart of Jesus over and above the official liturgical cult. In turn this implies that there must be skillful innovation and motivation throughout the entire pastoral and spiritual spectrum of our proclamation.

Hugo Rahner rightly insists on a new theological orientation: "What the cult of the Sacred Heart needs today is a new study of its theological foundations — which have been obscured, in part, by a shallow, insipid and emasculated piety. I mean the great mysteries of the Trinity and the Incarnation, which, in fact, are simply primal forms of the single mystery of love. Only under these conditions can Heart-of-Jesus spirituality become the 'synthesis of all religion', as the encyclical *Miserentissimus Redemptor* of Pope Pius XI puts it."[40] In addition to this Trinitarian and christological aspect, H. Rahner attributes an eschatological aspect to the Devotion when he says: "Every form of devotion shares with the Church that tension that arises between the disappointment of the present and the longed-for future." And "in future the Devotion, earthly as it is, will have to manifest itself more clearly as the eschatological cult of the human and saving love of God. . . . The more a sense of eschatological mystery penetrates our contemporary devotional forms, the more biblical, theological and hence fruitful they will be."[41]

The last great official utterance on the theology and devotion of the Heart of Jesus was the encyclical *Haurietis aquas* of Pope Pius XII in 1956. Its immediate aim was to refute current and growing errors threatening the devotion to the Sacred Heart and to reestablish the Devotion in the high regard due to it, a regard the Pope found lacking in otherwise good Catholics. Since the latter brought forward particular reasons for discountenancing devotion to the Sacred Heart, the Pope endeavored to show that the reasons were false. Such were the following: devotion to the Sacred Heart was not relevant to the distress of the Church and of mankind in present times; it was peripheral to Catholic faith and hence optional, the believer's private business; it was more something for women; it was too passive and therefore was of no use in

---

[40] H. Rahner, "Mirabilis progressio: Gedanken zur Geschichts-Theologie der Herz-Jesu-Verehrung" in *Cor Jesu,* vol. II (Rome, 1959), 55.

[41] H. Rahner, ibid., 57.

a modern revival of religion. In general the Pope attacks false views on the Devotion as being due to naturalism, sentimentalism, materialism and laicism. In conclusion he resists the idea that devotion to the Sacred Heart is permeated by an erroneous mysticism. The encyclical shows clearly that the inner essence of the Devotion is nothing but the veneration of the divine and human love of the incarnate Word, the love in which the heavenly Father and the Holy Spirit, too, envelop sinful men. For, it goes on: "*Augustae Trinitatis caritas humanae Redemptionis principium est.*" This love at the center of the Trinity has been poured out in abundance in the human will of Jesus Christ and in his adorable Heart. It was this that led him to give himself up for us in order to free us from sin.

According to *Haurietis aquas*, therefore, devotion to the Heart of Jesus is intended to lead us to the center of our faith and reveal it to our sight, namely, the love of the Trinitarian God for us men, the love which is the source of our salvation. To that extent the Devotion is totally adequate to the Christian religion — hence its wide popularity — because the latter is a religion of love. In the encyclical, the presupposition for devotion to the Sacred Heart is the Incarnation of the Logos; the Devotion is entirely based upon it. By means of the Incarnation the infinite love of God for us men is exhibited to us in a humanly intelligible form in the person of Jesus of Nazareth; we are shown that this love bears the imprint of the whole Trinity. Thus the Heart of Jesus also signifies this Trinitarian love, revealed in Jesus Christ. According to the encyclical, the symbol of the Heart of Jesus betokens "love, trinitarian love". Again and again it is pointed out that devotion to the Sacred Heart has no other origin and no other goal. It is meant to display the core of the mystery of our salvation and to lead toward it. The Heart of Jesus is, as it were, the "*vestigium Caritatis divinae*".

There is a final question here, which needs more than a glib answer. Why did this theological document of the Church have so little effect? Was the encyclical not understood, not adequately "translated" into the spectrum of the kerygma, and was thus not able to establish and revitalize the Devotion? Perhaps at this point we might suggest a word of Karl Rahner's: "Theology often lacks spirituality, but spirituality is often untheological." Throughout the course of history, many other forms of Christian piety experienced a *kairos*, a blossoming, only to be followed by decline and eclipse. What is important is that we should continue to strive for a dialogue between dogmatics and spirituality, for this dialogue is the very nerve of our Christian life in both these dimensions. The Protestant theologian W. Zeller puts his finger on it when he writes: "We know that theology has a duty to criticize spirituality, but people have not realized that spirituality also has a duty to criticize theology."[42] J. Sudbrack concludes that there must be self-criticism on the part of theology:

---

[42] W. Zeller, *Theologie und Frömmigkeit* (1971), 88.

Has it not become too cerebral? Has it not given meager rations to spirituality, which is the center of Christianity? . . . Nowadays for example we should be uninhibited enough to examine the theological and socio-psychological status of Heart-of-Jesus spirituality. A historical survey would show immediately that the Devotion has blossomed whenever theology and spirituality have diverged: Gertrude the Great comes at the end of High Scholasticism (1256–1301/2; Thomas Aquinas died in 1274); scholarship became embroiled in subtleties remote from reality, and spirituality looked for a concrete, visible object: the Heart. Margaret Mary Alacoque (1647–1690) also lived through a theological fin-de-siècle, at a time when lofty theology did not even throw a crumb to spirituality. The sociological role of the devotion to the Sacred Heart is plain: it puts a central element of the Christian faith into a concrete and practical form. . . . Where else can one find a symbol in which what has become popular in devotion to the Sacred Heart is expressed in a tangible form? Here again the tendency is unmistakable: the emphasis on the man Jesus in theology and exegesis (much more than in High Scholasticism and the theology of the baroque era) seems to eclipse the symbol of the Heart of Jesus. In that case Jesus' solidarity with mankind, particularly in death, would be the basis on which to recover a new understanding of representative atonement.[43]

It remains an open question whether we need a new *theologia cordis et affectiva* and whence it might come. Does the alienation of the idea of the Heart of Jesus mean that the world of imagery and symbolism related to the "heart" is effete and extinct? There are many indications to the contrary. Will theology once more find the way to move man's *heart*? These are questions which only the future can answer. In our view St. Augustine's dictum still applies: "*redeamus ad cor, et inveniamus eum*": Let us return to the heart so as to find him.

[43] J. Sudbrack, *Beten ist menschlich* (Freiburg, 1973), 229f.

JOHANN AUER

DEVOTION TO THE SACRED HEART
AND THE THEOLOGY OF CONVERSION

From the extensive literature on devotion to the Sacred Heart and through the papers we have heard, a very full picture of the Devotion has been made available to us. All that I can do here is clarify individual details and thus bring further questions into focus. This is how my remarks came to have the above title: having received the invitation to this congress, I took up Joseph Stierli's invaluable book[1] and Fr. Bea's two volumes[2] and looked through them carefully. Two sets of questions occurred to me: First, do these books really deal with all the Bible passages relevant to an understanding of devotion to the Sacred Heart? What about the *cor contritum et humiliatum*? This led to the second question. What of man's response, which is so important in the Christian life? What of conversion and penance? Cannot Christ, the God-Man, the sinless Lord, be the way, the truth and the life in this respect too? Must conversion remain a merely human act? Can there be anything "Christian" in the Christian without Christ? These questions led me to my topic. So, briefly, I will lay my thoughts and findings before you, and when I have finished I shall be glad if you set straight whatever strikes a false chord in you and supply what you find to be missing.

I shall develop my topic in four stages:

First, I will briefly list and evaluate the Bible passages that are most significant for devotion to the Sacred Heart.

Second, I will discuss the biblical idea of the *cor contritum et humiliatum* and show how it may be related to the Redeemer's Pierced Heart.

Next, I will take a quick look at what has been written to date on the "philosophy of the heart" and see how it bears on the issue of conversion and penance.

Finally, on the basis of the texts discovered so far, I will show the inner relationship between devotion to the Sacred Heart and the theology of penance.

At the back of my mind is the wish that no doubt animates all theologians who have grown old in their craft, namely, to be continually reflecting on the great tradition by which our faith lives. This is the way new connections, new

[1] *Heart of the Saviour* (Herder, 1957).

[2] *Cor Jesu*, 2 vols. (Rome, 1959), deals with the themes of the encyclical *Haurietis aquas* of Pius XII (1956).

questions, and hence new truths, come to light, not "imported" as it were from outside, but growing authentically from within, given to us as developments or deepenings of the revealed truth of faith, arising from the inner vitality of the truth itself.

I. Fundamental Scriptural Passages Cited in Connection with Devotion to the Sacred Heart

I can base my remarks on the excellent work already done and begin in a small way to apply it to our topic. First there are two fine articles in Fr. Bea's two-volume work. The fundamental idea of devotion to the Sacred Heart is to be found, as is well known, in the mystery of divine love. Here, in his study of "The Revelation of the Love of God in the Old Testament,"[3] J. Kahmann, CSSR, traces in detail the development of this idea through all the levels of Old Testament literature. Let us recall what he says: the prominent idea of the historical books is God's saving activity for the benefit of Israel: "This activity is presented as a creative work of deliverance, presupposing not merely Yahweh's love in general, but very often, and increasingly, his pardoning and bountiful love" (407). This belief in the love of God is deepened where we read of "The Lord, the Lord, a God merciful and gracious, slow to anger, and abounding in steadfast love and faithfulness, keeping steadfast love for thousands, forgiving iniquity and transgression and sin. . . ." His punishment extends only to the third generation (Ex 20:5f.; 34:6f.). In this way God shows himself "faithful to his covenant", which he made with Abraham, Moses and David.

In the prophets previous to and at the start of the Exile, especially in Jeremiah and Hosea, we see quite a new vision of the love of God as that which alone maintains the existence of the People of Israel in the past, present and future. In chapter 11 of his prophecies, Hosea sets the tone for the Old Testament "hymn of Yahweh's love".[4]

In the exilic and postexilic period, Deuteronomy endeavors to reconnect the theology of these prophets with the earlier theology of Israel's election as a historical fact. The Wisdom literature of the succeeding period, as well as many of the Psalms, deepen and expand Israel's existing faith in Yahweh's love, giving intensified expression on the one hand to Yahweh's individual love for each one of the elect" and on the other to his "universal love for all men, including those outside Israel".

---

[3] "Die Offenbarung der Liebe Gottes im AT" in *Cor Jesu* I: 349–410.

[4] Cf. H. Gross, "Zur Theologie von Hos 11" in *Mysterium der Gnade* (Regensburg, 1975), 83–91.

With regard to our present topic, it seems to me particularly significant that the love of God is "a creative, rescuing, pardoning love" that always remains faithful to itself, even when man is unfaithful (2 Tm 2:13). Fr. Criado, S.J.,[5] deals with the same topic of the love of God in the Old Testament, expressed in its lofty imagery and symbolism. He traces the following images through all the various levels of Old Testament literature: God as physician, as shepherd of his people, as the guest of the individual soul, as vinedresser, as father and as bridegroom. In the present connection the image of the "physician" has special meaning when we consider healing in its metaphorical sense, the healing of the guilt of sin, especially in the Prophets Hosea and Isaiah and in many of the Psalms, for Yahweh will "heal those who are brokenhearted" (Is 61:1; Ps 51). Later on we shall reflect on the relevant texts.

Now for the texts from the New Covenant: in his article "On the Biblical Basis of the Devotion", Hugo Rahner[6] first of all explicates the meaning of the word "heart", which occurs in the New Testament as καρδία, κοιλία or σπλάγκνα[7] and refers to the aspect of inwardness in whatever man does, just as, in the Old Testament, penitence or "circumcision of the heart" (Dt 30:6; Acts 7:51; Rom 2:29) is required before one can love God with all one's heart, all one's soul and all one's strength. Similarly, "justification" means nothing other than "believing with the heart" (Heb 9:14; 10:22; Rom 10:10). God has "poured out his love, his Spirit, into our hearts" (Gal 4:6; Rom 5:5) and our "love from the heart" is love in this same Spirit of God, in the Spirit of Christ, and it is this that constitutes the perfection of the Christian (Mt 22:37; 1 Tm 1:5). Thus Peter can call the Christian a "man of the inner heart" (1 Pt 3:4: ὁ κρυπτὸς τῆς καρδίας ἄνθρωπος).[8]

H. Rahner goes on to deal with certain messianic prophecies in which Christ's priestly love in his self-offering for us men is attributed primarily to his Heart. Thus Jeremiah 30:21 (JB): "I will let him come freely into my presence and he can come close to me; who else, indeed, would risk his heart [JB: "life"—Tr.] by coming close to me?" Jesus' dying prayer, Psalm 22:15, speaks in the same terms: "My Heart is like wax; it is melted within my breast." This is the word used to express the freewill sacrifice of Jesus in death, where Isaiah 53:12 says (in the great song of the Suffering Servant) that God will reward him "because he poured out his soul to death and was numbered with the transgressors". As the penitential Psalm 69:21 speaks of the dying Messiah being given vinegar to drink (and the Gospels recall this, Mt 27:34;

---

[5] Cor Jesu I: 413–60.

[6] "On the Biblical Basis of the Devotion" in J. Stierli, ed., Heart of the Saviour (Herder, 1957), 15–35.

[7] Ibid., 17.

[8] Cf. V. Warnach, Agape (Düsseldorf, 1951), 231.

Mk 15:36), so the preceding verse 20, found in the Good Friday Liturgy, refers to the Messiah when it says, "Insults have broken my Heart, so that I am in despair. I looked for pity, but there was none; and for comforters, but I found none."

But a special place, of course, belongs to the two passages from John's Gospel, which H. Rahner analyzes in detail. First there is John 7:37-41, Jesus' speech at the Feast of Tabernacles in Jerusalem, to which Rahner gives a new interpretation based on the new translation (cf. JB): "On the last and greatest day of the festival, Jesus stood there and cried out: 'If any man is thirsty, let him come to me! Let the man come and drink who believes in me!' As Scripture says, 'From his breast shall flow fountains of living water.' " Here "his breast" refers, not to the believer's breast, as in the older translations, but to the breast of Jesus, from whose Heart living waters flow. The phrase finds its interpretation in the context of the messianic prophecies of the Old Covenant (Is 12:3; Ez 47:1-12; Zec 13:1). That is why the people cry out "This is the Prophet, this is the Messiah!" (Jn 6:14; 7:41).

Finally, a word on the historical basis for devotion to the physical Heart of Jesus, John 19:34: "One of the soldiers pierced his side with a spear, and at once there came out blood and water"—which the Evangelist himself connects with the prophecy of Zechariah 12:10, "They shall look on him whom they have pierced." In his three-volume commentary on St. John's Gospel, R. Schnackenburg has recently made a thorough study of this passage.[9] Insofar as one may be allowed to glean "conclusions" from the cautious exegesis, the following is significant for our purposes: even if this account is exclusively Johannine, there is no reason to doubt its historicity. It may well be that John wanted to stress the truth of his account at this point precisely because the other Passion narratives make no mention of the event.

Perhaps, one day, it may be possible to cite the Shroud of Turin in support of this historical event, when the results of the exacting scientific examination performed on it in 1978 have been published.[10] No doubt the prophetic passages of Psalm 34:20 and Zechariah 12:10 are adduced by John simply as the scriptural basis for the meditations that follow. What is the meaning of this "piercing of the side of Christ"? It can hardly be a proof that Jesus was already dead, because we have no evidence that such piercing was customary at crucifixions. Rather we must ask whether God himself is not saying something to us here. If we see these passages together with John 7:38f., as it were stereoscopically, there is a strong indication that the opening of Jesus' Heart signifies the pouring out of the "Spirit of Christ and of God", from the innermost being of Jesus, which will fill the Church at Pentecost. The

[9] *Herder's Theological Commentary on the NT,* vol. 3 (Burns and Oats, 1979), 289f.

[10] Cf. M. Rinaldi, S.D.B., *La stampa,* supplement: "La sindone" (Aug.-Oct., 1978); Albin Michel, *Das Turiner Grabtuch* (1978).

reference to Zechariah 12:10, "They shall look on him whom they have pierced", is related to the account of the bronze serpent in Numbers 21:8. John 3:14 also refers to this passage, again in the context of a salvific event; the "healing" that is granted those who have been bitten by the snake if they raise their eyes to the Lord. Zechariah 12:10, taken together with John 8:28, may also imply a deeper knowledge of Christ: they shall know "that I am" (ἐγώ εἰμί). This passage from Zechariah is also used in Matthew 24:30 and Revelations 1:7 in the apocalyptic setting of the Lord's return as Judge, but it is less likely that it has apocalyptic meaning here in John, unless there is a prophetic hint of ultimate salvation. In his explanation of the passage Augustine recalls that "Here the door to life is opened at the very place whence the Church's sacraments flow, without which one cannot enter that life which is true life." Augustine also sees here an image of the opening of Noah's ark, and of the origin of Eve from the side of Adam, as the prefiguring of the Church's origin from Christ, the Second Adam.[11] It would be too great a restriction of the words water and blood to see them as signifying baptism and Eucharist. We shall have to return to these New Testament passages later on, in a larger context. For the present, let us turn to the second point in our reflections.

II. The *Cor Contritum et Humiliatum* in Scripture and in Its Possible References to the Redeeming Heart of Jesus Christ

We have set ourselves the task of reflecting on the connections between Devotion to the Sacred Heart and the theology of conversion. We may take as our starting-point the well-known verse from the penitential Psalm 51: "*Sacrificium Deo spiritus contribulatus* (*contritus* in the new translation); *cor contritum et humiliatum Deus non despicies*." It seems to me that these two expressions, *contritum* and *humiliatum*, have a clear connection with the words John uses in 19:36 in his meditation on the piercing of the Heart of Jesus: Psalm 34:20 says that none of the Victim's bones shall be broken. The word for "break" is *shabar*, here and in Psalm 51, that is, both heart and bones are "broken". In John the quotation from Zechariah 12:10 is "they shall look on him whom they have pierced", where "pierced" is ἐξεκέντησαν. The Septuagint, which is usually quoted in the New Testament, gives instead the splendid word κατορχήσαντο. κατορχέομαι means "to dance in mockery and spite, gloating over a person's misfortune, to treat him with scorn". This would definitely express more than the word we have in John. Here the piercing of Jesus' side would be an expression of scorn, not, for instance, a proof of his death. This would also fit with the vision of St. Margaret Mary Alacoque in

[11] In *Joh. Tr.* CXX, 2 (CC 661).

which the Pierced Heart of Jesus was crowned with the crown of thorns. Zechariah 12:10 also suggests this, for it continues, "They shall mourn for him, as one mourns for an only child". The enemies' spite is here contrasted with the mourning of friends.

However, the Hebrew text here has *daqar*. But the Hebrew word in Psalm 51 for ταπείνω, (humiliate), is *dakha*, often written with *qoph* instead of *kaph*, but never with a third radical *resh*; that is, it is a different word. Literally *daqar* means "pierce". A question arises regarding John's quotation from Zechariah, which comes from the Septuagint. Where did John get this word, which is not found in the Septuagint? The only other place in the Septuagint where *daqar* is translated in this way is in Numbers 25:8, where the Aaronite Phinehas heals Israel of its idolatry to Baal-Peor by piercing with a spear the offending man and woman, receiving great reward from God. Here *daqar* is translated by ἀπεκέντησεν, that is, corresponding to the ἐξεκέντησαν in John.

But let us return to the verse in Psalm 51, where the second word referring to the humble heart is given as ταπεινόω in the Septuagint, corresponding to the Hebrew *dakha*. In Kittel[12] *dakha* is only mentioned once in a note in the discussion of the word ταπεινόω, although elsewhere in Scripture it is used almost as often as *shabar* or *suntero*. The new *Theological Dictionary of the Old Testament* (ed. Botterweck, Ringgren)[13] discusses this word in detail and is useful for our purposes, as I shall show later. My aim, let me remind you, is simply to show that these two words from Psalm 51 also occur in the two quotations that John includes in his meditation on the pierced side of Jesus, at least as far as their content is concerned. Thus I want to build an exegetical bridge for my topic, in three stages:

1. First, a few thoughts on the *cor contritum*, which Kittel discusses thoroughly under the entry on συντρίβω, and which the new *Theological Dictionary* discusses in connection with the Hebrew word *dakha*, with numerous examples. It is to be observed that *contritum et humiliatum* is a hendiadys: the two words *shabar* and *dakha* are used here metaphorically as synonyms, even if we can make a distinction between contrition and humility. Taking the two words together, they no doubt signify what revelation generally means by "turning", "conversion", that is, what the New Testament calls *metanoia*, that change of heart we want to examine in the context of devotion to the Sacred Heart. In trying to appreciate better the meaning of the *cor contritum et humiliatum* of Psalm 51:17, it is helpful to take Psalms 32–34, which according to Bernhard Bonkamp's still very valuable commentary[14] came into being prior to 587 (i.e., before the Exile), together with

---

[12] *Theological Dictionary of the NT,* ed. Friedrich (Grand Rapids, 1972).

[13] *Theological Dictionary of the OT,* ed. Botterweck-Ringgren, vol. 3 (Grand Rapids, 1974–75), 195–208.

[14] *Die Psalmen nach dem hebräischen Urtext* (Freiburg, 1949), 174–76, 246–48.

Isaiah 1:2–20, where the Prophet puts forward his famous critique of sacrifice. According to Psalm 33:18, it is they who acknowledge and admit their guilt before God who find salvation, just as Psalm 32:5 says, "I acknowledged my sin to thee, and I did not hide my iniquity." Psalm 34:18 puts it like Psalm 51:17: "The Lord is near to the brokenhearted, and saves the crushed in spirit" (*contritos corde — humiles spiritu*). The same thought is expressed in Psalm 147:3, Daniel 3:39 (JB) and a similar one in Isaiah 57:15 and 66:2. Here we ought also to mention the other places where συντρίβω is used actively: if man does not repent, is not converted, God will crush him (cf. Ps 37:17: "for the arms of the wicked shall be broken"; or Is 21:9: "the images of her Gods he has shattered to the ground").

2. Now it is very significant that this same language occurs also in prophetic texts concerning the Messiah. Isaiah 61:1 says of the coming Messiah: "The Spirit of the Lord God is upon me, because the Lord has anointed me to bring good tidings to the afflicted; he has sent me to bind up the brokenhearted, to proclaim liberty to the captives, and the opening of the prison to those who are bound." This recalls the first Servant Song, in which (Is 42:3) it is said that the Messiah "will not break a bruised reed". Thus what is said of Yahweh in the penitential Psalm 51 is here applied to the Messiah, namely, that he will heal those who are brokenhearted. According to Luke 4:17–19 Jesus reads this passage in the synagogue at Nazareth with the observation that this prophecy has begun to be fulfilled in him. But it is very noticeable that in many, mostly the older manuscripts (χBDLW) the phrase "to bind up the brokenhearted" is missing; only in the later manuscripts of the fifth century (AQΨ, etc.) is it inserted. Since Luke in particular is usually meticulous in his quotations, one would very much like to know why this phrase "to bind up the brokenhearted" was omitted. However, asking is much easier than answering, and often our answer can be no more than a suggestion. First let us hear the exegetes. Joseph Schmidt deals with Luke 4:18 at some length in his commentary[15] but does not mention the omission. R. Schürmann does refer to the omission,[16] but regards the phrase as originally part of the Lukan text, supposing that it was omitted at a later date because of the fact that Jesus performed no miracle in Nazareth. It seems to me, from manuscript evidence in the first place, that the verse must have been reinserted later. In that case why did Luke leave it out? The text itself suggests the following explanation: Luke did in fact know of the piercing of the Heart of Jesus, but to him this "piercing", in the sense of the quotation later given in John (the quotation from Zechariah 12:10), was an action of spiteful mockery, as we have already seen in the Septuagint in the expression κατορχήσαντο.

---

[15] RNT (Regensburg, 1949), 87.
[16] *Herders theologischer Kommentar*, vol. 16 (Freiburg, 1969), 229.

Luke omits it, just as, in comparison with Matthew 27:27–31 and Mark 15:16–20, he omits the scene in the Passion in which Christ is mocked. Is he perhaps trying to deal gently with the Romans, to exonerate the vast mass of the people? He does not want to accuse mankind of scorning the Messiah. In a similar way he takes up a different position at the death of Jesus vis-à-vis Matthew and Mark: in Luke's account the centurion "praised God" and the multitude returned home "beating their breasts" (Lk 23:47f.). If this theory is correct, it provides a (albeit negative) testimony to the piercing of Jesus' side in Luke as well.

3. Here let me quote what the new *Theological Dictionary of the Old Testament*[17] has to say on this problem of the connection between conversion and the Pierced Heart of Jesus: "In the theological reflection of exilic and postexilic prophecy, especially in Trito-Isaiah, the idea of being broken takes on an added dimension that is then preserved in Lamentations (e.g., Lam 1:18, 20; 3:40–42; 4:22) and especially in the individual Penitential Psalms. The suffering of man, whether it be the individual or the nation, is ultimately and properly separation from God. In affliction at the hand of enemies, in sickness, and in nearness to death, he experiences remoteness from God and abandonment by him at the deepest level. He recognizes that the reason for this is sin, his sins against God and man. These stand clearly before the eyes of the Psalmist (Ps 51:5; cf. Is 59:12); they weigh down heavily upon him like a heavy burden (Ps 38:5; cf. Ps 32); they hang over his head (38:5). The Psalmist sees his sin radically interwoven with his existence (51:8; cf. Gn 8:21; Jer 17:9; Jb 14:4; 15:14f.; 25:4ff.; Ps 143:2). Standing under the heavy burden of sin, he turns to Yahweh with an unrestricted confession of his guilt and a prayer that it might be blotted out (Ps 51:3; cf. Nm 5:23; Is 43:25; Ps 109:14) and cleansed (51:9). Coupled with this petition is another for a wonderful new creation, for a clean heart and a steadfast spirit (Ps 51:12; cf. Jer 24:7; 31:33; 32:39; Ez 11:19; 36:25ff.). Only God's free, creative act (cf. Is 65:18) can overcome the intolerable situation of man's separation from God through sin and renew the heart of man. This new disposition of the man who has been set free from sin and guilt and reconciled to God consists in a complete surrender to Yahweh with a broken spirit and contrite heart, which is much more acceptable to Yahweh than all sacrifices (Ps 51:19; cf. Am 5:22; Is 1:11; Jer 6:20; etc.).

The idea of man's complete surrender to Yahweh with a broken spirit and contrite heart finds a distinctive development and new significance in the figure of the Suffering Servant of the Lord (Is 52:13; 53:12). It does so through its combination with the motif of vicarious suffering. This Servant takes upon himself the sin of others and sickness and suffering as its consequences. He who is disfigured by sickness and bowed down and bruised by the burden

[17] *Theological Dictionary of the OT* III: 207–208.

of an excruciating suffering bears the sin and guilt of others and thus procures salvation for them by his vicarious atonement. Yahweh shows favor to the "one he has bruised" (53:10), causes his work to prosper (52:13), ". . . and will lift up this bruised and broken one".

Having done our exegetical preparation, we shall turn to the theological treatment. Beforehand, however, a brief note on the concept of "heart".

III. Some Observations on the Concept "Heart" and Its Significance in Connection with "Penance and Conversion"

Whereas Karl Richstätter, in his valuable work *Die Herz-Jesu-Verehrung des deutschen Mittelalters* (Engl. transl. *Illustrious Friends of the Sacred Heart*),[18] only refers to the concept "Heart" incidentally, Karl Rahner, in his paper "Some Theses on the Theology of the Devotion" in *Heart of the Saviour* (ed. J. Stierli) [19] takes up the encyclical *Caritate Christi compulsi* of Pius XI (May 3, 1932) and discusses in detail all the possible meanings of the word "Heart". Rahner comes to the very firm conclusion that in connection with devotion to the Sacred Heart this word "Heart" primarily refers to the "Person of Jesus" as the center of the various activities (not merely the attributes) of the God-Man Jesus. Rahner again deals in detail with this question in the collection entitled *Cor Jesu*, edited by Fr. Bea.[20] Quite another direction is taken by the Munich philosopher Dietrich von Hildebrand's work, *The Sacred Heart: An Analysis of Human and Divine Affectivity*,[21] a book which first appeared in America. A deeper study is the *Philosophia Cordis* of Anton Maxsein,[22] which portrays "the nature of personality in Augustine" and sees *cor* as the personal center of the human being. In particular what he says of the *cor confitens* as the organ of personal openness[23] is important in our context, as we shall see. What is essential is that *cor* does not indicate the seat of the emotions that are aroused by man's various experiences of reality; rather, it must be conceived as the personal center that is operative in action, judgment and decision, in fundamental personal attitudes within social interaction and above all in love —things that are ultimately revealed in the deepest possibilities of human self-transformation and self-giving.

However, now let us turn at last to the theological questions that will bring together what we have said so far. By way of introduction, and as a way of

---

[18] (Regensburg, 1924) 267–70; *Illustrious Friends* (London and St. Louis, 1930).

[19] "Some Theses on the Theology of the Devotion" in *Heart of the Saviour*, 131–55.

[20] "Zur Theologie des Symbols" in *Cor Jesu*, 461–506.

[21] *The Sacred Heart: An Analysis of Human and Divine Affectivity* (Baltimore and Dublin, 1965; German ed. Regensburg, 1967).

[22] (Salzburg, 1966).

[23] Ibid., 281–92.

pointing out that a great deal of our subject is beyond all speech and explanation, I will relate the fairytale of the Mother and the Lost Son, which my
own mother told me when I was a boy.

> Once upon a time there was a mother who had a son, whom she treated with great
> love, indeed with nothing but love. The son grew up into a good-for-nothing and
> finally, on account of a degrading love affair, killed his mother. But in his confu-
> sion he tore his mother's heart from her body, thinking to bury it in the garden near
> his house. As he went down the hillside he stumbled and fell, and his mother's
> heart rolled away downhill. When the son, injured, got up and ran after the heart,
> what did he hear but the heart calling to him: "Son, did you hurt yourself?"

Behold the mystery of love!

IV. Theological Reflections on the Pierced Heart of the Redeemer and Man's *cor contritum* in Scripture, and the Connection between Devotion to the Sacred Heart and a Theology of Human Conversion

1. *A summary of the biblical material:*

The *cor contritum et humiliatum* is the presupposition for God's forgiveness of
sin. But in the Christian understanding this is not primarily man's work but
divine grace, which has its source in the Heart of Jesus the Savior.

The aspect of grace, which in the Old Testament is seen exclusively as God's
activity, is understood in the New Testament as the special activity of the Messiah, Jesus Christ. According to Zechariah 12:10 and the tradition of the Church,
the Messiah's love is above all to be seen in the Pierced Heart of the Redeemer.

The fact of the piercing of the Redeemer's Heart is reported in John 19:34
and perhaps also indicated by the omission in Luke 4:18.

In John 7 the Redeemer's Heart appears as the well whence flow "rivers of
living water", symbolic of the Spirit, in whom Christ has given us himself
and his grace in perpetuity.

In all this the Heart is not a conceptual symbol but rather the physical
Heart of Jesus, according to Tertullian's *caro salutis est cardo*,[24] that is, the
bodily flesh (in Christ, the incarnate Son of God) is the hinge upon which
hangs the door to salvation (opened to us in Christ).

2. *A summary of the theological ideas developed by devotion to the Sacred Heart*

The Church was born from the Wound in Christ's side.

Jesus' Wound is the source of the sacraments, above all baptism (water)
and the Holy Eucharist (blood).

---

[24] Tertullian, *De resurrectione carnis* 8, 2 (PL II, 806a).

Christ's Spirit, too, is emitted from the Wound in the side of Jesus, the Spirit in whom Christ has given us himself and all graces. The theology of the Middle Ages took up these biblically based truths and developed them thus:

Frederick Barbarossa returned from the Second Crusade with the point of a lance, which was initially kept in the castle of Hagenau in Alsace, where, in 1153, it became the focus for a new development of devotion to the Heart of Jesus for the Germanic peoples, with their concrete, historical and subjective way of thought. This lance point influenced the *Parzifal* of Wolfram von Eschenbach and the Legend of the Grail, and the first Hymn to the Heart of Jesus of Walther von der Vogelweide.[25]

Karl Richstätter[26] has traced the further development of this devotion to the Heart of Jesus, in particular in the convents of nuns of the Middle Ages: the physical Heart of Jesus becomes a historical symbol for the whole mystery of the divine love. The western devotion to the Sacred Heart continues to unfold, under the influence of the Christ-mysticism of St. Francis of Assisi and the fourteenth- and fifteenth-century mysticism of suffering.

A new theological idea enters the Devotion through the visions of Margaret Mary Alacoque. In the spirit of St. Francis de Sales' theological psychology she insists that the redeeming love that issues from the Heart of Jesus must meet, in man, reparation in the form of love of this Heart. This is the only valid response to Christ's redeeming love. These ideas are developed in particular in the context of the eucharistic piety of Corpus Christi.[27]

I began by observing that, to date, as far as I can see, the idea of "conversion and penance" is not really rooted theologically in devotion to the Sacred Heart, although conversion is both the beginning and the center of all Christian life, and all Christian life must find its basis and pattern in Christ. So, initially, we can say this: if it seems difficult to see the interplay of devotion to the Sacred Heart and human conversion, it is probable that either our idea of conversion, or our theological understanding of the Heart of Jesus needs to be corrected.

3. Devotion to the Sacred Heart and the theology of conversion

I should like to develop my thoughts on this matter in three stages:

1) Man's *cor confitens* is the organ of his personal openness to God and is thus also the foundation and the source of life of his *cor contritum;* 2) The *cor contritum* is the response to and the means of participation in the love of Christ's *cor perforatum;* 3) *Contritio* and *conversio* draw their life from the Christian's *conversatio* with the *caritas Christi urgens nos.*

[25] Cf. Medard Barth, *Die Herz-Jesu-Verehrung im Elsass* (Freiburg, 1928).
[26] *Die Herz-Jesu-Verehrung des deutschen Mittelalters (Illustrious Friends of the Sacred Heart).*
[27] *Leben und Werke der heiligen Margareta Maria Alacoque,* 2 vols. (Heidelberg, 1926).

First, however, a fundamental difficulty needs to be met. In a series of devotions, which appeared privately here and there and were explicitly rejected by the Magisterium, A. de Bonhome[28] refers to the "devotion to the penitent Heart of the Lord". At the outset, therefore, it might seem that linking devotion to the Sacred Heart with the theology of conversion is yet another erroneous cul-de-sac. I reply to this difficulty with two points:

1. In its long history, theology has become accustomed to unfold Jesus' simple call for "repentance" (Mk 1:15: *metanoeite*) in lengthy psychological, ethical and anthropological treatises, distinguishing clearly among conversion, sorrow for sin, penance, satisfaction and reparation. Nowadays a genuine religious approach must try to see how, in our world, which is often atheistic in practice, we can enable this biblical call for simple conversion to be heard in the interests of the Christian kerygma. It may be a sign of the times that the new *Lexikon für Theologie und Kirche*, in the article on "conversion", presents no biblical or dogmatic treatment but only deals in terms of the history and psychology of religion, and of fundamental theology.[29]

2. The history of spirituality within the Church shows that new forms have always been needed to express the same spiritual content in a new era. When Margaret Mary Alocoque enriched devotion to the Heart of Jesus with the idea of "atonement", she was opposed by a budding rationalism that could not be called atheistic in the modern sense, although it was beginning to destroy the Christian faith with its doubts. Modern atheism does not spring from critical thought in opposition to Christianity; it is an existential denial of God and faith, an aggressive atheism that employs economic, social and political means to promote its struggle — and we all live in this context. Is not *metanoia*, conversion, in the original biblical sense, more important for us today than "atonement"? Indeed, can there be any genuinely Christian "atonement" today without the prior requisite of *metanoia* and conversion? Anyone who shares this view of our times will also understand that forms of spirituality that submitted to the Church's critique in the past, in entirely different historical circumstances and atmospheres, must submit to new and necessary questioning now. The decision remains with the Magisterium. But the preparation for such a decision, now as always in the history of spirituality, lies with the *pars sanior* of the people and the conscientious deliberations

---

[28] DSp, vol. 3 (1957), 778–95: 781, "Dévotion à Jésus pénitent" — condemned on July 15, 1893. The visions of Mathilde Marchat, from Loigny in the Diocese of Chartres, were not recognized because the otherwise approved theme of *Jésus pénitent pour nous* was connected with political ideas (concerning a son of Louis XVII). Moreover Mathilde Marchat wanted to found an "Order of the Most Sacred Penitent Heart of Jesus"; here we are only concerned with the idea of Christ's atoning penance for our sins. (On this theme cf. *Nouvelle Revue théologique* 25 [Louvain, 1893]: 496–507.)

[29] LThK II (1958): 136–38. By contrast there is plenty of biblical and systematic material in RGG III (1957): 976–84.

of theologians. Now, let us turn to our three propositions regarding devotion to the Sacred Heart and the theology of conversion.

a. Man's cor confitens *as the organ of his personal openness to God and as the foundation and source of life of his* cor contritum

In his excellent book *Philosophia cordis*[30] Anton Maxsein has dealt with this subject, among others, in detail. I have nothing to add to his presentation but will simply summarize those points that are especially relevant for our topic. When we speak of conversion, we are not referring to a psychic act, let alone an emotional phenomenon. Conversion, repentance, penance refer to a fundamental attitude of the person, a personal decision and activity; it is not something embryonic or intentional but has about it something final and decisive that includes the future. It is important to understand that, through the *confessio* (the confession of sin), penance and conversion somehow attain freedom and independence and begin to mature. In the *confessio*, *contritio* attains self-expression and thus discovers its own actual center of being. The *confessio* shows that genuine contrition is impossible if man only turns into himself, revolves around himself, merely sees his own reflection in his attitude to law and determines the lawfulness of his own actions. What he must do is go beyond the law to the Lawgiver, who alone can correctly interpret the law. Religious thought is not concerned, ultimately, with man and his preoccupations; it concerns man's relationship with his personal God. It is only when man discusses his life in conversation with his God that it becomes clear what a religious life is, what sin and penance are and must be if they are to be understood religiously and not merely ethically.

Following Augustine, Maxsein makes the following points about this *cor confitens*: *confiteri* is a personal act, an act inspired by God himself, an act of what we generally call love. At its deepest it is a dialogue of love with God, an act that manifests God's call and hence leads, through dialogue with God, to self-knowledge. It is insight into the way to give shape to one's life, and since we are creatures made in the image of God, only the Creator can give us this shape. Hence *confiteri* is the way to purification by God; it empowers us to give ourselves entirely to God. Thus in the *confessio* man is seen to be the spokesman for the whole creation in its profession of faith that for man's sake has been subjected to futility and that longs for the glorious liberty of the children of God to be manifested in man (cf. Rom 8:19–30).

Hence *contritio* is not really the path to conversion; the reverse is the case: conversion is the root that can cause *contritio* to spring forth, that *contritio* that has its historical origin in the Cross of Christ, the response to man's sin.[31] From an ethical point of view, human sin may be regarded as man's negative

[30] 241–92.
[31] J. Ratzinger, LThK IX (1964): 1158.

act, calling for a positive act of reparation on his part; but from a religious point of view, it must be insisted that the forgiveness of sins and everything that leads to it is first and foremost the act and the gift of God's love.[32]

b. Man's cor contritum *is the response to and the means of participation in the love of Christ's* cor perforatum

If we are to understand this properly, we need first of all to take another brief look at Christ's *cor perforatum*. We have already tried to get a clear picture of the theological and religious ideas symbolized in this Heart through examining the history of the Devotion. If we see the Pierced Heart of Jesus as a symbol of divine love, which is full of understanding and which can make of us a new creation (in contrast with our human hearts in their sorrow for sin), there are three things that must be borne in mind, three determinants of this contrite human heart: sin as the denial and vitiation of the divine order of the world; suffering and evil as the result of sin; and the guilt of sin, as the creature's personal decision against the Creator God.

1. With regard to the first element of sin: Christ is not only the sinless one; he is totally free from sin's contamination. At the same time revelation makes it plain that he died not simply "for our sins" as a legal proxy and representative; no, his "representation" is at a deeper level, much deeper than we are willing to countenance on the basis of our Christology, which dates from the fourth century. The Apostle dares to clothe this fact in these striking words: "For our sake he made him to be sin who knew no sin, so that in him we might become the righteousness of God" (2 Cor 5:21). The Apostle is endeavoring to show how we have a genuine "reconciliation" ($\kappa\alpha\tau\alpha\lambda\lambda\alpha\gamma\acute{\eta}$) in Christ and how we can therefore become a "new creation" in Christ (2 Cor 5:17; Gal 6:15). Sometimes I think we make things a little too easy for ourselves with our way of looking at "representation".[33]

2. The fact that, in some way or other, Christ actually took upon himself the disorder that sin has brought into God's world is made manifest to us in the reality of his suffering and dying, his "Cross".[34] What the final Servant Song (Is 53:1–9) says about the cost to the Messiah for this "representation" for our transgressions has become a historical reality in the Gospel Passion narratives. Perhaps, too, we ought once again to take seriously what the Shroud of Turin means to us; perhaps we ought to face up to the deeply moving images

---

[32] A contrary view in P. Eder, "Der gerechte Ausgleich" in *Sühne* (Vienna, 1962), 205ff.

[33] Cf. J. Ratzinger, "Stellvertretung" in HThG II (Munich, 1963): 566–76.

[34] On the theology of the Cross, cf. P. Stockmeier, *Theologie und Kult des Kreuzes bei Johannes Chrysostomos* (Trier, 1966); W. Hülsbusch, *Elemente einer Kreuzestheologie in den Spätschriften Bonaventuras* (Düsseldorf, 1968); M. Flick and Z. Alszeghy, "Il mistero della croce", *Bl. di teol. contemporanea* 31, (Brescia, 1978); *The Acta of the International Congress of Passionists "La sapienza della croce oggi"*, Rome, October 13–18, 1975 (ed. Rome, 1978). Cf. also the publications of the International Association "Stauros", Leuven (Belgium), Leopoldstraat 12.

presented to us in, for instance, the baroque meditations on the Passion vouchsafed to St. Bridget of Sweden, to the Spanish Franciscan María de Agreda and others. We theologians in particular have got used even to seeing the Cross "symbolically", just as early Christianity enveloped this sign of redemption with gold and precious stones. In view of the fact that even after Christ's redemptive act sin has not simply disappeared (and we may even have to say that, precisely because of the new revelation of the love of God in the suffering of his Son, the reality of sin in the world has become in many respects more grave and terrible—think of the shape taken by modern atheism), the realization of our own sin ought to make us take Christ's suffering and Cross more seriously. Perhaps the spirituality of the baroque era was more than a "phenomenon" in the history of civilization; perhaps it was expressing a reality that we have largely forgotten.

3. What is decisive about our sin, however, is our "personal guilt": *Tibi soli peccavi et malum coram te feci*. In some way or other every sin embodies the creature's arrogant turning away from the Creator to what is perverse and spoiled—the perpetual result of sin in this world. Christ is the guiltless one, untouched by sin. How can we speak of "guilt" in his case? Repentance and conversion presuppose a personal sense of guilt that must be unknown to Christ. This truth has been a clearly understood part of our Catholic view of Christ since 325 A.D., and the solemn proclamation of the "two wills in Christ" in 680 naturally did nothing to change this.

In view of what we have said about "representation" and "the Cross of Christ", however, has this dogmatic pronouncement said all that needs to be said? In the preceding section we expressly spoke of the soul and foundation of man's *contritio* not as a feeling but rather as the sinful creature's openness to dialogue with his Creator, and as his confession of guilt before God. Perhaps we must go a little deeper: in our times, people are endeavoring to express human personal existence not solely metaphysically, but rather in the categories of psychology and psychotherapy. Shouldn't we learn from this to complement the metaphysical statements of our Christology with the kind of psychological insights that are substantially available in the simple terms of Scripture? For instance the "human I of Jesus" is unmistakable in Scripture.[35] An earlier paper, by H. Urs von Balthasar on "The Work and Suffering of Jesus: Discontinuity and Continuity", placed this reality vividly before our eyes. Why do we always have to overlay the moving words of Jesus in his Passion, his urgent beseeching in Gethsemane that the cup should pass from him or the baffling words from the crucified Son of God, "My God, my God, why hast thou forsaken me?"—why must we always overlay these words with masterpieces of interpretation, which convince no one, which we

---

[35] Cf. J. Auer, *Person: Ein Schlüssel zum christlichen Mysterium* (Regensburg, 1979).

only accept as an expression of the "mystery" that we cannot grasp? Surely we should be able to see, in the divine-human Person of Jesus that is mediated to us by the deeper metaphysical insight of our faith, the psychic, human Person of Jesus that is rooted in consciousness—the human person whom God the Father sends out into the night (the mystical "Dark Night") of suffering so that he really can take our guilt upon himself. For it is here that he experiences suffering entirely and exclusively as "his own human suffering" by really taking "human sin" entirely and exclusively upon himself. This is what is expressed in his cry for help, in mortal anguish, from the mysterious Psalm 22, in the words "My God, my God, why hast thou forsaken me?"

We cannot cease to be moved, whenever we pray the whole of Psalm 22, by the way in which it gives a prophetic picture of the entire suffering of Jesus as a "human suffering, borne in an ultimate human trust in God". May we not take these prayers of Jesus in Gethsamane and on the Cross as the expression of the *cor confitens* of one who was really (and not merely legally or in appearance) "wounded for our transgressions, bruised for our iniquities" and by whose Wounds we have been healed (Is 53:5)? Why are we so timid when it comes to taking seriously the reality of "Incarnation" (ἐνσάρκωσις, Jn 1:14) and hence the reality of redemption through the bodily dying of Jesus? For the Apostle himself writes: "For God has done what the law, weakened by the flesh, could not do: sending his own Son in the likeness of sinful flesh and for sin, he condemned sin in the flesh [of Christ]" (Rom 8:3). There is no question of making God a sinner; it is a matter of coming to grips with the representation that Christ has performed for us sinners. This could surely be a great help toward a Christian understanding of "conversion, penance and atonement".

Now let us turn to the second concept in our proposition, the *cor contritum*. First, genuine sorrow for sin, as an element of genuine conversion, is neither merely a matter of rational thought nor merely a matter of evaluation and judgment; it is a matter of personal knowledge, acknowledgment and decision, in some way an ultimate, internal, personal act.

Second, this inner act on the part of man is not something self-destructive. It is not something undertaken by a man against himself. It is only authentic when it includes two further orientations: *contritio* is essentially a new opening of oneself to the real order of being instituted by the Creator; it only involves inner upheaval because this true reality has come into the field of vision again. This was recognized by the pagan philosopher Epicurus, who introduced the word *contritio* into philosophy.[36]

Third, as person, man seeks ultimate reality outside and beyond himself in the form of a Person with whom and in whose presence he can look for and

---

[36] Cf. W. Schmidt, "*Contritio—ultima linea rerum in neuen epikureischen Texten*", *Rheinisches Museum* 100 (1957): 302–27.

attain this experience of being and of reality in a new way. The very word for sorrow for sin (German *Reue*, cf. English *rue*—Tr.) can tell us something in this connection: the original meaning of συντρίβω or *contero* is held by modern semantics to mean making fire by rubbing or spinning one piece of wood against another. Thus *contritio* comes about in a profound, dialogic relationship between persons. In the religious and Christian sense *contritio* is not simply man's act, but rather a collaboration between God and man, between Christ and the Christian: it is both a response and a participation. Hence, of itself it involves forgiveness. The plea of the penitential Psalm 51:10, "*cor mundum crea in me Deus, et spiritum rectum innova in visceribus meis*", is not only the other side of the "*cor contritum et humiliatum, Deus, non despicies*" (v. 17). God with his grace initiates my coming in sorrow to lay bare my sin, but he does not violate man's freedom; he calls to it, pleads for it.

Surely it is at this point that our theology of contrition, in which repentance and conversion are so deeply operative, needs to go far beyond the psychological and philosophical ideas that are still the stock-in-trade of so much of our theology. Surely, if we are to regain a deeper theological understanding of repentance, penance and contrition in our time, it is particularly important to contemplate Christ, to contemplate the picture of the crucified Lord, in the way the sermons of the baroque age exhort us to do.[37] Once we understand it properly, the old prayer "Look, O merciful and most sweet Jesus . . ." has a great deal to say to us men of the twentieth century.

At this point we can make some observations on the pictorial portrayal of the Heart of Jesus in our time, which may also be relevant to Central and South America. St. Paul does not grow tired of developing the idea of the Heart of Jesus, if I may speak of it thus, in his "in Christ"[38] and "with Christ" theology (Phil 1:1, 23; 1 Thes 4:17), continually endeavoring to put into words the reality of our redemption in and through Christ: "But if we have died with Christ, we believe that we shall also live with him" (Rom 6:8; 2 Tm 2:11). "I have been crucified with Christ; it is no longer I who live, but Christ who lives in me" (Gal 2:20). "But if Christ is in you, although your bodies are dead because of sin, your spirits are alive because of [his] righteousness" (Rom 8:10; cf. 2 Cor 5:21).

Bearing this in mind, it may be apposite nowadays to expand the picture of the Heart of Jesus beyond the symbol of the Heart alone, beyond the portrayal of Jesus alone, to include the relationship of the Heart of Jesus to man. Three historical pictures suggest themselves:

The first picture is drawn from the great Cistercian mysticism of the

---

[37] Cf. P. M. Zulehner, *Umkehr, Prinzip und Verwirklichung* (Frankfurt, 1979)—more orientated to psychology and sociology.

[38] Cf. G. Heyder, Paulus-Synopse (Regensburg, 1949), 133–38.

fourteenth and fifteenth centuries: Christ on the Cross releases his left arm and points to the Wound in his side, while St. Bernard is transfixed by the sight of it.[39]

A second biblical image, treated in a deeply religious and artistic manner, likewise from the late Gothic period, is that of the "Risen Lord who seizes the hand of Doubting Thomas and places it in his wounded side".[40]

The third picture, which seems to me to be particularly valuable for today, is that of the "Mother of Sorrows with the dead body of her Son at the foot of the Cross, pointing with her right hand to the Wound in Christ's side". We should see the Mother as the symbol of the Church, helping our age, which causes her so much pain, to visualize the love of God in the redemptive suffering of her Son.[41]

I think that these biblical portrayals could revitalize the mystery of the spirituality of the Heart of Jesus, which has become associated with a symbolism unintelligible to our contemporaries, and make of it once again a religious, spiritual and lived reality. Now let us gather together all that we have said and try to draw the conclusions.

c. Contrition and conversion as the Christian's conversation with the "caritas Christi urgens nos" *(2 Cor 5:14)*

If repentance, conversion, penance and contrition are to again become what they mean in the Christian understanding, if more than bringing an inner peace to man is at stake (as M. Scheeler illustrates in his valuable contribution "Reue und Wiedergeburt" ["Contrition and New Birth"]),[42] and instead a turning away from what is past by a turning toward the new, the whole, which comes as gift through the Yes of God's love in Christ Jesus, if all this is to happen once more, the two sides of this process of repentance and contrition, the *personal* and the *dialogic* side, need to be better understood. A particular way, often perhaps the only way, of doing this is to contemplate the *cor perforatum Christi* as we meet it in the theology of St. Paul and in the Church's Liturgy. As far as the Liturgy is concerned I only need to refer to the Improperia of Good Friday: *"Popule meus, quid feci tibi . . .",* a text with a long and great history.[43]

From the theology of St. Paul I will suggest only two of the more significant texts for special reflection. First of all there is 2 Corinthians 5:14–21.[44] It will suffice to quote a few sentences:

---

[39] Cf. E. Gilson, *The Mystical Theology of St. Bernard* (London, 1940).

[40] W. Mersmann, *Der Schmerzensmann* (Düsseldorf, 1952); Lex. Ch. Ik. vol. 4 (Freiburg, 1972), 87–95.

[41] J. Neuhardt/W. Schütz, *Die Pietà* (Freilassing, 1972); Lex. Ch. Ik. IV: 450–56.

[42] "Reue und Wiedergeburt" in *Vom Ewigen im Menschen* (Leipzig, 1921), 5–58.

[43] "Improperien" LThK V (1960): 640f.; prototype in 5th Book of Esdras. Cf. P. Riessler, *Altjüdische Schriften ausserhalb der Bibel* (Augsburg, 1928), 310ff.

[44] For Paul as the preacher of Christ's reconciling act, which makes everything new, cf. J. Sickenberger, *Die Briefe des heiligen Paulus an die Korinther und Römer* (Bonn, 1932), 115f.

> For the love of Christ controls us, because we are convinced that one has died for all; therefore all have died [in him]. And he died for all, that those who live might live no longer for themselves but for him who for their sake died and was raised. . . . God was in Christ reconciling the world to himself, not counting their trespasses against them, and entrusting to us the message of reconciliation. . . . For our sake he made him to be sin who knew no sin, so that in him we might become the righteousness of God.

What is involved here is not just man burdened by his sin, not just Christ who died for our sin; what is involved here is God who, because of our sins, has made Christ "to be sin", and for the sake of our redemption has raised Christ from the dead (Rom 5:1–21).

If our devotion to the Heart of Jesus is to be authentic and apt for the times in which we live, we need to see in the *cor perforatum Christi* not only God's love but also the denial of God, the perversity of our sin. We cannot take the love of God seriously unless once more we take our sins utterly seriously. Only when Christ's Cross and the Pierced Heart of the Redeemer have revealed to us a little of the mystery of sin shall we be in a position to appreciate that other solemn saying of St. Paul concerning our confidence in God through Christ—which by no means implies the cheap assumption, so often heard in our theology of late, that no one can be lost since Christ has died for all. This attitude is not a real Christian trust in God but rather the purely human insouciance and superficiality that refuses to take seriously the actual reality at work here.

The other Pauline text I wish to mention, Romans 8:31–39,[45] makes it clear that genuine, Christian confidence in God presupposes human suffering and sin. Again I will quote just a few sentences from it. It is preceded by the great discussion of the Spirit and the flesh (8:1–30), which means nothing other than the opposition between the careless life of guilty man-in-Adam and the committed existence of the child of God who strives to live by God's Spirit. For Christian existence is always "existence in patient hope for the fulfillment that God alone can give". Only the Christian can say with Paul:

> If God is for us, who is against us? He who did not spare his own Son but gave him up for us all, will he not also give us all things with him? . . . Who shall separate us from the love of Christ? Shall tribulation, or distress, or persecution, or famine, or nakedness, or peril, or sword? As it is written, "for thy sake we are being killed all the day long; we are regarded as sheep to be slaughtered" [cf. Ps 43:22]. No, in all these things we are more than conquerors through him who loved us [Aorist: who has once and for all loved us and always loves us]. For I am sure that neither death, nor life, nor angels, nor principalities, nor things present, nor things to come, nor powers, nor height, nor depth, nor anything else in all creation, will be able to separate us from the love of God in Christ Jesus Our Lord.

[45] A hymn in praise of the certainty of salvation, ibid., 245ff.

This is not some general love of God, the Creator's love of the creature: this is the historical love of the God of history in the historical Lord Jesus Christ on the historical Cross, made known to us in his Pierced Heart.

Let us then enumerate our conclusions:

1. The mortal suffering of Jesus is not an atoning suffering for our sins, arranged by God in some non-historical realm; it is the suffering of the incarnate Son of God through our sins, sins that have not come to an end as a result of his sacrificial death on the Cross. It is not without reason that the Apostle says, "God made him to be sin so that we might become in him the righteousness of God." Christ is our representative in God's presence. Christ's sufferings are not only physical, bodily sufferings: the whole God-Man Christ suffered. The piercing of his Heart by the soldier's lance expresses this: the Person of Jesus, his entire personal being as God and man, has suffered for us and through us. The man Jesus came to a unique awareness of this in Gethsemane and on the Cross. The crucified Jesus shows us what sin is: God-forsakenness. It can only be overcome by God himself in his love, not by a merely human act.

2. Perhaps, in asking why the Incarnation was necessary for our salvation, we need to bear in mind the fact that Christ suffered not only "for" but also "through" our sins. However profound and inspired the Scotist notion is that Christ would have become man even apart from our sins, since he is the fulfillment of human nature on earth, it would not be acceptable to Pauline Christology, nor is it compatible with the magnificent christological hymn of Colossians 1, which itself raises problems with regard to other Pauline statements.

3. Our penance, repentance is not merely an act to be interpreted at the level of psyche: it must be understood as a work of the grace of God and of Christ in us and together with us. Nor can our penance and contrition be seen simply as the result of a feeling of compassion that arises when we contemplate the suffering Lord. They must be understood as our response to what the suffering Christ tells us: the sufferings of Christ speak to us of the reality and havoc of sin, and in our contrition we are encouraged to confess the same with regard to our own sin. Initially it is not a question of the righteous and the unrighteous: it is a question of being close to God and being far from him.

4. We can see our repentance and penance as the fruit of Christ's suffering through our sins in an even deeper sense if we reflect that all that we do as Christians is done in the grace of Christ or by participation in the gracious work of Christ. "It is no longer I who live, but Christ who lives in me" and "I have been crucified with Christ" (Gal 2:20)—these are not mere pious metaphors; they seek to express a mystical but real dimension of our Christian existence. The man who no longer suffers with Christ through sin no longer knows what sin is.

5. We must go further and think at least briefly about the mystery of evil and sin. Like grace, sin is a mystery of faith, and we are ultimately dependent on revelation if we are to understand it. If my reading of theology is correct, we have to say this: all the mysteries of our faith are rooted in the mystery of God, and since God himself is triune, all our mysteries of faith somehow have a triune structure. I have tried elsewhere to develop the implications of this for the mystery of evil and sin.[46] Perhaps I may put the results thus: what revelation presents to us in the account of the first sin (Gn 3:1–6) is, as far as content goes, what operates in every man as "original sin" (in exact theology the *fomes peccati* of Augustine); it is the structural background behind each individual sin and has the following three elements: in this historical world, man, the creature of God, made in his image (like the angels), is always in danger of 1) *forgetting God*. This leads him to a 2) *self-glorification* in which, deprived of his true, God-given dignity and greatness, he is inclined to become 3) *swallowed up in the subhuman*. Sin in the Christian sense must be seen in this context of the drama of salvation, and not only in terms of the individual Ten Commandments.

6. If this view of sin is correct, then what we have termed "repentance, penance, contrition, atonement" must also be characterized by three elements or processes: man's return to himself from the subhuman world in which he had been lost; man's entry into the depths of his own being in which he knows himself to be a creature of God, made in God's image, that is called to be and to become the child of God; and finally the turning of man, the creature, in total self-surrender to God the Creator, who has given man not only his dignity, which is superior to the subhuman world, but also everything man himself is and has (cf. 1 Cor 4:7). Only when these three elements are joined do they yield the complete subject matter of a "theology of repentance". Now these three elements are forged into a unity in the Christ-event and expressed theologically in the symbol of the Heart of Jesus. We shall illustrate this unity of man's processes with the Christ-event by examining, in the context of the Sacred Heart symbol, the three structural elements of Christ's "dying" that can be identified theologically in his redeeming death.

7. We can consider the Heart of Jesus as the physical organ of his bodily life, the spiritual organ of the human Person, and finally as the center of the God-Man Jesus Christ. It follows that:

a. According to the view current at the time, his death was primarily a failure of the heart. The issue of brain versus heart, which was already raised in the eighteenth century in the disputres about the cult of the Sacred

---

[46] Cf. J. Auer, "Die Bedeutung des Immaculata-Dogmas für unsere Zeit", *Tagung der Arbeitsgemeinschaft marianischer Vereinigungen in Deutschland, Cologne 1979* (ed. Leutesdorf, 1980): 37–54.

Heart, can be put to one side. The Pierced Heart is first of all a sign of the death of Jesus. Now from a theological point of view physical death, for every man, signifies the end of that earthly life that endangers his relationship with God. In death we are abandoned by everything that was ours in the world; in death each man comes to himself.

b. The human Heart of Jesus, that is, the Person of Jesus insofar as he can be understood from the point of view of the human "I", had already consented, in the ultimate surrender of love, to this death for our sins at his very entrance into this world (cf. Heb 10:6; Ps 40:7ff.: "Lo, I have come to do thy will, O God"), so that, in John, Jesus can say on the Cross "It is finished" (Jn 19:30) and the piercing of the Heart (Jn 19:34) can be seen as a ratification of these words. This event expresses the total self-surrender of Jesus, of his human "I", to the will of the Father; it expresses the radical overcoming of all human "self-glorification".

c. But when we come to consider the death of Christ in the perspective of the Author of the letter to the Hebrews, it is the divine-human Heart, that is, the divine mystery in Christ, which is at work: Christ has "through the eternal Spirit offered himself without blemish to God", to "purify your conscience from dead works to serve the living God" (Heb 9:14–28). Thus he, the God-Man, has become "the mediator of a new covenant". Here God himself is at work in Jesus. "God so loved the world that he gave his only Son, that whoever believes in him should not perish but have eternal life" (Jn 3:16). Here man's "forgetfulness of God" is overcome by the action and being of God himself.

In conclusion we can say that the Christian understanding of all genuine "conversion and repentance" is concentrated in a historical and real way in the theological understanding of the "Sacred Heart". This is where a theological and moral understanding of repentance, contrition, penance and atonement must begin. Here, then, is my attempt to answer the question posed at the outset, as to the relationship between devotion to the Sacred Heart and the theology of conversion.

NORBERT HOFFMANN

ATONEMENT AND THE SPIRITUALITY OF THE SACRED HEART: AN ATTEMPT AT AN ELUCIDATION BY MEANS OF THE PRINCIPLE OF "REPRESENTATION"[1]

1. *Perspectives*

The very way in which theologians speak of their topics reveals their contemporary theological status. The very deliberate caution evident in the more recent studies of "atonement" — as compared with the treatment of devotion to the Sacred Heart[2] — and the deep concern for the integrity of Christian faith and practice, plainly indicate the real theological nub of the problem.

Some, of course, deny that atonement is possible at all for a human being,[3] but in any case it is characteristic of the current mentality to insist on the merely *analogous* nature of the "atonement" performed by the Christian,[4] and to ask whether it is still possible or right to use the term "atonement" — which has a precise meaning in the New Testament — both for God's saving

[1] What follows is a substantially expanded and annotated version of a paper on "Christology and Devotion to Christ" given on April 11, 1980, in Munich. I have taken account of the more significant remarks and criticisms that arose in discussion on that occasion.

[2] Cf. H. Küng, "Die Kirche des Evangeliums" in H. Häring, J. Nolte, eds., *Diskussion um Hans Küng "Die Kirche"* (Freiburg-Basel-Vienna, 1971), 175–221. Thus 193f.: "Congar values very highly the patristic (but by no means simply Johannine) idea of the Church as the New Eve, sprung from the wounded side of the sleeping Savior under the symbolism of the water and the blood; but, as a theologian speaking to modern men, I confess that this means as little to me as devotion to the Sacred Heart or the constant repetitions of the Litany of Loretto. Nor do I regard this as a sin. . . . These and similar things are not essential Christian issues."

[3] Cf., e.g., K. Barth, "Antworten auf Grundsatzfragen der Gefangenenseelsorge" in U. Kleinert, ed., *Strafvollzug: Analysen und Alternativen* (Munich, 1972), 48: "Atonement is not a human possibility but a deed performed by God in Jesus Christ. . . . Atonement and reparation have been superseded by Jesus Christ" (Quoted by L. Winner, *Sühne im interpersonalen Vollzug* [Paderborn, 1978], 12); E. Lohse, *Märtyrer und Gottesknecht* (Göttingen, 1963), 203: "No atoning value attaches to the suffering and dying of Christians, because the death of Christ has effected complete and eternally sufficient atonement"; ibid., 199: "According to the witness of the New Testament, atoning power belongs exclusively [sic] to the death of Jesus Christ. . . ."

[4] Cf. P. Neuenzeit, "Sühne" in HThG II: 594–96. There is a noticeable tendency to interpret Christian sufferings in terms not of expiation and satisfaction but of eschatology and martyrology: cf. ibid., 592f.; E. Lohse, op. cit., 196, 200, 202f. For the moment we leave it an open question whether the aspects of atonement and witness are mutually exclusive (cf. n.260 below).

activity, through the atoning death of his Son, in healing man's guilt, and also for individual or vicarious attempts to make reparation on the part of Christians.[5]

This concern is understandable. To speak of atonement is to touch the main soteriological nerve of the deposit of Christian faith. All the same one wonders whether this caution does not itself show a certain *lack of caution* in its unquestioning assumption that the New Testament concept of "atonement" is irreconcilable with human attempts at reparation. Are these attempts simply to be put under the heading of the history of religions as methods of "self-redemption" on the basis of "human retributive justice", distinct from "the unique approach of the Christian revelation"?[6] If not, the way may be open to a better understanding of that *ambivalence* that is undeniably present in the history of Christian atonement theology: on the one hand the emphasis on the unique "atoning act of Christ's sacrificial death", and on the other the conviction of the "expiatory effect of the martyr's death", including the sufferings and sorrows of everyday Christian existence.[7] We may be able to see that what we have here is not some imbalance[8] in the Christian consciousness but an ambivalence that can take us more deeply into the very structure of New Testament atonement.

We do not need those current new interpretations of the Christian message of redemption, which question or actually reject the idea of Christ's death on the Cross as being an "atoning sacrifice"[9] to make us aware that there are layers of problems associated with the phenomenon of "atonement" and that the nub lies not in the area of devotion or discipleship but in the heart of the mystery of redemption itself. The impression is almost irresistible that the topic of "atonement" has always been troublesome in Christian dogmatics.[10] The emphatic reserve vis-à-vis reparation-spirituality seems

[5] P. Neuenzeit, op. cit., 586. Our interest is not primarily historical; we are inquiring whether there is a dogmatically valid concept of atonement that can be of use in evaluating data from the history of spirituality and theology (e.g., P. Neuenzeit, op. cit., 586–96).

[6] Ibid.

[7] Ibid., 594.

[8] Ibid., 593.

[9] A brief report in H.-J. Lauter, "Brauchen wir ein Sühnopfer?" in *Anzeiger f. kath. Geistl.* 89 (1980): 75ff.; literature: ibid., 77 n.1.

[10] This is connected, perhaps, with the fact that on the one hand, dogmatics endeavors to understand as much as possible, whereas the doctrine of redemption, "by contrast with other comparable convictions of faith, remained much longer at the prereflexive level of direct biblical proclamation, liturgical celebration and faith-experience" and thus could "exhibit a high degree of diversification, indeed, of rank growth": G. Greshake, *Wandel der Erlösungsvorstellungen* (Freiburg, 1973), 69f.; cf. M. J. Scheeben, *Handbuch der kath. Dogmatik* V/2 no. 1254; H. Kessler, "Erlösung als Befreiung?" in StZ 192 (1974): 7. On the state of OT research into "atonement", cf. K. Koch, "Sünde und Sundenvergebung" in EvTh 26 (1966): 218: "This is a

strikingly to correspond to an unmistakable (though mostly unacknowledged) embarrassment with regard to the concept of atonement. By keeping to the (theologically speaking) relatively preliminary areas of the history of religion and culture or to ethical and juridical categories, or by adopting a positivist stance and being too quick to invoke the ineffability of the divine saving plan,[11] certain writers create the impression that — at least regarding the aspect of atonement — redemption, even if in fact it "has a precise meaning in the New Testament",[12] has not been adequately dealt with by theology as such,[13] so far as theology can "deal adequately" with anything. This impression is not removed by rhetorical reference to the love of God. Is God really so "manifest"[14] as love in the death of his Son? Can this "manifestly" be love, when it has something so terrible, not only as its symbol, but also as the locus of its fulfillment? Love too needs its "Logos"! But what kind of love is this, which is expressed in the "Logos of the Cross" (cf. 1 Cor 1:18)?

It seems that, in spite of many attempts to define it either formally[15] or biblically,[16] the current concept of atonement is remarkably vague, lacking conceptual definition and also a genuine theological identity.[17]

---

scandalously neglected area of a discipline in which otherwise we have been so active and productive." For an account of NT research into this topic cf. E. Lohse, op. cit., 9 n.1.

[11] This applies even to M. Schmaus, *Kath. Dogmatik,* vol. 2: *Gott der Schöpfer und Erlöser* (Munich, [3/4] 1949), 495, 806.

[12] P. Neuenzeit, op. cit., 586.

[13] What J. B. Westermayr wrote more than 40 years ago is still true: "As yet, the concept, legitimacy and meaning of the religious idea of atonement have hardly received any systematic treatment by technical theology": "Sühne" in LThK IX: 884–86.

[14] M. Schmaus, op. cit., 497, 496.

[15] Cf., e.g., M. Schmaus, *Der Glaube der Kirche* I: 502: "Atonement is to be understood as the freewill acceptance of some suffering as a penance for sins committed." Cf. ibid., II: 470; idem, *Kath. Dogmatik* II: 805 n.11; L. Winner, op. cit., 30f.: "Atonement denotes the active efforts toward redress, undertaken by a rational being who has incurred guilt in an interpersonal relationship, together with the active effort to come to a critical acceptance of the objective side of his guilt."

[16] We find this necessary (methodological) limitation, e.g., in the studies of J. Gnilka, "Wie urteilte Jesus über seinen Tod?", K. Kertelge, "Das Verständnis des Todes Jesu bei Paulus", R. Pesch, "Das Abendmahl und Jesu Todesverständnis", in IKaZ 9 (1980). These writers restrict themselves to demonstrating the fact of the unique atoning quality of the death of Jesus.

[17] If one tries to find a precise definition of the concept of atonement, in the context of other basic terms in the Christian doctrine of redemption such as forgiveness, reconciliation, satisfaction, conversion, penance, the elimination of guilt (i.e., of the penal consequences of sin), or contrition, its rather vague and indistinct quality becomes evident. Cf. J. Gnilka, op. cit., 41: "Atonement is initially a general and easily misunderstood concept. . . ."

On the semantic history of the German "Sühne" (Old High German *sona, suona,* Middle High German *suon, suone, süen*[e]) cf. *Deutsches Wörterbuch* by J. Grimm and W. Grimm, 10/IV (Leipzig, 1942), 1012–28; *Trübners Deutsches Wörterbuch,* ed. W. Mitzka, vol. 6 (Berlin, 1955), 683–84; L. Winner, op. cit., 30 n.8: the usage includes the meanings "judgment",

Let us put it quite bluntly: does the idea of "atonement" accepted in Christian *soteriology* arise *out of* Christian *theo-logy*? Is it orientated toward it? Or does its vagueness come from the fact that it is not sufficiently transparent in relation to the concept of God? And is not its lack of "theo-logic" ultimately responsible for the fervor with which more recent authors feel they have to try to liquidate "atonement", "satisfaction" and "sacrifice" as primitive religious categories that cannot be reconciled with the God of the New Testament, God the "Father"?[18]

Thus, further reflection on the soteriological heart of the whole concrete Christian reality of the "atonement" (which is also the heart of man's relationship to God in justification) must be accounted one of modern theology's desiderata.[19]

But, unless we are unaware of the implications of our topic and imagine we have no need to substantiate the claims it makes in the context of modern theological thought, we must actually undertake this reflection. Only by reaching a valid concept of the "atonement" that is Christ can we ensure a genuinely Christian answer to the question as to how far and in what sense being a Christian also involves "atonement". Only in this way, perhaps, can we decide whether atonement per se exhibits a specific relation to the notion

---

"sentence", "settlement of a lawsuit", "treaty", "peace", "reconciliation", "pardon", "satisfaction", "reparation" and "punishment".

[It will be clear from the foregoing that, although there is an overlap of meanings and associations, the German "Sühne" is in no way equivalent to the English "atonement". In the latter, the root sense of "at-one-ment", i.e., reconciliation, creating unity and harmony, predominates, and, in the absence of further qualifications, no specific theory of atonement is implied (cf. "At one", *Oxford English Dictionary* [1933], vol. 1). The legal and penal connotations of "Sühne" would suggest that "expiation" would be a more appropriate translation. However, just as "Sühne" is used in German theology as an umbrella term (to which the author of this article is attempting to give greater precision), so "atonement", though different in its connotations, is used in English. — Tr.]

[18] Cf., e.g., P. Fiedler, "Sünde und Vergebung im Christentum" in Conc 10 (1974): 569: "This is a question of theo-logy with far-reaching consequences. Jesus had proclaimed the Father's unconditional will to forgive: Was the Father's grace then insufficiently bountiful and, indeed, sovereign, that he had to insist on the Son's atonement all the same?" Cf. ibid., 570f. A critique of this in R. Pesch, op. cit., 185f. Cf. also R. Schwager, *Brauchen wir einen Sündenbock?* (Munich, 1978), 211: "The idea of a God who demands satisfaction is . . . of pagan origin"; ibid., 212; "A genuinely Christian doctrine of redemption must be purged of any suggestion that God's action must be matched by an action of ours."

[19] Current theology is "at a loss . . . as to how the message of redemption by Jesus Christ can be made credible and intelligible under the present circumstances" (G. Greshake, "Erlösung und Freiheit" in ThQ 153 [1973]: 324). R. Pesch, op. cit., 186, in agreement with P. Fiedler (cf. n.18 above), thinks that the question of the kind of atonement achieved by the death of Jesus has far-reaching consequences for theo-logy, and that its "elucidation is a task *laid upon* Christology and soteriology (and pneumatology too)" (our italics). Cf. H. Schürmann, "Jesu ureigenes Todesverstandnis" in *Begegnung mit dem Wort* (Bonn, 1980), 305.

of the "Heart", whether the actual conjunction of "atonement" ("reparation") and "Heart" in the Devotion[20] corresponds to a similar conjunction in the theological subject matter itself, and hence whether there is in fact any thematic unity in the present study.

What we are undertaking is a deliberate theological experiment. The "attempt" referred to in our subtitle is not that of a new definition of the conceptual components of "atonement" so much as a new transcendental rationale aimed at laying bare its theological core.[21] As a methodological key we shall consistently use the principle of "representation", tracing it back to its Trinitarian roots.

This approach, then, is characterized by a strict application of the systematic concept. We accept the fact that, as a primarily hypothetical treatment, "representation" is limited and one-sided; this is justified by the large internal dimensions, the many layers and the complexity of the topic. We cannot directly show the principle of "representation" to be a universal hermeneutical category contained in revelation;[22] but we shall attempt to justify it indirectly by showing how it can handle and illuminate the concepts "atonement" ("reparation") and the "Heart of Jesus". We shall attempt to show that the idea of "representation" can help to open up a whole horizon of understanding, within which the individual data of the distinct soteriological phenomenon of "atonement" can be integrated into a synthesis. We shall endeavor to reveal the a priori basis of the saving events of Christianity, tracing the Cross as the evidence of the atoning back to its theological essence and showing "representation" to be the key to the coherence of soteriology and theo-logy. These reflections are markedly systematic and speculative. What they produce is more in the nature of a theological intuition, initially vulnerable and in need of thorough testing by the specialist disciplines.[23]

2. The fundamental meaning of atonement in Christology and soteriology: Christ and "atonement"

2.1. "Atonement" as evidence of salvation history and its ambivalent structure

First of all we need deliberately to shake off the ready-made definitions of "atonement", and in particular the ideas associated with specific spiritualities,

[20] Cf. Pius XI, Encyclical *Miserentissimus Redemptor*, AAS 20 (1928): 169, 172f.; Pius XII, Encyclical *Haurietis aquas*, AAS 48 (1956): 312, 342, 347, 353.

[21] We are not really attempting to standardize the use of terms and concepts. Our main concern is not terminological intelligibility but theological understanding: we need an idea of atonement that not only is logically in focus but also is illuminated by the mystery of God.

[22] This is undertaken in N. Hoffmann, " 'Stellvertretung', Grundgestalt und Mitte des Mysteriums. Ein Versuch trinitätstheologischer Bergründung christlicher Sühne" in MThZ 30 (1979): 161–91. This study is essential for a full understanding of the following remarks.

[23] References to matters of exegesis, biblical theology and the history of dogma are not meant to be exhaustive; they only signify that these speculations are in touch with the reality of revelation and the theological tradition.

with their devotional expressions and practices,[24] in order to be uninhibited in uncovering the basic meaning of "atonement", authentically fulfilled in salvation history.[25]

Our fundamental conviction is that it is God who is working our "salvation" in history, liberating us from "perdition"[26] in a way that accords with the actual constitution of the world and of man. The situation of evil has its roots in "sin".[27] So God saves by redeeming us from sin.

But how does God redeem us from sin? This question goes to the heart of our problem: that the event of the Cross is the acme of God's redemptive work is beyond dispute, but the *interpretation* of the Cross is hotly contested. Naturally the Cross is the climax, but in what sense? The climax of what manner of redemption?[28]

It is not our intention to engage directly with those new interpretations that more or less deny the "atonement" character of Christian redemption, that see the death of Jesus for instance as the unmasking and exposing of a scapegoat mechanism that permeates all civilization and religion[29] as the triumphant and irreversible proclamation of an absolute (and absolutely unqualified) will on God's part, to give grace and forgiveness,[30] or that see Christ's death much more indefinitely as the "offer of salvation" or mere "solidarity".[31] Our basis is the New Testament in its totality.[32] At the same time, and with

---

[24] Without intending in the least to disparage or reject them, it is quite probable that many a despised trickle of popular piety, aside from the swelling tide of official theology, has been of service to the Church down the ages in preserving the genuine substance of faith — albeit perhaps in a limited form.

[25] As is necessary in any task of this kind, we shall start with a fairly general notion, e.g., "atonement" as a "way of eliminating sin" (K. Prümm, "Sühne. I. Religionsgeschichtlich" in LThK IX: 1152; cf. n.15 above).

[26] The German pair of opposites "Heil/Unheil" has to be rendered by "salvation/perdition" or some other pair of concepts not etymologically related in English as they are in German.

[27] On sin and guilt, as the deepest motive for man's need of redemption, cf. K. Rahner, "Salvation. IV. Theology" in SM 5 (Herder 1970): 425ff.; F. Bammel, "Erlösung. I. Religionsgeschichtlich" in RGG, 3rd ed., II: 584f.; A. Grillmeier, "Erlösung. IV. Systematik" in LThK, 2nd ed., III: 1024.

[28] Cf., e.g., H.-J. Lauter, loc. cit.; O. Knoch, "Zur Diskussion über die Heilsbedeutung des Todes Jesu" in ThPQ 124 (1976): 3–14; idem, "Die Heilsbedeutung des Todes Jesu", ibid., 221–37.

[29] R. Schwager, op. cit., 143ff. Critique in H. U. von Balthasar, "Die neue Theologie von Jesus als dem 'Sündenbock' " in IKaZ 9 (1980): 184f.; H.-J. Lauter, op. cit., 76f.

[30] K. Rahner, *Foundations of Christian Faith* (Seabury Press, 1978), 282ff. Cf. H. Schürmann, op. cit., 288f.

[31] E. Schillebeeckx, *Jesus: An Experiment in Christology* (London, 1979), 310; idem, *Christ: The Christian Experience in the Modern World* (London, 1980).

[32] Its contents are full of tensions; we have no intention of filtering out of the NT, on the basis of an a priori understanding of God, suspiciously univocal and plausible affirmations. We share with H.-J. Lauter, op. cit., 77, the conviction that redemption is a mystery and hence "is not only a deed done by God, but its significance must also be interpreted by him".

an eye to the discussion just mentioned, we wish to take the New Testament interpretation of the Cross together with an emphasis on its Old Testament presuppositions: the Cross is not an isolated element in the world but the meridian in a continuum of salvation history.[33] If constant factors can be identified in the concrete expression of salvation history in connection with the process of cleansing from sin, they may well indicate a hidden purposefulness in the divine drama of redemption. They may provide valuable assistance as we seek to go beyond the fact of the Cross, subject as it is to a variety of interpretations, to what is actually going on deep down within it.[34]

2.1.1. *Ambivalence in the Old Testament process of cleansing from sin*

If for the moment we put the problems associated with "atonement" to one side and look simply at the way redemption from sin is in fact carried on in the Old Testament, we discover three undeniable factors in this complex process:[35] first, Yahweh's absolute sovereignty,[36] second, his unmistakable and remarkable involvement[37] with man, and finally, his

---

[33] H. Schlier, "Die Anfänge des christologischen Credo" in B. Welte, ed., *Zur Frühgeschichte der Christologie: Ihre biblischen Amfänge und die Lehrformel von Nikaia* (Freiburg-Basel-Vienna, 1970 [QD 51]) 27: according to 1 Cor 15:3–5, "the death of Christ is set forth as an atoning death" and "takes its place as the fulfillment of salvation history. . . ." Cf. H. Gross and F. Mussner, "Die Einheit von Altem und Neuem Testament" in IKaZ 3 (1974): 544–55. As opposed to the view "that the Old Testament has been so totally and absolutely overtaken by the New that it could be cast aside without losing anything of substance", H. Gross is convinced "that the Old and the New Testaments form an indissoluble unity" (ibid., 544). According to F. Mussner, while there is "no unproblematical continuum" between the two, there is "the constant factor of God's will to save the world, a continuity in the area of soteriology" (ibid., 550), and the early Church "affirms a continuity of God's action, from the creation to the Resurrection of Jesus Christ from the dead" (ibid., 551). Cf. H. Haag, "Vom eigenwert des Alten Testaments" in ThQ 160 (1980): 2–16. On Christ as the fundamental exegetical principle of the Old Testament, cf. A. Vögtle, "Der verkündigende und verkündigte Jesus 'Christus' " in J. Sauer, ed., *Wer ist Jesus Christus?* (Freiburg-Basel-Vienna, 1977), 27–91, esp. 31f. On the significance for the NT of OT references to atonement and the forgiveness of sin, cf. K. Koch, "Sühne und Sündenvergebung" in EvTH 26 (1966):239 (see n.114 below).

[34] Such factors would be indirectly of significance in the current discussion of atonement insofar as it pursues a theo-logical line.

[35] On the many forms taken by the Old Testament phenomenon of "forgiveness" cf. W. Eichrodt, *Theology of the Old Testament*, vol. 2 (London, 1967), 443ff. G. von Rad, *Theology of the Old Testament*, vol. 1 (London, 1962 and 1975), 269: "What were the special features of the concept of expiation in the Old Testament? . . . No adequate answer has as yet been given." A detailed exmination is needed to ascertain whether the present presentation of the Old Testament conception of atonement, at the level intended, is correct.

[36] Cf., e.g., F. Maass, "Sühnen" in THAT I: 842–57, esp. 851, 853: "God is the one whose actions are decisive, who makes atonement possible"; P. Neuenzeit, "Sühnen" in HThG II: 589; J. Scharbert, "Vergebung" in HThG II: 741.

[37] Cf. A. Deissler, "Gottes Selbstoffenbarung im Alten Testament in MySal II: 226–71, esp. 267ff. ("Jahwes Eifer und Zorn"); W. Berg, "Die Eifersucht Gottes" in BZNF 23 (1979): 197–211; R. Guardini, *Die existenz des Christen* (Munich-Paderborn-Vienna, 1976), 275ff.

strikingly firm insistence that the guilty man should play his part in the process of forgiveness.[38]

While scholars on all sides emphasize the sovereign transcendence of God, they scarcely pay attention to the stubbornness with which Yahweh insists on the active participation of the one making atonement, beyond noting the fact.[39]

By contrast, we wish to devote special attention to this very aspect of the divine saving economy, in the hope that it may show itself to be of decisive significance in uncovering the deeper dimensions of redemption. This hope will be justified if it transpires that the three factors referred to are not an arbitrary selection from the multiplicity of Old Testament data but a consistent and coherent constellation of three characteristic features, in which case one would have to speak of the process of cleansing from sin as having a threefold shape. From a soteriological point of view this would repay attention, for the inner essence of redemption might then be seen to be articulated in the structure of the external events.

Indeed Yahweh neither is nor can be in any way the "object" of human attempts to change his mind,[40] and he does not first have to be put into a conciliatory mood. But, always exhibits and unswervingly[41] he *is* eternal, anticipatory willingness to forgive and power of forgiveness. *All the same* these inherent qualities of God *are not yet*, in and of themselves, the reality of forgiveness. And this is an assertion that merits great emphasis. Redemption does not simply exist: it is something that *takes place*.[42] How does it take place?

Redemption does not occur as a mere act of revelation, manifesting something that already is the case; it is not a Platonically conceived epiphany, in time, of what is eternal and unchangeable. Nor does God's "will to forgive" effect "forgiveness simply 'vertically from above', equally and directly at all time-space intersections".[43] The release from guilt takes place as an

---

[38] Cf. F. Maass, op. cit., 854: "The person making atonement is required to do something on his side. It cannot be shown to be a striving for self-redemption, but it does involve renunciation and sacrifice." Cf. ibid., 847; J. Scharbert, op. cit., 743; E. Lohse, op. cit., 110: "And although the Jewish faith can say a great deal about the grace of God, it remains a fact that there can be no forgiveness unless there is a demonstrable effort on man's side." Cf. ibid., 19, 27, 48. However, we are not so much concerned with the guilty person's involvement in the cultic sense as with the total claim which Yahweh makes on him in his forgiving action; cf. Eichrodt, op. cit., 465f.

[39] With the prominent exception of H. U. von Balthasar!

[40] Cf. W. Joest, "Versöhnung" in RGG VI: 1378f.; E. Lohse, op. cit., 145f., 153.

[41] Cf. H. Vorgrimler in MySal V: 354f., 355: "Fluctuations of mood . . . are to be found only on man's side." Cf. 2 Cor 5:18ff.: God reconciles us with himself. Cf. on this issue F. Büchsel in ThWNT I: 255 (καταλλάσσω).

[42] Cf. H. U. von Balthasar, *Theodramatik* II/2: 106 ("The recovery of the dramatic").

[43] K. Rahner, "Erlösung" in SMI: 1170; cf., ibid., 1163.

interpersonal event, in the personal theater of action between God and the sinner. True, God is not the object but the subject of reconciliation. But he is this—in the freest autonomy, of course—in the tension between himself and the sinner, as one who stands over against him in the personal mode.[44] God is encountered as the divine thou,[45] in the context of that unique "covenant" relationship,[46] which is meant to be characterized by deep *reciprocal*[47] love and faithfulness.[48] Already on the basis of the amazing fact that the God of the Old Testament does not reign in Olympian aloofness above the world but is "existentially" involved in its destiny and loves it,[49] we must no longer be amazed that, as revelation describes it, he is affected by sin, hurt by it, and consequently strives, with zeal and unconcealed "self-interest", to eliminate it. His very zeal emphasizes the qualified way in which the sinner is addressed as a subject,[50] a relationship summarized by the fundamental Old Testament word *šûb.*[51]

The seriousness of man's status as (qualified) subject is plain from the fact that, for sin to be taken away, the correlation between "forgiveness" (on Yahweh's side) and "repentance" (on the sinner's) is absolutely essential.

Corresponding to the "synthetic view of life" of the people of antiquity,[52] however, where "sin" was felt to be a complex of the evil deed, the guilt and the consequent punishment, the process of *metanoia* too is felt to be a layered process, governed in totality by the dynamic saving activity of God.

Yahweh insists on "repentance", but not only in the sense of merely distancing oneself from the evil deed and thought (i.e., by not turning back to

[44] Thus Yahweh is not, as it were, a "transcendental a priori" looking over man's shoulder; nor does he make his presence felt merely as a "moral order". Cf. R. Stadler, "Der neue Gottesgedanke Fichtes: Eine Studie zum 'Atheismusstreit' " in ThPh 54 (1979): 481 541, esp. 491.

[45] Cf. K. Barth, *Church Dogmatics* II/1 (Edinburgh, 1957), 13ff. on the "objectivity of God".

[46] Cf. A. Deissler in MySal II: 243ff.; H. Mühlen, *Der Heilige Geist als Person,* 241ff.

[47] Cf. Ex 6:7; Lev 26:11f.: "I will be your God and you shall be my people."

[48] On the marriage covenant as an illustration of this relationship cf. A. Deissler, op. cit., 262f.; H. Mühlen, op. cit., 247f. The fact that Yahweh, in the free and causeless initiative proper to God, "guarantees the covenant as the utterly superior covenant-Lord" (A. Deissler, op. cit., 250) does not contradict the fact that he "courts the trust of the people with living warmth of feeling and looks for a response that is spontaneous and from the heart" (W. Eichrodt, *Theology of the Old Testament* I: 52.

[49] R. Guardini, *Theologische Briefe an einen Freund: Einsichten an der Grenze des Lebens* (Op. posth. Munich-Paderborn-Vienna, 1976), 10, 19–28; idem, *Die Existenz des Christen* (op. posth. Munich-Paderborn-Vienna, 1976), 277. Cf. K. Barth, *Church Dogmatics* II/2 (Edinburgh, 1957), 8, 25f., 92f.

[50] Cf. W. Joest, "Versöhnung", 1378: God does not treat "man as the mere object of his almighty power. . . ."

[51] Cf. W. Eichrodt, *Theology of the OT* I: 357f.; ibid., II: 466; R. Schulte in MySal V: 120ff.

[52] Which, according to G. von Rad, *Theology of the OT* I: 265, presupposes "the closest possible correspondence between action and fate". Cf. W. Eichrodt, *Theology of the OT* II: 426.

it):[53] it is not enough for the sinner simply to cease his wrongdoing: he must bring it to bear in his *metanoia*. Of course the deed is done and cannot be undone. But what has been perpetrated and set in motion by it transcends both deed and doer and has somehow acquired an existence of its own, so that, whether or not the perpetrator's subjective will has undergone a change, it is *there* now and is continuing to exert a "power proper to it"[54] in the sinner and his world, affecting God too. This is the sin that must be "wiped out", "put away",[55] "carried away".[56]

Now this injunction receives all its force in connection with the very fact that seems to nullify it, namely, the massively documented autonomy of Yahweh's will, a will that is independent to the point of apparent arbitrariness, according to which he grants or withholds pardon[57] in response to human attempts at repentance (sacrifice, pleading, intercession).

Thus, when there is increasing emphasis on a real taking-away of sin (particularly at the climax of Old Testament teaching on redemption in Isaiah 53),[58] we must take this, not as evidence of a magical ritual or even ethical retributive concept, but as the result of Yahweh's entirely personal, deliberate, free decision.

So, for our purposes, we need to closely examine what Yahweh so obstinately insists upon: the inner process betokened by the notion of "carrying away" sin. First, we must notice that the "original meaning of '*nassa awon*' is not to 'carry away' (= 'take away') guilt, but . . . to take it upon oneself and 'carry' it",[59] to endure it.[60] So our interest focuses on what is actually to be "borne" in this way.

Initially, doubtless, there are the earthly effects of sin — misfortune, trouble, all kinds of hardship. Yet, corresponding to its radically theological understanding

---

[53] Cf. G. von Rad, op. cit., 264f.: It is only our coarse modern understanding of sin which "narrows the meaning of sin . . . down to affect only the individual and his spiritual life, and confines the evil that accompanies the sin . . . to the evil act itself". [Slightly altered — Tr.]

[54] Ibid., 265.

[55] Cf. W. Eichrodt, *Theology of the OT* II: 423, n.8; Th. C. Vriezen, *Theologie des AT in Grundzügen* (Neukirchen, 1956), 246 n.3; J. Scharbert, op. cit., 741.

[56] Cf. F. Stolz, *nś'* "lift, carry" in THAT II: 109–17, esp. 113.

[57] Cf. Th. C. Vriezen, op. cit., 250, 253f.; J. Scharbert, op. cit., 748.

[58] Cf. Th. C. Vriezen, op. cit., 256f.; J. Scharbert, op. cit., 743; P. Neuenzeit, op. cit., 589.

[59] A. Deissler, "Hingegeben für die Vielen", loc. cit., in MySal II: 341; cf. F. Stolz, op. cit., 113.

[60] According to the Priestly Document, "this was as a rule effected by way of channeling the baneful influence of the evil into an animal that died vicariously" (G. von Rad, op. cit., 271; cf. L. Winner, op. cit., 135). Corresponding to the theistically purified conception of God in Israel, these rites are thought of "sometimes more, sometimes less explicitly, as a transaction between two persons" (W. Eichrodt, *Theology of the OT* I: 159; cf. ibid., II: 444, 465; F. Maass, "Sühnen" in THAT I: 846; Th. C. Vriezen, op. cit., 252; L. Winner, op. cit., 147ff.). G. von Rad, op. cit., 270f.: the priests who consume the sin-offering "deal in Yahweh's stead with the entire removal of the evil which has been laid upon the animal".

of existence,[61] Israel, as its religion becomes less a matter of things and more personal, experiences these consequences of sin more and more clearly as effects of a disturbed relationship with God.[62] They are expressions of Yahweh's "anger".[63] Therefore, what is actually being "borne"—in the destruction of earthly existence, even to death itself—is the breaking of the "covenant", Yahweh's self-concealment from his people, the suffering involved in being far from him who *is* life and happiness.[64]

However, Yahweh's anger, the "epitome" of what, "in his love for his creatures, he does not wish",[65] "never becomes an independent power of destruction".[66] "Even the severest punishment" serves "the purpose of conversion".[67] Yahweh rebukes and chastises only to persuade the sinner "to create on his side the conditions necessary for forgiveness".[68]

But it would not satisfy the "radical seriousness" of God's zeal for salvation (expressed anthropomorphically in the term "anger"), a zeal "in which God fulfills his election . . . carrying through his plan with maximum energy",[69] if the only change were to be the fundamental *metanoia* in the personal center of the sinner's will.[70] God's anger only "turns",[71] "stands still" (cf. 2 Mc 7:38),

---

[61] Cf. G. von Rad, op. cit., 262ff.; W. Eichrodt, *Theology of the OT* I: 160: "The divine 'thou shalt' drives home the fact of a God whose personal will is present to control all human conduct." Ibid., II: 433: The evil consequences of sin are so related to sin itself that they reveal sin as "an infringement of that divine purpose that embraces and sustains the whole of life". Cf. ibid., 426.

[62] Cf. W. Eichrodt, ibid., 431, refers to the "vividness with which men were aware of God's punishment as the operation of a personal relationship between God and man". Ibid., 432: above all it is the prophets who "make it their business to convey to men that punishment is the annulment of a wholly personal relationship between God and man. . . ." Ibid., 433: "the divine love that woos a return of love from man must make it plain that to reject God's love is to forfeit the only salvation."

[63] Cf. W. Eichrodt, "Zorn Gottes" in RGG VI: 1930; J. Fichtner, *Der Zorn gottes im AT*, 399–402, 405; R. Schwager, op. cit., 219ff.

[64] Cf. G. von Rad, op. cit., 155: God cursed Cain "away from the fertile, arable lands. So Cain went away from the presence of Yahweh." On the connection between "God's anger" and "distance from God" see J. Fichtner, op. cit., 402; W. Eichrodt, *Theology of the OT* II: 432. On Israel's corresponding idea of death, cf. G. von Rad, op. cit., 387f.; ibid., 388: "Death begins to become a reality at the point where Yahweh forsakes a man, where he is silent, i.e., at whatever point the life-relationship with Yahweh wears thin." On the cult as the "center and source" of the world of the living, see ibid., 389.

[65] H. Brandt, "Zorn Gottes IV. Dogmatish" in RGG 3rd ed., IV: 1932–33.

[66] W. Eichrodt, "Zorn Gottes" in RGG VI: 1930; cf. H. Brandt, op. cit., 1932: Yahweh's anger is not an "autonomous direction or quality of his will" independent from or opposed to his love. J. Fichtner, op. cit., 410: the anger of God as the "obverse of his love for Israel"; cf. ibid., 404, 408–10.

[67] W. Eichrodt, *Theology of the OT* II: 459.

[68] J. Scharbert, op. cit., 742.

[69] W. Eichrodt, "Zorn Gottes", 1930.

[70] With K. Rahner, "Ablass" in SH I: 31 ["Indulgences" in SM 3: 126ff.], one can speak of an "initial conversion" in this phase of *metanoia*, to which our theology assigns the elimination of the *reatus* of guilt.

[71] J. Scharbert, op. cit., 741; cf. W. Eichrodt, *Theology of the OT* I: 160; J. Fichtner, op. cit., 408 (Is 51:17, 22).

when sin is overcome in all its consequences, when the sinner is really "cleansed" and "healed"[72] from it and forgiveness is fully achieved. At this point the dialectic of grace and punishment in God's saving activity begins to make deep sense.[73] Thus, even if "there is absolutely nothing in the thought of the Old Testament that generally corresponds to the distinction we make between sin and penalty"[74]—because of the Old Testament's unique, dynamistic perspective on existence[75]—yet the Old Testament does at least occasionally make a clear distinction between "forgiveness" in the modern (more restricted) sense (remission of the *reatus culpae*) and the "remission of punishment".[76]

We can see that the religious practice of the Old Testament was clearly aware of the distinction and the connection between (initial) forgiveness and the suspension of punishment, by the different value placed upon the way the punishment of sin is "borne": if this is done not in resistance and stubbornness but "in pious submission",[77] what we have, in our view, is the very heart of what the Old Testament calls "atonement".

In the whole process of *metanoia*[78] this doubtless presupposes an "initial conversion" and its corresponding "forgiveness": the sinner *has* repented of his sin, he *has* turned back from his path, has humbled himself before Yahweh, has submitted to his will in obedience and self-abasement;[79] now he lays hold, in penitence, of the means of atonement offered by Yahweh[80] and is ready to make reparation.[81]

In the Old Testament view, then—and this view has not perhaps been fully worked out theoretically—atonement is performed by someone who, as far as his innermost will is concerned, is *no longer a sinner*. Only the converted man, once again turned to God and loving him, *can* "Bear sin" in such a way (i.e., under the form of suffering) that, in the very act of his doing so,

[72] Cf. J. Scharbert, ibid.; K. Rahner, "Sündenstrafen" in SM IV: 761–66.

[73] Cf. J. Scharbert, op. cit., 742: "Even though Yahweh is a gracious God, he does not 'acquit' the sinner, i.e., he does not entirely absolve him from punishment" but permits "the calamitous consequences of sin to take effect as punishment".

[74] G. von Rad, Op. cit., 266; cf. W. Eichrodt, *Theology of the OT* II: 413: "The Hebrew had no particular interest in making a sharp conceptual distinction between sin and guilt."

[75] Cf. R. Knierim in THAT I: 546, 255.

[76] Cf. J. Scharbert, op. cit., 742.

[77] W. Eichrodt, "Zorn Gottes", 1930.

[78] Cf. K. Rahner, "Busse" in SH I: 652 ["Penance" SM 4: 385ff.; "Contrition" SM 2: 1ff.].

[79] Cf. W. Eichrodt, *Theology of the OT* II: 445, 460, 465; ibid., I: 159f.; J. Scharbert, op. cit., 742; E. Lohse, op. cit., 23, 27. Ibid., 22: The sins through which a man "had injured his neighbor could only be expiated provided he had already become reconciled to him". "According to the rabbis, the expiatory power of the Day of Atonement was only effective if the sinner had turned from his way."

[80] Cf. W. Eichrodt, *Theology of the OT* II: 444, 446, 459; E. Lohse, op. cit., 20.

[81] Cf. W. Eichrodt, *Theology of the OT* I: 164; J. Fichtner, op. cit., 401f., 406: God's anger also strikes the righteous.

sin is wiped out.[82] Hence atonement would be the bearing of sin by the one who has turned away from it. On the basis of the Old Testament, then, we can say that atonement concerns the one for whom sin (Yahweh's "anger", his self-concealment) has become a great suffering. *Atonement is sin changed into the suffering that results from distance from Yahweh.* This understanding includes the realization that atonement and sin are not contradictories but contraries; the realization that "conversion" does not simply mean turning away *from* sin but is also a turning round *of the sin itself*, that is, of the sinner, who for his part is the object of the divine anger ("Yahweh is afar off") on account of his guilt. Yet paradoxically this very distance *turns him* back to Yahweh in a way that is *unique* to the sinner, namely, in the mode of a suffering love, stigmatized by the pain of sin.

Even if Old Testament thought had not advanced to a reflexive understanding of such a concept of atonement,[83] we may still see it as part of the horizon of understanding within which Israel sought atonement, at least to the extent that it helps us to understand an indubitable historical fact: the firm and widespread belief in the special intercessory power of the *Godfearing* man, the phenomenon of the *representative* atonement of the *righteous*.[84]

Consider, if people were convinced "that sin is not forgiven as a matter of course but as a result of the offering of a *pure and innocent* life as expiation for the guilt-laden life of the offerer",[85] and that "God ascribes" to the intercessor "atoning value sufficient for the removal of guilt" *because*, in "his own longing that God's salvation shall be fully revealed", the intercessor has become "one with the will of God *to the point of self-sacrifice*" and thus "his own existence is offered for the redemption of the one threatened by the wrath of God".[86] Can we not continue this line of thought? Can we not see the righteous man's power of *atonement* as a power of *transformation*, inasmuch as his righteousness (longing for God) enables him to change sin (i.e., the "forsaking of Yahweh" or "being forsaken" by him) into the painful renunciation of God's nearness?

[82] Cf. K. Rahner, "Opfer. V. Dogmatisch" in LThK VII: 1174–76; 1175: "Man can come to an awareness of himself as a sinner standing under the judgment of God, which threatens his whole existence, and can hand over a gift (thus withdrawing it from his own use—this is brought out by the 'destructive' aspect of sacrifice), as an expression of the fate that he deserves and of his contrite and willing acceptance of it: this is what expiatory sacrifice means. . . ."

[83] Cf. W. Eichrodt, op. cit., I: 166f., mentions "the absence of any theory of atonement properly so-called" in the OT; E. Lohse, op. cit., 21: "In late Judaism, as in the Old Testament, hardly anyone wondered why and in what way the sacrificial cult was able to effect atonement."

[84] Cf. W. Eichrodt, op. cit., I: 167; ibid., II: 462; E. Lohse, op. cit., 66ff., 78ff., 94ff.; L. Winner, op. cit., 141ff. On the climax of the OT doctrine of forgiveness and atonement (Is 53 and Zec 12:10–14) cf. J. Scharbert, op. cit., 743; P. Neuenzeit, op. cit., 589; L. Winner, op. cit., 147ff.; Th. C. Vriezen, op. cit., 255–59.

[85] W. Eichrodt, op. cit., I: 166.

[86] Ibid., II: 450.

There can be no doubt that such a conception, as a result of its origin, guarantees that the process of atonement shall be an interpersonal event of unique dimensions. And seen under the aspects of "substitution" and "reparation"[87] —far beyond all attempts to measure and quantify punishment—atonement is most closely correlated with Yahweh's holy and injured love. It is this love that brings itself to bear on the sinner in the form of the saving burden that, in atonement, is "borne" as "wrath".[88] God's love, wounded by sin, corresponds in the sinner to atonement, seen as sin transformed into the suffering of love.

If, against the background of this understanding of atonement, one accepts the fact (vouched for by the whole of the Old Testament), that Yahweh is the "subject", not the "recipient" of atonement (cf. Lv 17:11; Dt 21:8)[89]—in the sense that both the relevant cult[90] and the disposition to conversion[91] come as gift and grace from him, that is, that "God himself has created and enjoined the means of propitiation"[92]—then it is clearly right to say: "Expiation was thus not a penalty but a saving event."[93]

Essentially, "atonement" (on man's side) cannot be understood in isolation from the idea of "forgiveness" (on God's).[94]

There can be no doubt that the attempt to clarify the relationship between "forgiveness" and "atonement" is made more difficult by the lack of conceptual distinction in the Old Testament between the "sinful act", the "reatus culpae" and the "reatus poenae". Quite apart from this, however, we can detect in the contents of the two ideas a characteristic and considerable fluid overlap, mirroring—as we are convinced—the unfathomable mysteriousness of what actually occurs in the depths of the process of atonement between God and man.

Naturally enough, a juridical understanding of atonement or forgiveness (as "remission of punishment") cannot do justice to the specifically personal quality of this process.[95] Even the formula that describes atonement as "a means employed by God's purpose of forgiveness"[96] leading to a reopening of divine fellowship[97] seems too anemic; it does not express the characteristic and

[87] Cf. ibid., I: 159.

[88] Yahweh's injured love for Israel as the central motive of his anger: J. Fichtner, op. cit., 404, 409.

[89] G. von Rad, op. cit., 270: in the Priestly Document, too, "although the priest actually performs the actions for expiation, in the last analysis it is Yahweh himself who offers or refuses expiation." Cf. Th. C. Vriezen, op. cit., 247.

[90] W. Eichrodt, op. cit., I: 163; ibid., II: 443f.

[91] Ibid., II: 459f., 465f.

[92] Ibid., I: 163.

[93] G. von Rad, op. cit., 271.

[94] W. Eichrodt, op. cit., II: 443-48.

[95] Cf. ibid., 453 (". . . men have been released from a penal sentence"; "punishment . . . compensation fitted to the offense"); 455.

[96] Ibid., 446.

[97] Ibid., 455.

incomparable relationship between Yahweh and the sinner, the unique interpenetration of forgiveness and atonement.

Yahweh forgives the sin (in the full Old Testament sense) *by allowing* the sinner to atone for it:[98] it is only because of the *love* the sinner has received in the (initial) forgiveness, and in virtue of the "initial conversion" wrought by it, that he is able to "bear" his sin under the form of suffering. Although Yahweh in "anger" withdraws his presence from the sinner, he graciously draws the sinner to himself in such a way that he experiences this withdrawal as the pain of love and is able to "wipe out", kill and transform the sin into its opposite under the form of suffering.

Presupposing a metaphysical basis and the holistic and dynamic concept of forgiveness, we can go even further in our examination of the relationship between forgiveness and atonement and — using the Thomistic-Aristotelian doctrine of the "motus"[99] — dare to see them as identical (bearing in mind their different relational perspectives). That is, when sin is changed into the pain of God's distance then, forgiveness and atonement are one and the same reality — it is called "atonement" insofar as it is found in the sinner (as his act and disposition), and it is called "forgiveness" insofar as it is obtained from God.[100] More exactly: Yahweh's eternal power (actuality, "*actus*") of forgiveness takes effect *in* the sinner here and now as forgiveness ("*actio*") *in* the act *of* the sinner[101] himself. Under the influence of grace he achieves initial conversion in the forgiveness of the *reatus culpae*, and then — by virtue of the love thus granted — the full coversion that embraces the sinner's whole personal being. Consequently, it is God who converts;[102] he enables the sinner to atone. But he does this in such a way that the sinner can act *as* a free subject vis-à-vis Yahweh: he draws him out of his sinful self-preoccupation and to

---

[98] This is an unbreakable principle; thus, it applies also in the case of vicarious atonement: the person concerned must acknowledge his proxy, must ask him to atone, and must involve himself in the atonement. Cf. J. Scharbert, op. cit., 743; idem, *Heilsmittler im Alten Testament und im Alten Orient*, QD 23/24 (Freiburg-Basel-Vienna, 1964): 298, 310. Cf. H. Vorgrimler, "Busse und Krankensalbung", HDG IV/3 (Freiburg-Basel-Vienna, 1978): 129: "The Fathers were of the opinion that men's penances [subjective penance] lead to forgiveness by God. . . . Taking up the patristic view, the majority of early scholastic theologians teach that contrition alone deletes man's guilt . . . and even later the view is put forward that the man who comes to receive the sacrament of penance comes as someone already justified through contrition."

[99] Cf. B. Lonergan, *Divinarum Personarum conceptionem analogicam* (Rome, 1957), 246.

[100] Ibid.: "Iam vero ille unus idemque actus qui a movente producitur et in mobili recipitur duplicem habet relationem: aliam nempe ad movens a quo est; aliam vero ad motum in quo est." Cf. K. Rahner, "Penance", SM 4: 386 [idem, "Penance" in *Encyclopedia of Theology*, ed., K. Rahner (London, 1975), 1188]: "Precisely as God's gift, penance is a human act. . . ."

[101] The sinner's atonement is required as the "*terminus ad extra*" (*creatus et contingens*) in order to vindicate what is contingently affirmed of God ("he forgives"). Cf. B. Lonergan, *De Constitutione Christi ontologica et psychologica* (Rome, 1956), 51f.

[102] Cf. R. Schulte in MySal V: 125.

himself, but in the mode of freedom, so that it is the sinner who turns round and endeavors to put his sin right in the sight of Yahweh.[103] In this sense it is true that the sinner's *conversion*, which attains its radical fullness in atonement, *is* Yahweh's energetic and sovereign response to sin. But he responds in such a way as to posit the sinner as a free person over against himself, in the mode of conversion and atonement that is appropriate to one who has been harmed by sin.

Let us summarize: in spite of the great variety and mutability of its concrete forms, one can detect in the Old Testament, with increasing clarity, a process of atonement that is characterized by three elements: the sovereignty and affectivity of Yahweh and the involvement of the sinner. These elements are consistently and deliberately developed, resulting in a clearly contoured structure in which Yaweh's utter autonomy is shown by the very fact that, with passionate and even emotional insistence, he causes the sinner to pursue his conversion within a relationship of free partnership with him.

As a result, however, "atonement" emerges as a historical process of very striking ambivalence; and this ambivalence is noteworthy, among other things, in that, far from being this time an unbalanced form of a Christian piety of reparation, it bears the stamp of the authentic, official, saving activity of Yahweh himself.

2.1.2 *The atonement of the Cross in the New Testament: the heightened ambivalence of forgiveness becomes a* skandalon

In the course of Old Testament salvation history, in spite of the incessant sacrifices of atonement, there is a growing sense of powerlessness against the superior power of sin;[104] the question of a final appeasement of the divine anger becomes more and more pressing;[105] there is an increasing need for redemption,[106] until, in the prophets, forgiveness is set in the perspective of

---

[103] Thus G. von Rad's assertion, op. cit., 270, with regard to Dt 21:9, that "the one who receives expiation is not Yahweh but Israel", seems a somewhat crude conclusion with regard to the theological essence of atonement as understood in the OT.

On the relationship of "forgiveness" and "atonement" in the OT, cf. K. Koch, op. cit., 218: "Atonement is . . . closely allied to forgiveness, and often identical with it"; Th. C. Vriezen, op. cit., 245f.; the distinction, which in Christian theology is sharply drawn, "between reconciliation (*reconciliatio*, καταλλαγή) and atonement (*expiatio*, ἱλασμός) is also present in the OT. Yet here the two concepts are not clearly separated from one another. Thus, e.g., the word *kipper*, which originally means *expiatio*, is sometimes used in the sense of *reconciliatio* or in the sense of forgiveness and the obtaining of forgiveness"; St. Lyonnet, "Sühne", 631f. M. J. Scheeben, *Handbuch der kath. dogmatik* V/2, no. 1245, distinguishes κατάλλαξις as *reconciliatio* (the change of inner disposition achieved in and among mankind by God in Christ) from ἱλασμός as *propitiatio, placatio* (the "softening of God's anger" achieved by Christ). In what follows we shall attempt to investigate this overlapping of the two terms.

[104] Cf. W. Eichrodt, op. cit., II: 396f., 455ff.: E. Lohse, op. cit., 110.

[105] Cf. J. Fichtner, *Der Zorn Gottes*, 401, 406.

[106] Cf. W. Eichrodt, ibid., 460.

eschatology[107] and people yearn for an ultimate act of redemption,[108] and, on the horizon of the longed-for salvation, Deutero-Isaiah discerns the mysterious figure of him who, as the Ebed-Yahweh, will achieve universal atonement once and for all.[109]

Probably no one disputes these facts. Yet it is questionable whether people are sufficiently clearly aware of what these facts presuppose, that is, the continuing and undiminished validity of the picture and structure of the divine saving activity that we have just recognized. The Old Testament's unique sense of futility, its melancholy awareness of the disappointment of its most fundamental desire, arises *because* it knows that forgiveness must take place in the form of atonement; it is an unshakable law: sin must be "borne" ("transformed", "converted"), but every attempt to "bear" sin in this way failed to get off the ground. The "Advent" theme is present in the Old Testament precisely because this "law" is valid and immutable.

If then — which again no one doubts — the whole New Testament sees itself as the fulfillment of the Old Testament promise of redemption,[110] surely the formal reason lies in its claim to be the fulfillment of that same *basic Old Testament law*, that is, in the conviction that in the Christ-event, the "bearing" of sin, which time and again had proved an impossibility, had now been achieved, finally and absolutely. Surely a "fulfillment" can never negate the fundamental sense and intention of what it fulfills. Is it possible for a person to insist exclusively that "Jesus performs his service *as commissioned by God*, and not *over against* God"?[111] Or could a person believe that God is "the author, not the recipient of atonement" and that the death of Jesus only *manifests* the inscrutable saving will of God,[112] *and* at the same time believe that the Christ-event is

---

[107] Ibid., 457; cf. H. Gross, op. cit. (see n.33 above), 546: "In its real, inner essence" the OT revelation "is the word, full of both doom and promise, which envisages the future as God wishes it, piecing it together in a multicolored mosaic".

[108] W. Eichrodt, op. cit., 460.

[109] Cf. L. Winner, op. cit., 147ff.; J. Scharbert, "Vergebung", 743; G. von Rad, *Theology of the Old Testament* vol. 2 (London, 1962 and 1975), 260: the Servant Songs "go far beyond the description of anyone who might have existed in the past or the present. The picture of the Servant of Yahweh, of his mission to Israel and to the world, and of his expiatory suffering, is prophecy of the future, and, like all the rest of Deutero-Isaiah's prophecy, belongs to the realm of pure miracle, which Yahweh reserved for himself." Ibid., 262: "the tremendous new factor which [Deutero-Isaiah] introduced . . . was the universal sweep of his prediction." K. Koch, "Sühne und Sündenvergebung", 235: In the fourth Servant Song "Deutero-Isaiah portrays an immense eschatological atonement rite, which applies not only to Israel but to the 'many', i.e., the nations, as well (52:15)."

[110] Cf., e.g., P. Bläser, "Erfüllung der Schrift" in LThK, 2nd ed., III: 983f.; F. Mussner, "Jahwe. II. Im Neuen Testament", ibid., 624f.

[111] W. G. Kümmel, "Jesus und Paulus" in ThBl (1940): 203–31, esp. 225 (quoted in E. Lohse, op. cit., 121, n.3 above).

[112] E. Lohse, loc. cit.

the climax and fulfillment of salvation history? In denying inappropriate "influence" on God, do not these views also rule out genuine interpersonal exchange?[113] If God's initiatory power is conceived in such a way that, instead of enabling personal relationships with the creature, it absorbs them; if the drama of the Cross and its constitutive dialectic (i.e., the divine, transcendent will to forgive and man's participation in atonement) is dissolved, does this not automatically dissolve and "empty" the Cross itself?

As E. Jüngel says in a rather different context, "there is no gospel apart from the whole severity of the law. . . ."[114] What the gospel proclaims is inconceivably new, but it does so in fulfillment of what is old. Indeed, if the Old Testament manner of forgiveness with its threefold structure is compared with the phenomenon of the Cross, it is almost impossible *not* to see that the Cross is by no means the abrogation of this law but is instead its eschatological affirmation. The law according to which forgiveness is carried out "not as 'mere forgiveness' but as atonement",[115] so that—as Anselm insists—"the freedom and autonomy of man in the process of redemption is preserved"[116] and man himself, in the power of God, nullifies sin: this law is fulfilled in the New Testament in a way undreamt of by the heart of man, namely, by the "Father" "sending" the "Son".

It is important at this stage to weigh each of these three concepts carefully (God's sovereign autonomy, God's affective involvement and man's participation), for it is here, in the New Testament, that they are given their definitive

---

[113] We can only emphasize what W. Joest says in this regard in "Versöhnung", 1379: "The biblical message of the Cross unanimously describes God as the One who reconciles men with himself. He gives his Son as a reconciliation on the Cross (2 Cor 5:18ff.; Rom 8:31f.); nor does he first need to be persuaded to love, for his motive is always love (Rom 5:8; Eph 2:4; Jn 3:16)." All the same, if we are to grasp reconciliation in its specifically Christian sense, we must add with equal force: "Of course the one who reconciles is ultimately God, but now he performs this reconciliation unambiguously in the one whom he surrendered to death: the Son, who now, as the man Jesus, has conclusively proclaimed his solidarity with sinners", (H. U. von Balthasar, *Theodramatik* II/2: 109). For the OT and specifically the postexilic period "it is God who takes the initiative in showing men ways and means of performing the required atonement. No doubt this is a paradox, since it presupposes a God who is *already* reconciled and yet *nonetheless* requires something from man before the reciprocal reconciliation (καταλλαγή) can take full effect; this is called atonement (ἱλασμός), brought about by the means of atonement (ἱλαστήριον)" (ibid., 107 [our italics]).

[114] E. Jüngel, *Gott als Geheimnis der Welt: Zur Begründung der Theologie des Gekreuzigten im Streit zwischen Theismus und Atheismus* (Tübingen, 1977), 510. Cf. K. Koch, "Sünde und Sündenvergebung", 239: "Some people dismiss what the OT has to say about atonement and the forgiveness of sins as 'mythological' or 'magic'. But what is left of the NT if all this is jettisoned? When the NT speaks of the death of Christ 'for us' (ὑπέρ ἡμῶν), is it not committed to the view that sin is a reality within the history of mankind, and that the One making atonement does so as a representative of the whole of humanity?"

[115] Cf. R. Guardini, *Der Herr*, 358.

[116] Cf. G. Greshake, *Erlösung und Freiheit*, 338.

shape: here "atonement" no longer takes place as a merely human act, guaranteed and made effective by God's grace; atonement is no longer only the sinner, made free by God to perform atonement. Now atonement *is the only Son*, he who has "come" in sinful flesh.[117] The Crucified is therefore pure grace, a testimony both to God's sovereign power to forgive and to his unfathomable love, because in him the Son has taken up the sinners' cause and has become really and truly *their* atonement. God does not just give us some means or other of wiping out our sins: in Christ, God himself is not merely the liquidation of our sins but *our* liquidation of sins.[118]

Now therefore, in his zeal for salvation, God not only gives the means of atonement, sacrifice, contrition, the spirit of penitence, but also—directly and without mediation—the absolute transcendence of his most personal Self, yet in such a way that the human partner does not forfeit his participatory role. Thus while it is true that on the Cross God's salvific sovereignty and man's efforts are both "stretched to the limit by their *ekstasis*"[119]—so that we have to say that the action of the *man* Jesus on the Cross *is* the personal intervention of God the *Father*,[120] that is, that, in the Crucified, God is established as the One who gives his only begotten Son for us (Rom 8:32; Jn 3:16)[121]—it does not mean the suspension of personal reciprocity in an exclusively divine scenario. Katabasis does not swallow up anabasis.[122] The

[117] The expression ἐν ὁμοιώματί in Rom 8:3 in no way weakens the truth of this "coming" but, according to H. Schlier, *Der Römerbrief*, 241, stresses "that there is identity in non-identity" in the sense that (as in 2 Cor 5:21) "the Son knew ἁμαρτία but not from personal experience". More precisely, perhaps, we should add that he did not know sin from personal experience to the extent that he did not commit it. Cf. idem, *Grundzüge*, 139 (see n.159 below).

[118] According to M. J. Scheeben, *Handbuch der kath. Dogmatik* V/2, no. 1258, "It is part of the specific character" of Christ's mediatorial, saving work "that he also acted as a representative of men needing reconciliation . . . so that men themselves, in him and through him, should win God's favor and obtain their salvation". Cf. *Missale Romanum* (*Typis Polyglottis Vaticanis*, 1971), 414: here the Sunday Preface (III "*Per Annum*") is headed "*De salvatione hominis per hominem*", and in the text itself we find this: "Ad cuius [Dei] immensam gloriam pertinere cognoscimus ut mortalibus tua deitate succurreres; sed et nobis provideres de ipsa mortalitate nostra remedium, et perditos quosque unde perierant, inde salvares. . . ."

[119] R. Pesch, "das Abendmahl und Jesu todesverständnis", 186. On the significance of the Incarnation for the event of the Cross, cf. N. Hoffmann, op. cit., 171ff.

[120] Correspondingly there is such an interpenetration of "forgiveness" as a divine act and "atonement" as a human deed that one can say, with R. Guardini, *Der Herr*, 357, that, "through his own destiny", Christ has effected the forgiveness of the Father in heaven. Cf. ibid.: "He is live, living forgiveness." Naturally this applies to forgiveness in the "objective" sense.

[121] Cf. E. Jüngel, op. cit., 510: "the self-surrender of the eternal Son of God takes place in the temporal existence of a man, of this crucified man Jesus."

[122] Cf. J. Ratzinger, "Sühne" in LThK IX: 1157: since "in the Christian dispensation God himself is the subject of atonement . . . the Cross must be understood initially as a movement downwards from above. . . . Yet atonement also includes a genuinely human component, resulting from the true humanity of Jesus Christ, by virtue of which he can be equally a representative of humanity before the Father."

"law" of partnership in the cleansing from sin in the Old Covenant is not disavowed. On the contrary, it is definitively ratified; human efforts are not rejected, rather, they are finally and decisively lifted up from their situation of powerlessness and futility.[123]

And that is not all. The Cross itself, the meaning of which, taken as a mere fact, is by no means obvious,[124] only lets its fundamental significance shine through when it is illuminated by the "law" and its requirements; only in the perspective of the Old Testament can we appreciate the staggering newness of what is specific to the New Testament. We begin to see that the original personal polarity, "God-Sinner", far from disappearing in the New Covenant, is unimaginably radicalized. Amazingly—and we must say this, inconceivable though it be—this polarity is somehow transposed into the relation of Father and Son *in* God himself[125] and thus mysteriously made part of the life of the Trinity. The atonement process, having retained its interpersonal quality throughout every stage of revelation, here attains its ultimate concentration and, transcending itself in the Christ-event, actually impinges on the inner-Trinitarian economy of Persons. Our atonement, the atonement of us sinners with God the Father, is his *crucified* Son!

The "ambivalence" of our starting point, the remarkable contrariety of divine omnipotence and human act in the structure not only of atonement-spirituality but also in the public and official working out of salvation, is incarnated as a Person in Christ and thus is underwritten christologically in a totally unexpected way. So it appears to be part of the plan that God has resolutely been carrying out. But this "answer" only throws us back all the more painfully to the nagging question, "Why?" Particularly in the light of the Old Testament, the Cross poses the question, and a question of a decidedly theo-logical kind. The Cross asks: Is God still "God" if he lets sin go as far as the Cross?

If "atonement" is the counter-response to sin, which "converts" it, why is the atonement for *human sin* the death of the *Son of God*? What can lead God to invest his Trinitarian life in the elimination of human sin? Where is the sense of proportion here?

Here at least, finally, the stubborn ambivalence we have already met provokes more than a merely theoretical θαυμάζειν. The Gospel, which does not

---

[123] Cf. J. Ratzinger, "Is the Eucharist a Sacrifice?" in Conc 3 (1967): 39: "Christ's life and death exemplify the authentic aim of Old Testament cultic worship. . ."; R. Guardini, *Der Herr*, 564: "Pagan cults are foreshadowings of the real cult, before it has been proclaimed."

[124] Cf. H. Schlier, *Grundzüge*, 133: the "inner structure of the Cross cannot be seen simply by looking at the course of the external event. . . . The external event can be interpreted in many ways. . . ."

[125] E. Jüngel, op. cit., 510, puts it rather too starkly when he says that "God is distinguished from God by the severity of the law, shown in the anger of God toward the sinner."

exist "apart from the whole severity of the law", becomes a σκάνδαλον (1 Cor 1:23) to the pious people of the Old Testament and of ancient paganism, precisely because they are concerned about God!

And as for *Christian* thought, if it realizes the grotesque truth of the Cross at all — perhaps with an eye to the way it causes the ancient world to stumble — it cannot avoid being drawn into the questioning of the Anselmian "*Cur Deus homo?*" Anselm's dialogue partner Boso puts the central issue thus: "Why, in order to save man through his death, did God become man, when obviously he could have done this in some other way?"[126] This "he could have", however, is not the expression of an unreal, hypothetical theology; rather, it is evidence of "the believer's astonishment".[127]

The believer knows, through his very astonishment, that at the bottom of the event of the Cross, which comes to him "out of the blue", nothing is arbitrary. He cannot make a positivistic retreat and simply embrace the divine will and decree. He must look for the meaning (Logos) of what has taken place, like the philosopher who, illuminated by the radiance of what is as yet unknown to him, seeks Being itself above and beyond the marvels of what exists. If the philosopher is given this light of Being — in the ὡς ἔστιν ("that IS is") of Parmenides[128] — can we not say that the believer too is granted an (albeit only) analogous light, illuminating the world of his faith?

This is our conviction. In our view, this light of the Logos, so greatly longed for, is evident in the principle of "representation".[129]

2.2 The divine logic revealed by the concept of "representation" within the ambivalence of atonement by the Cross

2.2.1 The ternary structure of "representation"

Analyzing the events and processes of salvation history, we are led to a discovery of their structure which, on account of its universal application, has the status of a fundamental law. This structure can be called the principle of "representation".[130]

---

[126] G. Greshake, *Erlösung und Freiheit*, 325.

[127] Ibid.

[128] H. Diels, *Die Fragmente der Vorsokratiker*, ed. W. Kranz, vol. 1 (Berlin, 1954), 232 (B, 8, 2); cf. H. Krings, "Vom Anfang der Philosophie: Gedanken zu Parmenides" in H. Kuhn, H. Kahlefeld, K. Forster, eds., *Interpretation der Welt: Festschrift für Romano Guardini zum achtzigsten Geburtstag* (Würzburg, 1965), 17–31, exp. 21ff.

[129] Cf. the author's study "Stellvertretung" (n.22 above), the results of which are adopted at this point.

[130] Cf. L. Scheffczyk, "Substitution" (Representation) in SM 5: 391f. [idem, "Sacrifice. II. Substitution (Representation)" in *Encyclopedia of Theology* 1491–92]; idem, "Die heilshafte Stellvertretung als missionarischer Impuls" in GuL 37 (1964): 109–25, esp. 111–15; J. Ratzinger, "Stellvertretung" in HThG II: 566–75; A. Deissler, "Hingegeben für die Vielen: Stellvertretung als Prinzip der Heilsgeschichte" in LS 30 (1979): 339–45.

Far more important, however, than the correct term is a correct grasp of what is specific to it. In our view, what is decisive and distinctive about this structure is not simply that someone acts "in place of" another (for him), but that he acts in the "place" of the other in such a way that, far from "dis-placing" him, he actually "em-places", posits, establishes him. He does not drive him from his place, he liberates this "place" for him from the powers of negativity, so that his own self can take possession of it; he enables him to be himself.[131]

Formally, therefore, the essence of "representation" exhibits three interpenetrating elements:[132] the active, enabling movement of the positing subject, the passive receptivity of the posited "other",[133] and the "repercussive"[134] effect on the former.[135]

Mutatis mutandis, this ternary structure stays remarkably constant throughout the historical development of "representation", not only in the personal destinies of the individual protagonists in salvation history but also in the ontological and historical shape of the fundamental saving events themselves.[136]

But the most radical and far-reaching theo-logical implications of this structure lie, in our view, in the fact that it shows "representation" to be a feature inherent in the Trinity.

2.2.2 *The immanent Trinity as the prototype of "representation"*
On closer scrutiny it is not difficult to see that the principle of "representation" cannot be limited to the area of salvation, to the so-called economic

---

[131] We can discern this structure not only in the heroic action of a Maximilian Kolbe but also in so many everyday experiences, in many professions, for instance (the soldier, the politician, the doctor); those in particular who help in the developing countries and fight for the rights of the oppressed are performing "representative" service.

[132] N.B. the correspondence to the threefold structure of atonement in OT and NT.

[133] This aspect of representation, whereby the positing subject liberates the self of "another", is especially significant in our context.

[134] This term is meant to express the effect on the subject of action undertaken on behalf of another (in the way of self-development and self-affirmation), cf. Mt 10:39. The acting subject posits not only the "other" but in a certain sense himself too. In some way or other this factor of repercussion is present in all forms of representation, even if only as a category of our thought ("*ratione*"). In the case of creation, for instance, God is the recipient of this repercussive effect.

[135] The three aspects could be described by the following pairs of concepts: the "initiatory/originative"; the "consecutory/obediential"; and the "aspirative/mutual".

[136] Creation, grace, redemption (cf. N. Hoffmann, op. cit., 176f., 164ff.) and Incarnation are so many analogous variations of a process that is formally identical, namely, the creation of a "place" in which the "other" (the world, man, the sinner, the human nature of Christ) can develop (or regain) its true self, as a result of a corresponding personal initiative on the part of God.

In the interests of what is specific to the Christian revelation of God, we are obliged to maintain that God's relation to the world is somehow or other real and concrete, while naturally remaining autonomous and self-determining. We are aware of the theo-logical problems that result from this (cf. N. Hoffmann, op. cit., 164–66, 187ff.; H. Pfeil, "Die Frage nach der Veränderlichkeit und Geschichtlichkeit Gottes" in MThZ 31 [1980]: 1–23).

Trinity, but extends to the inner depths of the Divine Being.[137] It is here that God's saving activity has its ontological roots: the three elements that are manifest in salvation history are, in their prototypical origin, *Trinity*.[138] Here the sovereignty of the positing subject is radicalized as "fatherhood".

Giving away his own nature in the self-transcending act of generation, the positing subject enables a being, who is *other* in person but *identical* in nature, to *be*; this being's otherness vis-à-vis the positing subject — an otherness "greater than which cannot be thought"[139] — arises specifically from his total dependence on the Father as his origin and goal.

The form of self-involvement or self-participation implied in this process is pure and unconditional; so much so that it is here that the First Person posits himself, not only as "Father" but as personal Self. Here, then, we have self-affirmation through the radical generative relation to the Other. This orientation to the Other is what formally constitutes the Self as such.[140] The generative principle is "God" ("Person"), but only as "Father". For his part, the Second Person acquires his identity (in absolute otherness and in distinction from the First Person) through the absolute refusal of self-dependence: the Second Person is "God" and "Person", but only as "Son".

Thus, with regard to the relationship of both Persons in God, we can say that there is absolutely *no* difference "*in absolutis*", but an *absolute* difference "*in relativis*", that is, the only difference is that of absolute relation ("*relatio subsistens*")! And as for ambivalence: here we encounter it again at the very heart of Being! But it is an ambivalence that causes the meaning of Being to blossom; it so perfects it that this very ambivalence is drawn to aspire beyond

---

[137] Cf. N. Hoffmann, op. cit., 185f.

[138] It will not be surprising if, on the basis of everyday usage, there is a certain amount of resistance to speaking of "representation" in the context of the inner-divine life. The everyday meaning of the term needs to be refined and the formal (metaphysical) essence of "representation" laid bare, eliminating those aspects of ordinary usage that refer exclusively to intramundane affairs and thus cannot be applied to God.

We must ask whether — as in the case of the concepts "being", "love", "activity" and "life" — attention to the Trinity may not help us to discern the formal content of the concept of "representation" in its analogous intramundane variations. Thus for instance we are enabled to see the real essence of "instrumentality" (*causalitas efficiens*) through observing its purest form in creation; only then can the Scholastic maxim *actio est in passo* mean anything to us.

We see the formal conceptual content of "representation" in that a positing principle, through its own self-investment (self-sacrifice), creates a "place", a locus, in which the posited "other" can express its own self. Hence the Trinity would be the prototypical matrix of all representation.

[139] Cf. H. Mühlen, *Der Heilige Geist als Person*, 114.

[140] Of course, the First Person must always be held to be the "*fons trinitatis*", yet in such a way that he exists only as the principle of the Second and Third Persons. This aspect of reciprocal "dependence" will yield its significance later on in our discussion, when we come to explain how God is affected by sin and atonement.

itself, affirming itself personally in the Holy Spirit, the *"jubilus Patris et Filii"*, the jubilant affirmation that Being itself, Being *as* Being, is, eternally, love.

For our present topic, however, this Trinitarian ambivalence is of central importance to the extent that it can be shown to illuminate theologically that other "ambivalence" that we find in the *skandalon* of the Cross that "atones for our sins".

2.2.3 *Jesus' atonement on the Cross is the extension of Trinitarian Sonship as conditioned by the fact of sin*

2.2.3.1 *Creation as the positing of "sons"*[141]

In actual fact there is a connection between the existence of our world and the triune nature of God. The world exists as a "creation in Christ" (Col 1:15ff.; Jn 1:1–14; Heb 1:3f.). What we have to do is fully realize the consequences of this truth.[142] Out of the divine depths of his "fatherly" affectivity, God prepares a "place" for man, a place not only in being, not only in freedom ("free-being"), but also — in all truth — in the Trinitarian "locus" of the Son. But this means that, in his love for the only begotten Son (Eph 1:6), he establishes man in his irreplaceable, creaturely self in such a way that, by that very fact and with a daunting seriousness, he posits man as a "son" in relationship with himself.[143] He wants and loves man, not in the way he wants and loves the creatures below man, but as a *subject*, by whom he wishes *to be loved* in return, as Father.[144]

2.2.3.2 *Sin as the "son's" refusal of sonship*

If, however, God posits ("poses") himself as Father over against a creature, this means (since the creature's freedom is finite and defectible) that he also "ex-poses" himself, that he somehow renders himself "vulnerable". From the human point of view this means that our being established as sons involves the first, real possibility of "sin" as it is understood in revelation. This is the dark shadow without which, evidently, there cannot be the light of God's fatherly love. Man, regarded as an ethical subject,[145] cannot "sin": sin is done

---

[141] Cf. N. Hoffmann, op. cit., 189ff.

[142] In preparation for an understanding of the correspondence of sin and atonement. Anselm's theory is often accused of "leaving guilt and expiation extrinsic to one another": H. U. von Balthasar, *Crucifixus*, 33; cf. K. Rahner "Erlösung", 1169; [idem, "Salvation. IV. Theology" in *Encyclopedia of Theology*, 1524].

[143] Cf. Eph 1:5: "He destined us in love to be his sons through Jesus Christ. . . ." On this passage, cf. H. Schlier, *Der Brief an die Epheser*, 54.

[144] On the reciprocity of love, cf. Thomas Aquinas, *S. Th.* II II q. 23 a. 2 c.; Duns Scotus, *Opus Oxoniense* III dist. 32 q un. no. 6.

[145] Cf. K. Rahner, "Erlösung", 1160; [idem, "Salvation. IV. Theology" in *Encyclopedia of Theology*, 1519]: " 'Sin' is the free No to God's direct, intimate love in the offer of his self-communication. . . ."

by the "son" as such; it is the son's rejection of sonship; it is an interpersonal event between "Father" and "son".

This lends us an insight into the idea of the "Trinitarian barb" of sin that wounds God: once God the Father has loved men in the Son, once it is true that we are sons "in the Beloved" (Eph 1:6; cf. Col 1:13; Rom 8:14–17, 29; Gal 4:5–7; 1 Jn 3:1f.), we have to ask whether it is enough to maintain that sin "offends" God only insofar as it injures the sinner.[146] Does not sin also have a "meaning" for God himself, to the extent that he is, and desires to be, the inner-Trinitarian Father? In its true dimensions, sin seems to be more than merely something affecting God's relationships "ad extra", more than mere resistance to his authority as Creator. As the "negative image" of that self-transcendence, which is of Trinitarian proportions, it affects, in a mysterious way, the very relationship between Father and Son in God himself. Its objective intentionality implies opposition to the inner-Trinitarian mystery of "representation" being extended into the creation. It signifies the refusal to allow one's own existence to be a "place" where the holy unity of Father and Son can become reality in this world, the refusal to participate in "representation". Fundamentally the sinner denies "Trinity"—not Trinity "in itself" but in its constitutional "for us".

Once the free creature has been established as a "son", once there is the possibility of sin in the full, revealed sense, an abyss yawns in created being in the genuine possibility of the "nihilum malum", the "evil void",[147] which is called "hell". This does not take place at the level of Creator/creature, where the creature tears loose from the Creator and descends to the "death of God". True hell can only exist where there is Trinity. Real hell is when the "Father" withdraws into absence from the "Son"; it presupposes Trinity. And sin is the fall into the "nihilum Trinitatis".

2.2.3.3 "Atonement" as the assertion of sonship against sin

When sin occurs, therefore, it is something monstrous. Its effects exceed the bounds of what is human and creaturely to the extent that the one who commits sin is more than a man, namely, a "child of God". The "consequences" of sin extend into the Heart of God. When there is real "sin", something happens that goes far beyond the powers of a mere man.

So too, if sin is to be "wiped out", "borne", "taken away", something far beyond human powers must take place. True, God is a match for sin, but only he is so.[148] Indeed, accepting with reverence God's revelation in word and deed, we can go on to say that, if sin is to be liquidated as a result of the

---

[146] Cf. Thomas Aquinas, C. G. III c. 122 init.: "non enim Deus a nobis offenditur nisi ex eo, quod contra nostrum bonum agimus." Cf. on this St. Lyonnet, De peccato et redemptione. I. De notione peccati (Rome, 1957—SPIB III), 88–90.

[147] R. Guardini, Der Herr, 474.

[148] Ibid.

fundamental thrust of "creation in Christ", that is, following the principle of "representation", only God as *"Father"* is a match for sin.[149]

Now the Father must re-instate the sinner in his "place" as a "son"; this time, however, it does not occur in the innocence of the "good" void [*"nihilum bonum"* — Tr.], that is, he cannot ignore and bypass the sin:[150] this re-instatement must be carried out in the face of sin and through sin; it must be won back from the depths of the "evil void", that is, according to sin's Trinitarian dimension, from the depths of "hell".

And, again presupposing that, in accordance with the law of representation, man's erstwhile established freedom shall be respected, this liquidation of sin, while it comes from God as grace, must be the sinner's own deed, must be "atonement", the "conversion" of sin into its opposite by the sinner himself[151] insofar as he is a "son". Moreover (always bearing in mind the fact that we are only trying to continue the lines of God's thought as they have been made known to us) we can ask whether, since man was created in the Son,[152] he should not be recreated—against his sins—by the Son.

Let us be quite clear that, although we are operating entirely within the light of revelation, reflections of this kind can never deduce a priori that the death of the God-Man on the Cross was the only appropriate and necessary way in which atonement could be made for human sin.[153] Quite apart from the fact that we only know about the triune God as a result of the actual historical Christ-event,[154] Incarnation and Cross are so far beyond anything that human beings could conceive, are so rooted in God's free graciousness,

---

[149] Ibid., 148.

[150] Cf. W. Joest, "Versöhnung", 1378: ". . . God is not indifferent to sin and does not ignore it. . . . To overlook sin without anger would not be love, but only the lofty equanimity of an infinitely superior being."

[151] Cf. G. Greshake, *Erlösung und Freiheit*, 338: according to Anselm, "satisfaction, that is, human effort, is required . . . so that, in fact, redemption is effected by the free human being himself." Cf. also Thomas Aquinas, *S. Th.* III q. 1 a. 1 s. c.: ". . . sicut Damascenus dicit, per Incarnationis mysterium monstratur . . . justitia . . . quoniam homine victo, non alio quam homine fecit vinci tyrannum. . . ." ["But, as Damascene remarks, through the mystery of the Incarnation the . . . justice . . . of God (is) shown . . . because, since a man had been conquered, he made the tyrant be conquered by none other than a man" (Dominican ed., London, 1920–1938)].

[152] For the moment we are prescinding from creation "in Christ" (the incarnate Word).

[153] So too the question whether God might pardon the sinner at all can only be answered on the basis of God's manifest will. Similarly, it is only revelation that justifies us in saying "that God simply permitted evil because he foresaw how he could set mankind free from its fetters, or rather, because he had already determined upon the Incarnation of the Logos and saw in it the possibility of a superabundant redemption" (M. Schmaus, *Kath. Dogmatik* II: 492 [cf. n.11 above]; cf., ibid., 491, 500f.; K. Rahner, "Erlösung", 1163, 3a/b; [idem, *Encyclopedia of Theology*, 1521]).

[154] R. Schulte in MySal III/1: 55, 60.

that, even if one had special knowledge of the mystery of the Trinity, they would not be deducible from it.[155]

At the same time, these mysteries are in line with what the fundamentally Trinitarian principle of "representation" leads us to expect. This is something we cannot construct a priori, but in retrospect we can see, at the vanishing point of these perspectives of salvation history, the Cross of Jesus. It is unimaginable, yet, illuminated by the inner-Trinitarian mystery of representation that is carried forward into the creation, it is intelligible as the unimaginably *meaningful* manifestation of this same transcendental-theological core-mystery of the Trinity, a manifestation that is by no means an arbitrary, historical a posteriori but is unexpectedly *suited* to the situation marked by sin.[156]

We have become too used to accepting the Cross as something done "on our behalf" and "for us". But unless our inner vision is illuminated by the light of Being, which radiates from that representation that goes on in God himself, the innermost nature of the representation contained in the Cross will remain hidden from us: we shall fail to see the Cross as the self-affirmation of the Trinitarian mystery of representation *ad extra*, confronting its negation in the form of sin.

The Logos enters sinful flesh, sinful nature (i.e., not only the realm of sin's infection)[157] and acts as "Son", is "Son", in the sinner's "place", that is, where the sinner is. Far from holding himself aloof from sinners, he, sinless (2 Cor 5:21; Heb 4:15; 7:26; 1 Pt 2:22), enters the Godlessness of their sin, yet as Son.

And this signifies the *conversion* of sin. For if "the Son" enters sin and absorbs it, sin has no choice but to become its own opposite: and as for the Son, in the Godless void of sin, all he can do is to become the nameless, yet somehow still personal, absence of the Father. Jesus' death-cry (cf. Mk 15:34) is the Son's cry of dereliction.

[155] As atonement, the Cross always lies beyond the boundary of what, according to the notion of "representation", God's reaction to human sin might be. The light that is granted to us in God's self-manifestation always preserves the mysterious nature of what is revealed; our thinking is never allowed to "encompass", "reproduce" or "reconstruct" the revelation from its own profound origins. Cf. E. von Ivánka, *Plato Christianus: Übernahme und Umgestaltung des Platonismus durch die Väter* (Einsiedeln, 1964), 56, 68f., 455; R. Schulte in MySal IV/2: 77.

[156] The concept of representation is not intended to "get behind" somehow the mystery of salvation, in a rationalistic sense, but to illuminate it in all its mysteriousness—for mysteries too have their splendor. It is a case of letting two mysteries shed light on each other by contact with the idea of representation—an idea which is itself arrived at only through the revelation of these mysteries. "Representation" helps us to see God as Trinity shining through the Cross.

[157] See n.117 above. Cf. N. Hoffmann, op. cit., 167ff.: M. Schmaus, *Der Glaube der Kirche* I: 494 (see n.15 above); H. U. von Balthasar, *Theodramatik* II/2: 221, 223; idem, *Crucifixus*, 34: "How far . . . can the Pure One penetrate into the other world of the impure. . . ? As far as the end-result of negation, refusal; as far as that turning-away, that alienation which stands as an objective reality between God and the sinner and affects both."

As the Son experiences the nature of sin, however, sin is converted in its very nature: the proud self-assertion against God, the sinful desire to be free from God, is changed into pain, a pain that is as great as this Son's love.[158]

"Sin" now means the crucified Son, dying in estrangement from the Father.[159] And the Cross of Jesus has a twofold meaning: it means the Son, made "sin" (2 Cor 5:21; Gal 3:13), and it means sin, transubstantiated into the Son's love-suffering.[160]

Thus it is on the Cross that the real transforming miracle takes place: by suffering, sin is transformed into its opposite: now it has become the negative image of love, suffering sonship. This is where sin is really "put away" (Heb 9:26), "killed" (Eph 2:16 [JB])[161] and "blotted out" (cf. Acts 3:19), unhinged, compelled to negate itself, paraded in public (cf. Col 2:15 [JB]).[162] Here, at last, sin is "borne" (Jn 1:29).[163]

Here sin has become *atonement*. In the Cross we see God manifesting in the eschatological way proper to the New Testament what the Old Testament expressed in terms of atonement: the Cross is the ultimate proof of sonship; on it Jesus demonstrates that he is the Beloved Son of God the Father.

In its innermost reality, the Cross is not something that takes place between Jesus and sinful men, as if they cast their evil deeds upon him, or as if he — as the "Lamb" — demonstrated to them their violence, wickedness and jealousy.[164] "The *world's* atonement" takes place through "Jesus bearing the

---

[158] Cf. M. Schmaus, op. cit., 494.

[159] Cf. H. Schlier, *Grundzüge*, 138: Paul means us "to see in this death the absolute forsakenness of the Servant". Ibid., 139: ". . . his exposure to utter nothingness and God-forsakenness is also exposure to the powers of sin and of 'the curse' "; physical death expresses the mortal nature of this God-forsakenness as it affects actual human existence. Cf. ibid., 137; M. Schmaus, op. cit., 494.

[160] Cf. M. Hengel, *Der stellvertretende Sühnetod Jesu*, 19: "In 2 Cor 5:21, too, we must understand the sinless Christ's being 'made sin for us' by God . . . in the sense that Christ was given up for our sake as the perfect sacrifice for sin." Cf. also M. J. Scheeben, *Handbuch der kath. Dogmatik* V/2 no. 1255 (quoting the Council of Toledo: "*Qui solus pro nobis 'peccatum est factus', id est, sacrificium pro peccatis nostris*", DS 539). The aim of the present study is to make it clear that the "Son" becomes a sin-offering by the very fact of entering sin.

[161] Cf. H. Schlier, *Grundzüge*, 135: "for our sake" means that "Jesus Christ has accepted . . . 'sinners' . . . by concretely taking their hostile deeds upon himself and enduring them in his own body . . . by concretely 'taking these deeds' into his death, concretely 'killing' them in his own dying." Gregory of Nyssa, *C. Eunom.* III 10: Christ "frees us from the curse by making our curse his own . . . taking the hostility upon himself and mortifying it within him . . ." (quoted in H. U. von Balthasar, *Theodramatik* II/2: 219).

[162] Cf. H. Schlier, *Mächte und Gewalten im Neuen Testament* (Freiburg, 1958 [Qd 3]), 43.

[163] [None of the familiar English versions uses this word in Jn 1:29; they all prefer "take away". The author's argument, however, is better illustrated by the English "bear, carry", equivalent to the Luther Bible's "tragen". — Tr.]

[164] Cf. R. Schwager, *Brauchen wir einen Sündenbock?*, 171f.; H. U. von Balthasar, *Crucifixus*, 30.

world's sin, something that happens between him and God the *Father*".[165] To try to interpret this process formally as "punishment"[166] or even in a less specific sense as "satisfaction" (the restoring of the injured divine "honor" by an act of infinite value) is to miss what is specifically Christian in the atonement of the Cross.

Atonement is the son's business qua *son*.[167] It cannot be performed by someone who incidentally *happens* to be a son: it must be done by *the* Son *insofar* as he is "son". Formally speaking, atonement is concerned with sonship,[168] the *assertion* of sonship against its rejection in sin.

Atonement expresses God's determination to adhere to the primal meaning of creation, namely, the extension outward of the inner-Trinitarian sonship.[169]

The Incarnation took place not simply *because* of sin—it certainly took place *against* it.[170] And when God's resolute plan to extend his fatherhood into the world through the mediation of Christ, the Son of God, takes shape in salvation history, what results is the "Cross". God provides the Son as an "expiation" (Rom 3:25), because those who are sinners are to become "sons"! Thus human beings (and this, surely, is beyond all doubt) are vitally involved in the atonement of Christ that takes place between Father and Son; this is where the "for us" is achieved, by him who has become man, who has come to stand by our side and who "bears" our sins. All the same, one would fail

---

[165] H. U. von Balthasar, "Die neue Theorie", 184 [our italics].

[166] H. U. von Balthasar, *Theodramatik* II/2: 222: "We must never forget that the christological atonement must in no way be interpreted as a penance imposed on the Son by the divine Father. . ."; cf., ibid., 221; idem, *Crucifixus*, 30. Among those who see Christ's atonement in terms of bearing the penalty for our sins are E. Lohse, op. cit., 143f., and R. Bultmann, *Theology of the New Testament*, vol. 1 (London, 1952), 297.

[167] In spite of their phonetical similarity, there is no etymological connection between "sohn" and "sühne" ("versühnen", "versöhnen", etc.).

[168] For the most part insufficient attention is paid to the deliberate way in which the word "Son" is used in Scripture, for instance, in Rom 8:3, 32; Gal 4:4.

[169] On the motive for creation and Incarnation, cf. M. Schmaus, *Kath. Dogmatik* II: 500ff. (see n.11 above); R. Schulte in MySal III/1: 57ff.; idem, MySal IV/2: 122ff.; H. Schlier, *Der Brief und die Epheser*, 39ff., 50f. (see n.178 below); H. U. von Balthasar, *Crucifixus*, 34: the relationship between God the Father and God the Son is "the presupposition for the existence of the world and of finite freedom (1 Jn 1:2; Eph 1:4ff.; Heb 1:3)". Idem, *Das Selbstbewusstsein Jesu*, 38: according to "the christological formula of Aquinas . . . the sending (*missio*) of the Son is only the prolongation into the world of his eternal proceeding (*processio*) from the Father. . . ."

[170] Cf. K. Rahner, "Salvation. IV. Theology" in *Encyclopedia of Theology*, 1521: "We are quite entitled to assume that (i) even divinizing grace as such was given from the start *intuitu Christi*, in view of Christ as the incarnate Word of God. This grace becomes forgiving because God's saving will, directed from the start toward Christ as its historical culmination, was (freely) *absolute*, even in face of sin. It is also possible to assume that (ii) sin . . . was permitted by God only *as* already transcended by his grace. He wished to manifest the victory of his own absolute love even over the refusal of his creature and in the deadly abyss of its futility."

completely to grasp what, at its deepest level, this "bearing" *is* if it were not seen as the realization of the eternal Father-Son relationship, transposed into the drama of sin and salvation history. For it is here, incarnate in creaturehood and in the arena of redemption,[171] that sonship proves itself: Jesus bears sins by enduring them: before the face of the Father the "Beloved Son" endures the sinful opposition of those who are created in him, and called in him, to be sons; he accepts their shame and disgrace as his own (cf. Rom 15:3; 1 Cor 4:10ff.; 1 Pt 2:19f.; Heb 12:2; 11:26; 13:13). He endures sinners.[172] At the focus of God's displeasure (for God's determination to be "Father" extends to his saving wrath) the Son endures those who do not wish to be sons. Thus what Christ does for us, he does "for the glory of God" (Rom 15:7), in obedience to God the Father and in fulfillment of his fatherly will: enduring the sinner, he endures the whole weight of the love of God the Father. For this is what happens when God as Father loves sinners: the Son takes his brothers' sinful estrangement into his own most intimate relationship with the Father.[173] Here the sin of these sons is fashioned as in a furnace until all that is left is the Son's pain, that is, that form of love that is the exact opposite of sinful rebellion, that it converts and nullifies, and for which it atones. Here we are faced with the staggering truth that the sinner has become "dear to the heart of God"[174] the Father. The crucified Son yields to the Father's love as it presses toward sinners: he occupies the "place of sinners" and allows God to be "Father" there; and he is "all the more" Son as he stands *in* their sinful estrangement from the Father and endures it. Here, then, are the refined and thoroughly personal features of what is really meant by "substitution", "satisfaction", "appeasement of the Father's anger" and "sacrifice".[175]

Since Jesus was "Son" as no one else ever was, Son through and through, since he never betrayed his sonship, he could "bear" sin as no one else could.

[171] Jesus' atoning function reaches its climax in his death, but it is not restricted to it: his cry of "Abba" indicates "what is the real mystery and center of Jesus' life": W. Kasper, "Neuansätze gegenwärtiger Christologie" in J. Sauer, ed., *Wer ist Jesus Christus?* (Freiburg-Basel-Vienna, 1977), 121–50, cf. 137. Cf. J. Jeremias, *The Prayers of Jesus* (London, 1967), 11–65.

[172] Cf. H. Schlier, *Grundzüge*, 135; idem, *Der Herr ist nahe: Advents-betrachtungen* (Freiburg, 1975), 54–56: ". . . he has accepted us by enduring us in love . . . taking our guilt and sin upon himself and bearing it. . . . The destiny of the cosmos, the destiny of history is laid upon him. He endures us."

[173] Cf. H. U. von Balthasar, *Crucifixus*, 33f.

[174] R. Guardini, *Der Herr*, 146.

[175] For a truly christianized concept of sacrifice, cf. J. Ratzinger, "Is the Eucharist a Sacrifice?", 39f.; H. Kessler, "Erlösung als Befreiung?", 7ff. On the concept of "satisfaction", cf. L. Hödl, "Genugtuung. I. Dogmatisch" in LThK IV: 683–85; F. Lakner, "Satisfaction" in SM 5: 433–35.

It should be pointed out that only in this filial perspective can the atonement performed by righteous men in the OT (the godly, the martyrs, the Suffering Servant) be seen in its true typological significance.

Since he had *no* sin to "repent of", [176] he could "atone" for *all* sins; thus he had the necessary power to put away *sin, all* sin, ἐφάπαξ "once for all" (cf. Heb 9:26; 10:10).

No doubt it will remain an impenetrable mystery just how anyone can atone for the sin of another. [177] At the same time we can say this: Christ's relation to us is not like that of any "other" person. For in him we are created. *"He* is our 'transcendental' locus". [178] If, "for the creature, God is not 'the Other' but the Creator, the One who enables the creature to attain its own meaning, then the more influence he has on it". [179] If, according to the fundamental meaning of "representation", God, the transcendental cause (*attingens ens qua ens*), far from opposing the creature's selfhood, actually liberates the creature's own self, enabling it to *be* and to be *free,* [180] should we not have the courage (basing ourselves on 2 Cor 5:17; Gal 6:15; Jn 1:3; Eph 1:4ff.; Col 1:16f.; Heb 1:3) to take Christ's atoning Cross literally as "new creation"? Can we not understand the Cross as the act of creation whereby the *sinner* is drawn back from the evil abyss (*nihilum*) and re-instated in his lost filial identity and selfhood?

If the biblical teaching on our creation in Christ is given its full weight and if we fully realize the truth that we are sons in the Son, we may tentatively put forward this view: in the full New Testament sense we human beings "sin" — speaking in the Pauline manner "as fools" — at the *Son's expense,* as it were, contained in the Son, desired and loved by the Father as sons in the Son. This is so much so that, conversely, Christ, the first born of many brethren, can "bear" and endure his brethren, sinners that they are, before the Father and recover them for sonship. In this way Jesus' atoning death, understood as sin transformed into the pain of his filial love, would be his way of creating from nothing, *ex nihilo,* from the *nihilum* that is sin.

Such a view could enable us to glimpse the breathtaking truth contained in those words of R. Guardini, which otherwise sound like the babblings of a

---

[176] Jesus was unable to experience μετάνοια. Consequently, if he is spoken of as a "penitent", the meaning of "penitence" will need to be modified. Jesus' atonement — unlike that performed by the sinner — is not the *terminus ad quem* of penitence in the sense of conversion or the return to sonship.

[177] On this, cf. H. U. von Balthasar, *Crucifixus,* 32ff.

[178] H. Schlier, *Der Brief an die Epheser,* 48. Cf. ibid., 50: "To the extent that we are in him, we always have been. Being in him is before everything, eternally; it is the first thing we were." Cf. n.201 below; L. Scheffczyk, "Die heilshafte Stellvertretung", 116: what guarantees "the solidarity of humanity and of the whole creation" is the christological fact "that the *whole creation* is centered on the *God-Man,* that it has its blueprint and goal in the Incarnate One".

[179] R. Guardini, *Die Bekehrung des Aurelius Augustinus: Der innere Vorgang in seinen Bekenntnissen* (Leipzig, 1935), 118.

[180] Cf. N. Hoffmann, op. cit., 176; Thomas Aquinas, *In I Sent.,* dist. 37, q. 3, a. 3: ". . . omnia entia sunt in uno loco, sc. in Deo, qui omnia continet."

madman: "To forgive, to forgive effectively, is in an absolute sense harder than to create. True, only God can create. But only a God who is—I almost want to say 'above God'—can forgive. . . . In fact Christ came for the very purpose of proclaiming to us this 'God who is above God'! Not 'the Highest Being', but the Father. . . . Men really had no notion that God is like this, as he *must* be if he is to forgive."[181]

We have already seen that God adheres to the fundamental law of representation and respects man's dignity as a partner[182] with both a divine sensitivity and an unswerving singleness of purpose; and so he forgives sins by enabling the sinner to atone for them. He returns them, as it were, to the sinner in the form of *his* atonement; but now we can go on to say this: the God who is Father forgives by giving to these sinful sons his own Son to be *their own*—a Son who goes so far in his sonship that he enters into their refusal of sonship, converting it into the unconditional Yes and Amen of his atonement, his filial suffering.

Again we come across the fluidity in the relationship between forgiveness and atonement that we have noted before. This time the context is "patrogenetic",[183] and the reason for it is plain: it is rooted in the Trinity like Father and Son, generation and birth. When the sins of the sons are to be blotted out, "forgiveness" and "atonement" are the names given to the act of Father and Son.

Atonement means being a Son to the very end (εἰς τέλος), the prevailing of sonship in the face of its extreme denial.[184] But being "Son" always means being dependent on the "Father" as source. So in Christ's atoning work God the Father is acting with his *generative* power: in the atoning Christ we see God the Father's *self-affirmation* as Father.[185]

---

[181] R. Guardini, *Der Herr*, 148 [our italics].

[182] Cf. L. Scheffczyk, op. cit., 117ff.; R. Schwager, op. cit., 219ff.

[183] This expression is used in the sense defined by R. Schulte in "Die Heilstat des Vaters in Christus" in MySal III/1: 49–84, esp. 52f. Ibid., 53: "In view of the Trinitarian and christological structure of the entire order of creation and salvation . . . it is helpful to use the dual term 'genetic/gennetic', familiar to us from the Trinitarian controversies, and to apply it, albeit now in a reverse direction, i.e., from the point of view of God the *Father*, to all things as proceeding from him, the *ex quo omnia*: God the Father is the source of the Word, the Son, whom he begets (γεννάω), and hence he alone, the ἀγέννητος, the only begetting One, is Father; thus the Son's relation to him is seen to be 'patrogennetic'. . . . But since God the *Father* is always the *ex quo omnia* with regard to creation (and its maintenance), it follows that all created reality must be seen and understood in a 'theo*genetic*', indeed 'patro*genetic*' (γίγνομαι), way. . . . Clearly, then, every person and thing must be held to be patrogen(n)etic ('*ad intra*' as well as '*ad extra*'), dependent on God the *Father* as their origin and originator."

[184] Here we glimpse the "Easter" quality of atonement: as a journey of conquest through fundamental negativity, it manifests a structure of "resurrection".

[185] Scripture expresses this indirectly. The Resurrection of Jesus is only rarely ascribed to his own action; mostly he is spoken of as being raised (passively) by the Father. Cf. W. Kasper, *Jesus the Christ* (London and New York, 1976), 144ff. Cf. also 1 Pt 1:3.

Summing up the argument so far: having followed the idea of "representa-tion" to its Trinitarian and patrogenetic origins, we have reached the basic christological and soteriological meaning of atonement: what we see in Christ's atoning work on the Cross is the affirmation of sonship in the face of its denial in sin. This is effected by the Father's generative power and carried out by the incarnate Son in free, obedient love. Thus we have arrived at a basis in Christology for a definition of the nature and meaning of an atonement-spirituality that will be faithful to revelation.

3. The pneumatological and ecclesiological dimension of Christ's atonement: the Christian and atonement

Here, once again guided by the idea of "representation", we are endeavoring to find out whether, if we acknowledge the paramount and universal efficacy of Christ's work on the Cross, we are obliged to say that atonement is not something that the human being and the Christian can perform.[186]

3.1 Christ's representing of us is not a substitution, not an "ersatz", but an "enabling" work

Christ being "for us" means that, as "ἱλαστήριον", all his power is devoted to restoring sinners to their lost identity as sons of God (cf. Jn 10:10; 3:16; 12:24; Mk 10:45; 1 Tm 1:15; Gal 4:4f.).[187]

In the sacrifice of the Cross God is not operating a suprapersonal, forensic compensation scheme. The "God and Father of Our Lord Jesus Christ" (2 Cor 1:3; Col 1:1) is not interested in the bare formality of "honor restored" for its own sake. Certainly he does require satisfaction for sin, but what "satisfies" him is when he is able to reveal his fatherly nature in a personal way, and to the sinner in particular. But a view that restricts the event of the Cross to so-called "objective" redemption cannot do justice to the divine sav-ing will, which is urgent for the redemption of the individual.[188] The totality of grace is not revealed until this "objective" redemption has achieved its "subjective" goal.[189] There is this unavoidable personal difference—and not in spite of but because of Christ's unique communion with those who are his.

---

[186] See n.3 above. Cf. also R. Pesch, Das Abendmahl (Münster, 1965), 186.

[187] Cf. W. Thüsing, Per Christum in Deum, 117.

[188] Cf. R. Schulte, Die Umkehr, 173: "The redemptive events in Cross and Resurrection 'for many', fully valid as they are, have not immediately brought this redemptive work to bear on the individual, have not yet become reality in him."

[189] To ignore this would be to let the believer's status as subject be absorbed into Jesus, seen as the only genuine partner with God. This would result in a certain christological solipsism. Cf. G. Kraus, Vorherbestimmung: Traditionelle Prädestinationslehre im Licht gegenwärtiger Theologie (Freiburg-Basel-Vienna, 1977), 321f.

Precisely because of its particular creative and penetrative power, Christ's atonement situates each man in the "*ultima solitudo*"[190] of personal uniqueness. The "for us" is not an automatic process overriding the personal self, and "representation"—in spite of, perhaps, many widespread misconceptions —is not, in its innermost core, "substitution", "ersatz", but an action that enables the "other" to be himself.[191] And it would be more than strange if this basic law were to have an exception at the very place where God, as it were, exercises all his patrogenetic power, at the climax of representation in saving history, in the redemptive act of the Cross.

If God the Father has redeemed us by the representative atonement of his incarnate Son, this must imply—according to the inner intentionality of representation—that, in and through Christ, God has enabled us personally to share in Christ's atoning work.[192]

If we turn to revelation for an answer as to "how" the atonement of Jesus can enter intimately into the personal uniqueness of every redeemed person, we find ourselves pointed firmly toward a dimension we have so far more or less neglected: the dimension of the Spirit.[193]

---

[190] Cf. Duns Scotus, *Opus Oxoniense* III dist. 1 no. 17.

[191] Cf. G. Greshake, *Erlösung und Freiheit*, 345: "Thus in his work of representation Jesus is not a substitute who supplies what we are unwilling or unable to do. He is our representative [*locum tenens*—Tr.], i.e., he has made a place for us and is keeping it open, the only place where the world can find its identity." H. Volk, *Gott alles in allem: Gesammelte Aufsätze* (Mainz, 1961), 10–22, 149–56, emphasizes God's tendency, in governing the world, to let the creature "be", not taking him over but enabling him to cooperate. L. Scheffczyk, "Die heilshafte Stellvertretung", 118, notes "the principle adopted by God in the created order", namely, that of "elevating man in everything to the dignity of a partner and taking him seriously as such". This principle is essential if we are to understand the imperative aspect which permeates the NT message. Cf. R. Schulte, *Die Umkehr*, 199f. The Pauline διὰ πίστεως (e.g., Rom 3:21ff.) should also be mentioned in this context.

[192] Cf. L. Scheffczyk, op. cit., 119: Christ left his redemptive work "for his servants to complete. . . ." The redeemed "are to bring redemption to its fullness, as willed by God, through their own collaboration". Cf. also H. U. von Balthasar, *Theodramatik* II/2: 222; H. Schlier, *Grundzüge*, 175, 177; W. Joest, "Versöhnung", 1379; H. Volk, op. cit., 20: it remains a fact "that, according to the divine decree, the humanity of Christ, and hence the creature, is actively involved in the work of redemption." N.b. the difference in approach to the recipients of baptism and of penance. Cf. B. Poschmann, "Die innere Struktur des Bussakramentes" in MThZ 1 (1950): III, 12–30, esp. 23: because of the substantially greater wickedness of the sin of a baptized person, whose sin is an "injury to his relationship as a child of God . . . it is totally appropriate that his sin is now not simply forgiven (as at baptism), but, in order to receive forgiveness, he must 'atone' for it through temporal punishment, he must make satisfaction for it. . . ."

[193] Our particular interest is to see whether the idea of representation can shed new theological light on what Scripture has to say about the Spirit-dimension of Christian atonement.

3.2 *The Christian is one who atones in Christ through the Spirit*

Our neglect of the Spirit so far has been deliberate, for there is one respect in which all that we have said needs a more thorough theological grounding.

3.2.1 *The Creator Spirit*

This applies primarily to what we have said about Christ himself. His nature and work only become intelligible in the context of the Spirit. For Christ "not only renders present what always was in God; he is also its radically new, historical realization".[194] In him we meet not only the Logos, but the incarnate Logos, that is, the mediation that has already taken place between heaven and earth, between necessity and contingence. But if it is true that the world is not "self-explanatory" (in contrast to God)[195] and that it can only be made intelligible as a dependent reality in relation to God, the question arises whether, in God, it is the Logos who is the explanation of the world's existence (as possibility and as fact), and our answer must be No. As far as, in revelation, we are given a glimpse of the mystery of the Trinity, we must say that the procession of the Second Person in God, his begetting, has as its formal term his identity with the First Person in the divine nature. To that extent the Second Person witnesses to God's power of positing and affirming "*ad intra*".

In "Christ", however, the content of the "μυστήριον"[196] is realized in a new and typically Pauline sense that goes beyond the internal divine mystery of the Logos: for Paul what is essential is the unique relationship of the Logos to *created reality* ("*ad extra*"), a relationship implicit in the hypostatic union (but perhaps in a purely notional way). Thus the mystery of Christ presupposes that the divine power of "representation" in the begetting (*generatio*) of the Son is not exhausted in it: there must be in God another factor distinct from the Logos in order to yield the possibility of representation in the form of creation (*creatio*).

The testimony of revelation enables us to see this factor in the procession of the Third Person.[197] The Greek theology of the Trinity conceived the Holy Spirit as the "surplus and effusion of freedom in the love between Father and Son", as the One in whom "God's innermost essence . . . impels him outward", in whom God "has the possibility of producing something outside, that is, a creature. . . ."[198]

---

[194] W. Kasper, *Jesus the Christ*, 250.

[195] K. Hemmerle, *Franz von Baaders philosophischer Gedanke der Schöpfung* (Freiburg-Munich, 1963), 9.

[196] Cf. R. Schulte in MySal IV/2: 76f.

[197] W. Kasper, op. cit., 256. Cf. R. Schulte, ibid., 133, 123: "Created reality does not originate in nothing, but in the love of God the Father."

[198] W. Kasper, ibid., 250. It would be interesting to investigate Hegel's doctrine of the Trinity (does he preserve the personal integrity of the Holy Spirit? does he reduce the tri-Personality to a duality of Persons?) and to see how it is connected with his view of creation (is

Therefore, whereas God shows his power of "representation" "*ad intra*" in the eternal generation of the Son, positing a difference between God and the "Other" who is *also* God; in the spiration of the Spirit (equally eternal, necessary and terminating in a Divine Person) we see God's self-affirmation in the free exercise of his power of representation "*ad extra*", directed toward the *creaturely* "other". If the Spirit "is, as it were, the . . . transcendental condition of the very possibility of a free self-communication of God in history",[199] the mystery of Christ points to the Spirit as its precondition within the divine life, that is, Christology is only intelligible as pneumatology. The "sending" of the Son is only possible in the Spirit (cf. Lk 1:35).[200]

3.2.2 *The Spirit of sonship*
In accordance with his patrogenetic essence, however, when God creates he does not actually lay stress on the "creature" as such;[201] the "point" of creating is the glorification of his fatherhood by and in the created world. The Spirit's function, too, is subservient to this aim: he makes creation possible as a corollary of the mysterious fact that "the creature" is "son". He expresses the dynamism of his Trinitarian nature by carrying the inner divine processes of generation and communication forward into the sphere of the creature — as the overflowing of the love between "Father" and "Son" — and revealing the Father's love in sons who are not *the* Son, but sons by grace. In the Spirit, that is, the ecstatic principle which reaches out beyond the sphere of internal divine relations, God has the power to call into being things that are not (Rom 4:17) and to summon the one who is a "hired servant" to the dignity of the child.

The Spirit is the *Spirit of sonship* (Rom 8:15). As such he already makes himself felt in the God-Man's relation to God, by perfecting the divine sonship of *Jesus*, which arises from the hypostatic union, and making it into the sonship of the *Christ*.[202]

3.2.2.1 *The Spirit and the sonship of Jesus*
Within the terms of our inquiry (atonement as the affirmation of sonship) the following aspects of the New Testament message acquire special importance, perhaps unexpectedly:

---

he able to preserve God's freedom in creating the world?); on this, cf. L. Oeing-Hanhoff, "Hegels Trinitätslehre. Zur Aufgabe ihrer Kritik und Rezeption" in ThPh 52 (1977): 378–407, esp. 392ff.; W. Kern, "Dialektik und Trinität in der Religionsphilosophie Hegels: Ein Beitrag zur Diskussion mit L. Oeing-Hanhoff" in ZKTh 102 (1980): 129–55, esp. 146ff.

[199] W. Kasper, ibid., 250.

[200] The formula "The Father sends the Son" (see above) is — covertly — already Trinitarian.

[201] Cf. H. Schlier, *Der Brief an die Epheser*, 51: "For the Christian, who is in Christ, 'being' never means only being-in-the-world, only being a creature: it also means having been chosen by God before all things."

[202] Cf. H. Mühlen, *Der Heilige Geist als Person*, 170ff.

1. A somewhat surprising function is ascribed to the *Resurrection* of Jesus: it signifies his establishment in his sonship (Rom 1:4); it fulfills the promise of Psalm 2:7: "You are my son, today I have begotten you" (Acts 13:33; cf. Heb 1:5; 5:5).[203]

2. The Resurrection glory does not simply *make* Jesus "Son" but it does make him the "first born" of many brethren (Rom 8:29),[204] the new progenitor and the Second Adam (cf. 1 Cor 15:45; Rom 5:12ff.) who "brings many sons to glory" (Heb 2:10; cf. Jn 17:2,9, 11f.,24; 12:32; 1 Pt 1:3).

3. Jesus attains Resurrection, and the new sonship it involves, having *"made purification for sins"* (Heb 1:3; 5:7f.; 2:9, 10, 13; Phil 2:9; Lk 24:25).[205] It seems "not improbable" that in Romans 8:3, 32 Paul understands the "Son of God" as him "who obediently, that is, . . . in personal dedication to the Father, allowed himself to be sent to his death." The "Son's earthly obedience must be seen as preceding and grounding the exalted Christ's role as our righteousness according to 1 Corinthians 1:30."[206] Thus the sonship of "Jesus" is filled out into the sonship of the "Christ" by his obedient acceptance of the "representative" ministry of atoning suffering, which is the source of the "new birth" of the children of God (cf. Jn 3:3, 5, 7, 14, 16, 17.; Ti 3:5; 1 Pt 1:3).

4. However, the New Testament leaves us in no doubt that all this occurs *in the Spirit*:[207] vis-à-vis the Spirit, Jesus is not only, nor primarily, active;[208] prior to his becoming *"Kyrios"* and as such having authority over the Spirit, he himself is totally subject to and dedicated to the Spirit.[209] It is the Spirit who bears the whole destiny and being of Jesus. "Through the eternal Spirit" he offers himself to God (Heb 9:12–14), loves the Father and those who are his own "to the end" (Jn 13:1).[210] Jesus must first make

---

[203] Cf. W. Thüsing, *Per Christum*, 145. Everything said about Jesus' being "lifted up" (e.g., Jn 3:14; 12:32; Phil 2:9), his "going" to the Father (Jn 13:1) and his "glorification" (Jn 17:1, 5, 24) is in the context of sonship.

[204] W. Thüsing, ibid. Cf., ibid., 153f.; H. Schlier, *Der Römerbrief*, 272: Christ is the "first born among many brethren . . . not only with regard to the creation (Col 1:15) but also with regard to the Resurrection from the dead (Col:18; Rom 8:11; 1 Cor 15:22ff.; Rev 1:5)." Idem, *Über die Auferstehung Jesu Christi* (Einsiedeln, 1968), 51: "For Jesus Christ himself, his Resurrection results in the unveiling and fulfillment of his Person as Christ and Kyrios, as the formula in Acts 2:23 says, or as the acclamation in Rom 10:9 or the hymn to Christ in Phil 2:11, etc., put it. . . ."

[205] Cf. E. Lohse, op. cit., 167f.

[206] W. Thüsing, op. cit., 146. Following O. Cullmann, *The Christology of the New Testament* (London, 1959), 293: " 'Son of God' signifies God's redemptive action, the Son's obedience to the end."

[207] Cf. H. Mühlen in MySal III/2: 519ff.; W. Kasper, op. cit., 251ff.

[208] As J. Moltmann seems to suggest in "Gesichtspunkte der Kreuzestheologie heute" in EvTh 33 (1973): 346–65, esp. 359.

[209] Cf. H. U. von Balthasar, *Pneuma und Institution*, 224.

[210] Cf. ibid., 218–24; O. Michel, *Der Brief an die Hebräer* (Göttingen, 1949), 206: "Here too, in his sacrificial action, Christ is governed by the objectivity of the Holy Spirit (7:16; 9:14). The Holy Spirit is thus, not the 'possession' of Jesus, but the power that sustains his office and sacrifice."

himself totally available to the Spirit, endure the hell of separation from the Father in the strength of the Spirit, and, having become an atonement for sins, prove his sonship against the power of sin. Only then does he attain Resurrection,[211] become *Kyrios*,[212] "Pneuma" (2 Cor 3:17), "life-giving Spirit" (1 Cor 15:45), Second Adam[213] and thus perfectly a "Son".[214]

5. Moreover, Paul connects the Resurrection from the dead (effected by the Spirit), and the act of atonement that determines it, with sonship, understood not only messianically but as the eternal sonship of God,[215] that is, he is convinced that, through the Resurrection, men become sons of God in the sense of sharing in the eternal sonship of the Logos.[216] This being the case, and assuming that our being, given a share in his sonship, somehow perfects it, it follows that Christ's atonement on the Cross also perfects his eternal sonship and hence, in some manner, the sonship of the Logos. Not, of course, in the "immanent" but in the "economic" Trinity: if we are right to see the mysteries of the Incarnation and of grace as the prolongation and carrying forward of the eternal generation,[217] as an "uttering" of the eternal Word[218] into the outer world, if the Father "gives up" (Rom 8:32) his only Son so that men shall become "sons", then we can understand the atoning death of Jesus (in which sonship asserts itself against sin) as the perfection of that prolongation, of that utterance into the outer world. Then we can surely say that, in the atonement of the Cross, made effective by the Spirit, the eternal Logos proves himself *ad extra* as the One in whom (according to Col 1:17; cf. Heb 1:3; Jn 1:3) all things—including finite, defectible freedom—"hold together", even against sin! In the perspective of the Cross, it is because of the Logos that the risk[219] and responsibility of creation "by the Word" was undertaken at all. From this point of view of the economy of salvation, we can confidently put forward the following suggestion: Jesus' atonement on the Cross, made effective by the Spirit, brings the generation of the Logos to its

---

[211] On Jesus being raised by the Spirit, cf. W. Thüsing, op. cit., 153.

[212] On the relationship between *Kyrios* and *Pneuma*, cf., ibid., 154f.

[213] Cf. ibid., 207ff.; R. Schnackenburg in MySal III/1:333ff.

[214] Cf. W. Thüsing, ibid., 153f.: the pre-Pauline expression found in Rom 1:4, which connects the Resurrection of Christ with the Spirit, is "no doubt a stage on the way to Paul's understanding that Christ's function as Son (i.e., to draw all the elect into his sonship)" is dependent on the fact "that in his Resurrection Christ became a 'life-giving Spirit' (1 Cor 15:45)".

[215] Ibid., 145.

[216] Ibid., 145, 121–25.

[217] Cf. M. J. Scheeben, *The Mysteries of Christianity* (London and St. Louis, 1946) secs. 26–31, 55.

[218] M. J. Scheeben, in *Handbuch der kath. Dogmatik*, ed. M. Schmaus, vol. 2 (Freiburg, 1943), no. 1069.

[219] H. U. von Balthasar, *Crucifixus*, 34; M. Schmaus, *Kath. Dogmatik* II: 492, 501 (see n.11 above).

fulfillment; in it, the Father causes the Logos to be perfectly "Son", in the sense that this atonement perfects the utterance of the Word ("*dictio verbi*") into the outer world in salvation history. In this eternal generation, thus perfected, God expresses himself perfectly as Father.[220]

Summarizing we can say that, through the Spirit, the patrogenetic principle of representation is ratified in Jesus, who becomes "Christ" through his atoning work: this principle is the Father's power of enabling us to *be*, and to *be "sons"*, in the face of the sinful world.

3.2.2.2 *The Spirit and our sonship*

Through the Spirit Jesus is put in a relationship with men that is constitutive for him as the Christ.[221] Conversely, we must say that it is only through the Spirit, only through the Spirit of Christ in men[222] that they can be in relation to Christ, that they can be "Christians" and children of God in the full sense—which is of vital significance for the innermost quality of this "childhood".

The Pneuma is the "Spirit of sonship", but he communicates sonship as the Spirit of Christ, *the* Son. It is "in" and "through" the Spirit that Christ, the Son, is in us, so that through the Spirit we share in the sonship of Jesus Christ himself.[223]

Following Scripture (cf. Acts 10:38, 44) we must be more precise and say that the cooperation of Christ and Spirit is related to our sonship in such a way that the Spirit does not mediate *between* us and Christ: he is one and the same Spirit in us and in Christ.[224] The Spirit unites us with Christ in such a way "that we are not, as it were, sons of the Father 'alongside' the Son, but 'in' the Spirit of the Son".[225]

Here particular stress must be laid on the fact that the reciprocal (pneumatic) "Christ in us" and "we in Christ" (cf. Rom 8:10; Col 1:27[226] is a

---

[220] In this connection a certain theological profit can be drawn from the (objectively speaking, heretical and overstressed) co-ordination of *generatio verbi* and *creatio mundi*, i.e., of the λόγος ἐνδιάθετος and προφορικός in some of the early Fathers (cf. L. Scheffczyk in MySal II: 157–59, 163).

[221] In what follows we shall indicate the far-reaching consequences that this has for the possibility and the meaning of Christian atonement.

[222] H. Mühlen, *Der Heilige Geist als Person*, 256, 188. This statement is of great importance in showing how Christ's atonement affects the individual: it implies that the so-called "corporative" view alone (Christ as the juridical representative, the originator, the mediator of creation) is insufficient to account for the actual content of the representation actually achieved by Christ. "Christ is a 'corporate personality' . . . as the 'New Adam', endued with the power of the Spirit" (W. Thüsing, op. cit., 75; cf. ibid., 74, 72). This "New Adam", through his Spirit, unites "the members of the new humanity" to himself (ibid., 66) in an intimate and personal way (69, 75) and "draws them into his life" (66).

[223] Cf. H. Mühlen, ibid., 188, 254–57, 301; W. Thüsing, ibid., 152.

[224] Cf. H. Mühlen, ibid., 252, 187.

[225] Ibid., 257. Cf. W. Thüsing, ibid., 63–66, 116–18, 187; R. Schulte in MySal V: 145.

[226] Cf. W. Thüsing, ibid., 61ff., esp. 65, 152.

determinant of being and personhood. Paul does not hesitate to speak of a "new creation" (Gal 6:15; 2 Cor 5:17),[227] so intensively does it refashion our *being*, our *personal* being: by being in Christ through the Spirit and sharing in his sonship, we are and we exist with Christ in relationship to the Father (cf. Rom 5:1; 2 Cor 3:4; Gal 4:4ff.; 2:19f.; Rom 8:9–11),[228] we are adopted "into the inner-Trinitarian personal mystery of the mutual embrace of Father and Son in the Divine Spirit".[229]

To the precise degree in which this is—mysteriously—true; insofar as the primal personal word really is "I-thou" and "person" means "being-*in-relationship-with-the-thou*",[230] we can attribute to the (pneumatic) mystical union with Christ—albeit in a distant analogy—a personalizing effect on the believer that is like the effect of the hypostatic union on the human nature of Christ.[231]

Transposed into the terms of "representation": through his personal initiative in the sending of the Son (in Incarnation and Cross) and of his Spirit, the Father[232] establishes us permanently[233] and definitively in our filial selfhood: it is through and from the Father, not of ourselves, that we attain selfhood.

This must be kept before us when we come to inquire into the possibility and meaning of atonement in the Christian.

3.2.3. *Sonship in the Spirit and atonement*
Starting out from the idea of "representation", the inner logic of our reflections brings us to the insight that atonement in the Christian sense is only possible as "*grace*".

The same logic, however, shows that atonement—the gift of grace—is an essential determinant of Christian existence, not only as a possibility but also in fact.

3.2.3.1 *The thesis*
If it is true that "atonement" means "being a son in the face of sin", bearing sin as the suffering of filial love; if in Christ we are children of God by the Spirit; and if, moreover, "being-in-the-world" is an existential aspect of our sonship, and this world of ours is in a concrete, historical situation of sin: it follows that, as "sons of God", we are also involved in atonement.

---

[227] Ibid., 111.

[228] Cf. ibid., 117f., 187, 61ff. ("The theocentricity of being-in-Christ"), 151ff. ("Pneuma and theocentricity"); R. Schulte in MySal V: 144, 150–58; idem, in MySal IV/2: 124f. (The creature's participation in the πρὸς τὸν θεόν of the Logos.)

[229] R. Schulte in MySal V: 145.

[230] C. Schütz and R. Sarach in MySal II: 644.

[231] On the idea of a "personal causality", cf. H. Mühlen, op. cit., 249–53, 266–69, 272–77.

[232] Cf. R. Schulte in MySal V: 151, 143: the NT speaks of "being born again" or "being begotten again by God" "from above" (Jn 3:3; 1:13; Ti 3:5).

[233] Scripture speaks of God knowing and calling the individual "by name"; e.g., Is 43:1; Phil 4:3; Rev 17:8; 13:8; 3:5; Jn 10:3; Lk 10:20.

This conclusion, that our sonship as it were bears the stigmata of expiation,[234] simply makes explicit the ecclesiological and sacramental dimension of the New Testament message of redemption.

3.2.3.2 The proof: the Church is the mystery of Christ made present sacramentally and existentially as the process of atonement

In the divine plan, it pertains to the mystery of salvation that its realization in Jesus Christ does *not* "sublate it or bring it to an end": rather, it continues to "extend and carry forward the realization already achieved."[235] The "movement of God's eternal, salvific will continues beyond Christ's body on the Cross" in "the form and work of his . . . 'Mystical' Body",[236] the Church. With the Church, one and the same μυστήριον τοῦ θεοῦ (Eph 3:9f.) enters the "second stage" (phase) of its realization,[237] in the "era of the Church". For our purposes here we must note carefully that the Church is not only derived from Christ's atoning work but actually contributes to, and is constitutive of, the full reality of that work (the unsearchable riches of Christ: Eph 3:8). As Christ's σῶμα (Eph 1:23) and πλήρωμα (Eph 1:23; 4:13) it is to "*be*" the single, entire mystery [238] "with Christ and in dependence on him". There is a

---

[234] In our view, "atonement" must be seen primarily as an "objective" state of affairs prior to all reflection upon it. It is a modality that attaches to the child of God by nature, since that nature flows from the Cross of Christ, mediated by the Spirit. Existentially, of course, in a world imperilled by sin, it can be—must be—performed subjectively too, to a greater or lesser extent.

[235] R. Schulte in MySal IV/2: 78; cf., ibid., 79, 115.

[236] H. Schlier, "Die Kirche als das Geheimnis Christi nach dem Epheserbrief" in *Die Zeit der Kirche: Exegetische Aufsätze und Vorträge* (Freiburg, 1956), 299–307, esp. 303. According to the context, ibid., 302f., "Christ's body of the Cross" stands unequivocally for Christ as atonement.

[237] Cf. J. Heer, *Der Durchbohrte* (Rome, 1966), 123, 147, 160, 205, 275.

[238] R. Schulte, op. cit., 79. As an atoning sacrifice, the Crucified is related to the Church not only as efficient cause but also as a quasi-formal cause. Cf. R. Schulte in MySal V: 17 ("Conversion [*metanoia*] as the beginning and the form of Christian life"); ibid., 198 ("*Metanoia* as the permanent structure of Christian existence"); J. Ratzinger, "Das Geschick Jesu und die Kirche" in V. Schurr and B. Häring, eds., *Theologische Brennpunkte*, 2nd ed., vol. 2: *Kirche heute* (Bergen-Enkheim, 1969), 7–18: "When we speak of the Last Supper as the origin of the Church, it is clear that 'Church' is not founded by individual juridical acts but springs forth from the person of Jesus, from the mystery of his life and death. 'Church' is the concrete shape taken wherever the mystery of Jesus Christ's life and death is appropriated." Idem, "Der Weltdienst der Kirche: Auswirkungen von *Gaudium et spes* im letzten Jahrzehnt" in IKaZ 5 (1975): 438–54, esp. 452; idem, "Bemerkungen zur Frage der Charismen in der Kirche" in G. Bornkamm and K. Rahner, eds., *Die Zeit Jesu: Festschrift für Heinrich Schlier* (Freiburg-Basel-Vienna, 1970), 257–72. esp. 272; H. Schlier, "Das bleibend Katholische: Ein Versuch über ein Prinzip des Katholischen" in Cath 24 (1970): 1–21, esp. 15: "God's ultimate decision for the world, through his concrete Word and sacrament and through concrete ministry, has given man both being and existence in Jesus Christ and thus has established the Body of Christ, the Church, by the power of the Holy Spirit, as the *concrete presence* of the crucified body of the Exalted One" [our italics].

mysterious sharing of the same nature between the atoning Christ and the
Church.

Of course it is communicated through the sacraments, that is, as gift, particularly the fundamental sacraments of baptism and the Eucharist.[239] But
this "indicative" aspect must not blind us to the "imperative" aspect of New
Testament proclamation;[240] we must not forget that—corresponding to the
historic-dynamic character of sacramental reality as a life-process between
God and man[241]—the Church is meant to *carry out* the *mysterion*, which is
Christ "as its own nature".[242]

What must attain to "fulfillment in terms of personal life"[243] in the members
of the Church is *exactly the same* as what has occurred historically through
God's own saving action in Christ's Cross and Resurrection and has been en-
acted sacramentally in the event of baptism. While renouncing any false sacra-
mentalism, we must maintain that, as baptized persons, we participate in Jesus'
decisive destiny, in the "conquest of sin and death"[244]—not only symboli-
cally/mystically, in a merely parabolic sense,[245] but also in a "conversion" that
seizes our whole life in the concrete—so that contact with the "ἀπολύτρωσις of
the Cross", the "fundamental saving event"[246] performs in our personal existence what, in Jesus Christ, has taken place "for us".[247] But this means that
the baptized believer is involved in the struggle with sin, not as a sinless person

---

[239] Cf. J. Ratzinger, *Meditationen zur Karwoche*, 5th ed. (Meitingen-Freising, 1975), 11: the
"two fundamental sacraments of Eucharist and baptism" form "the actual context of the
Church *qua* Church. . . ." Idem, "Das Geschick Jesu und die Kirche" (see n.238 above), 14ff.

[240] Cf. R. Schulte in MySal V: 198ff. Scriptural references ibid., 200–202, 205–208.

[241] Cf. R. Schulte in MySal IV/2: 126ff.

[242] R. Schulte in MySal V: 198 [our italics].

[243] Ibid., 199; cf. 203.

[244] Ibid., 146; cf. 147.

[245] Cf. O. Casel, *The Mystery of Christian Worship* (Westminster, Maryland and London,
1962), 16.

[246] W. Thüsing, op. cit., 193f. (on Rom 3:24 and 1 Cor 1:30). Cf., ibid., 67ff. ("Being-in-
Christ" in its orientation to God: Rom 6:11 as a central text [". . . alive to God in Christ
Jesus"]); ibid., 68f.: "But according to v. 3 this surrender to Christ through baptism is
simultaneously a 'being baptized εἰς τὸν θάνατον αὐτοῦ'. Since in the surrender of baptism Christians are united with Christ himself, they are also 'implicated in his destiny', and particularly in
the fundamental element of it, i.e., his death on the Cross to destroy sin. . . . Baptism effects
the most intimate union with him who not only died once for the salvation of believers but ever
lives as the One who died, i.e., whose death is in a certain respect still a present reality." Ibid.,
69 n.28: "It must be kept in mind that θάνατος does not mean the *realm* of death but the *event* of
the death of Christ. . . ."

[247] R. Schulte in MySal V: 147. Ibid., 204: "If our existence is to remain Christian we must
perform the very *turning away* from sin and death that has occurred in Christ's Cross and is communicated through baptism; we must also *perform* that turning (back) to God that has taken
place *for us* in the Resurrection of Jesus Christ who was crucified for us, and that is intended to
be a reality which expands constantly toward fullness."

but in *metanoia*, as one who, though smitten by sin, is turning away from it and thus needs a physician (Mk 2:17), as one who enters into the redeeming act of him who has "borne" our sins.

In other words: participation in the Cross of Jesus means participation in his *atonement*, bearing sin in the form of "filial" pain, enduring God's absence in the form of Godlessness and the "death of God"—forms that are concrete and tangible in a world that is as it is precisely because it closes itself to God, insulates itself against his nearness, his reality: inhuman, dreary, boring, joyless, cruel, hard, haunted by despair and meaninglessness.

Being a "son" (cf. Phil 2:15) in this world, which has become what it is through its own sin and that of others, must be seen as the primary form[248] of atonement, of sharing in the atonement-destiny of the Son. Being a "son" is essential to genuine Christian existence. The sacraments must be understood as "enabling" and "empowering" us "to participate validly in the *metanoia-event* of the New Covenant",[249] meaning among other things that they make it possible to transform sin and its objective effects in one's own life and in the world into atonement, that is, to "bear" it as the Son bears his estrangement from the Father. In this view the believer is conformed (cf. Rom 8:29) by sacramental grace to the image of the "Son". Here this does not mean the eternal "Logos of God": the believer is drawn into the movement of the mystery called Jesus Christ,[250] involving the *complete realization* of the Son's "mission" in *sinful flesh* itself, in our world marred by sin.

Such a view of the sacraments, impressively supported by the Thomist doctrine of the "mission",[251] should allay any remaining suspicion that Christ's

---

[248] Which may naturally develop into atonement-spirituality.

[249] R. Schulte, ibid., 203. Cf. H. Schlier, *Grundzüge*, 168f.: "The righteousness of God, which is encountered in the Cross and Resurrection of Jesus Christ in the form of atonement, reconciliation and liberation from sin, death and the world's arrogance . . . announces God's claim upon us. Those who are open to receive this gift and to live by it can hear it and respond to it in simplicity here and now and in every way possible."

[250] Cf. R. Schulte in MySal IV/2: 131f.

[251] Thomas Aquinas, *S. Th.* I q. 43 a. 1 sqq. Ibid., a. 6 ad 2: "Sed tamen secundum illud augmentum gratiae praecipue missio invisibilis attenditur, quando aliquis proficit in aliquem novum actum, vel novum statum gratiae; ut puta cum aliquis proficit in gratiam miraculorum, aut prophetiae, vel in hoc quod ex fervore charitatis exponit se martyrio, aut abrenuntiat his quae possidet, aut quodcumque opus arduum aggreditur." ["Still there is a special instance of an invisible mission based on an increase in grace when someone advances to a new act or new stage of grace, e.g., to the grace of miracles or prophecy or to delivering himself in the fervor of his charity to martyrdom or to renunciation of all he possesses or to taking up any sort of heroic task." (Dominican ed., London, 1920–1938).]

With regard to our problem (Christ's atonement vis-à-vis the atonement of the Christian), the specific contribution of the Thomist teaching seems to be the way it facilitates an understanding of the necessary connection between Christ's presence as the One who atones in the believer and the latter's personal atoning efforts (which are therefore essential). According to Thomas the new manner of presence of a Divine Person ("mission") is dependent on a

representative atonement is an impersonal, automatic process over the head of the individual. It should make it clear that God's representative action really "bites", that it is not concerned with a "soul" beyond world and history but offers the human being in the locus of his existence, in the concrete conditions of his real world, a "place" as son; that the fundamental patrogenetic nature of the Divine Being and action, the absolute *sovereignty* that *lets the other as such be*, attains its ultimate manifestation in the encounter with the sinner. God's power is such that even the sinful self is not excluded, bypassed or made to feel small; it is not merely *dealt with* or overpowered by a magical forgiveness. In contact with the sinner, God's power *does* become a forgiving power, but it takes full effect in him in the mode of his own atonement. With inimitable sensitivity, God brings even the sinful self before him in its unique dignity, not belittling it but raising it from sinful degradation and empowering it to take action against its own sin; he speaks to it encouragingly and establishes it, by enabling it to convert its sin into filial pain and thus, by "bearing" it, to destroy it.[252]

In the atonement of the sons, as we have said, the *Son's* mission to sinful flesh is sacramentally implemented to its very last detail.

However, it is the *Spirit* who enables believers to share in the sonship that belongs to Jesus as the *Christ* (or: the sonship of the Jesus, who, through his atonement, has become "Christ").[253] What takes effect in the believers' atonement as a quasi-formal cause is the presence *of the Spirit*, sent as a result of Christ's atoning death.[254] Hence God's initiative in the world by way of Incarnation and the event of the Cross is carried through in an intimate and existential manner by the Spirit, prolonging Christ's power of filial atonement into the realm of personal, historical existence. Consequently we may and must say that the absolute

---

supernaturally effected change in the recipient of grace (cf. *S. Th.* I q. 43 a. I c; a. 2 c. and ad 2; a. 3 c.; a. 6 c. and ad 2). In this view, grace's gift of an atoning attitude and atoning deeds would be seen as this "change" in the recipient (*terminus*) of the divine visitation (*missio*), a change demanded by the new presence of the Holy Spirit as the Spirit of the atoning Christ. See n. 254 above.

[252] Here too, in blotting out sin, God remains faithful to the law whereby he is the cause of all creaturely action, in whatever mode is proper to the creature concerned. Cf. Thomas Aquinas, *S. Th.* I q. 83 a. 1 ad 3: Deus "movendo causas voluntarias non aufert, quin actiones earum sint voluntariae, sed potius hoc in eis facit; operatur enim in unoquoque secundum eius proprietatem." ["Just as his (God's) initiative does not prevent natural causes from being natural, so it does not prevent voluntary action from being voluntary but rather makes it be precisely this. For God works in each according to its nature" (Dominican ed., London, 1920–1938).] R. Haubst, "Gottes Wirken und die menschliche Freiheit" in TThZ 88 (1979): 175–93, esp. 185: "The higher the goal of man's free willing and doing, the more God enables him to strive toward it, the higher is the corresponding '*motio Dei*', and the greater is God's effect in man."

[253] Cf. H. Mühlen, *Der Heilige Geist als Person*, 187.

[254] Cf. R. Schulte in MySal IV/2: 133: "We must observe that the Spirit who animates the Church as the μυστήριον of God is the *same* Spirit who is sent from the Father by the dead and resurrected Son of God, so that, on the basis of *this* (saving) event and in an historically conditioned manner, he can he present in a totally new way."

ultimum of God's Trinitarian power of "representation", which is at work in the world, is not shown until the sending of the Spirit. Only by reflecting on the Spirit and the pneumatic prolongation of Christ's atonement into the existence of believers can we come to realize the creative and enabling power of Scripture's ὑπὲρ τῶν ἁμαρτιῶν ἡμῶν (1 Cor 15:3), which was achieved on the Cross to establish the sinner in his converted state. Only this can protect "representation" against being misunderstood as an automatic "for us".

3.2.3.3 *Conclusions*

A pneumatically proportioned understanding of atonement in which the Spirit mediates and activates Christ's atonement in the believer's existence sheds light on the ἀνταναπληρῶ of Colossians 1:24, going beyond pure exegesis[255] to a wider theo-logical context yielding a new interpretation.

The sufferings of Christians *"complete"* those of Christ, not in an additive sense, but by putting Christ's sufferings into effect. In no way can Christians' sufferings be viewed as something independent "alongside" or "beyond" the atonement of Christ, but only as the making effective, the gracious occurrence, of the *"for us"*, the "representation dimension" of Jesus' atoning act.

If it is true that the Christian's relation to Christ is constitutive of him, and that, conversely, Jesus' relation to the sinner ("for him") is constitutive of him as the "Christ" — since after all he is *the* Son through whose atoning death, in God's saving plan, the "many" are to be reborn as sons by personally participating in his atonement[256] — it follows that the atonement performed by Christians is an inner factor in the atonement of Christ: in it, Christ is constituted as the Atoner in his own *pleroma*; in us, Christ's atonement "blossoms". Our atonement is his glory.

Furthermore, within this horizon it ought to be possible to arrive at a precise theological understanding of what is meant by saying that the atonement of Christians is only "atonement" in an *analogous* sense.

It is beyond question that human atonement "must be preserved from any tendency to become autonomous". Christian atonement is only conceivable as something arising from our "participation in Christ's atoning work",[257] not separate from it.

Yet we must reach a correct understanding of the inner nature of this participation and its function in the totality of the saving events, and we must also appreciate its meaning for Christ's atoning work itself. K. Rahner writes

---

[255] Cf. J. Kremer, *Was an den Leiden Christi noch mangelt: Eine interpretationsgeschichtliche und exegetische Untersuchung zu Kol 1:24b*, BBB 12 (Bonn, 1956); E. Schweizer, *The Epistle to the Colossians* (London and Minneapolis, 1982), 99f.

[256] As the Christ, Jesus is envisaged in the Spirit from the very beginning as being "for us"; he *"is"* in order by the power of the Spirit to enable sinners to be "sons" (i.e., to be "atonement") and to assert their authentic, personal selfhood against sin.

[257] P. Neuenzeit, "Sühne", 596.

that Christ "has so made atonement to the Father . . . for our sins . . . that he willed us to have a share in him in the expiatory suffering for the sin of the world";[258] those who are well disposed toward atonement-spirituality may be gratified by such a positive statement, but in fact it is an anemic response to the real state of affairs.

Our participation rests primarily, not on the will of Christ, but on that of the Father; here in particular Christ is already subject to the *"mandatum Patris"*, to the control of the Spirit. Above all, however, this participation of ours is not an additional something granted us by the Father: it is at the very focus of his salvific will; it is the apex of representation in the redemptive process whose goal is sonship. God is so resolutely Father that he even grants sinners the opportunity of "being atonement". Now *atonement* is the way in which God causes *sinners* to be sons; atonement is the form taken by sonship in a sinful world. And Christ's death on the Cross testifies to God's determination to demonstrate his inner-Trinitarian nature as Father even against sin, through salvation history. Christ is atonement because he is the Son. But he is so in the mode of representation: he is not to substitute for sinners, to *replace* them, but to *em-place*, to establish them as sons (and hence as atoning sons). In and through Christ, the great Atoner, sinners too are to be sons and atoners—for this is the only way sinners can be sons. In Christ, the Father enables the sinner to be a son in a way that is appropriate to him as a sinner, and that respects his personal dignity (even as a sinner), namely, in the mode of a love that is deprived of the Father's nearness.

Christ *is* uniquely and inimitably "atonement": but so are we, really and truly. The specific quality of Christ's atonement is that, through it, we are enabled genuinely to perform atonement (just as really and genuinely as we are "sons" in him).

Certainly, in comparison with Christ, the Christian "is" atonement only in an analogous sense; yet this is true of his sonship too; the Christian is only analogously a son, yet formally and really he *is* a son.

However atonement may have been understood in present or past theory or praxis, it can hardly be doubted that the concept of atonement, which results from the idea of representation, can[259] and must [260] be subsumed under the clearly definable New Testament umbrella concept of atonement.

---

[258] K. Rahner, *Theological Investigations*, vol. 3 (London and Baltimore, 1967), 346f.

[259] Cf. P. Neuenzeit, "Sühne", 586.

[260] Cf. N. Brox, *Zeuge und Märtyrer: Untersuchungen zur frühchristlichen Zeugnis-Terminologie* (Munich, 1961 [StANT vol. V]), 217: According to Ignatius of Antioch, martyrdom "stands in a more direct relationship to the Passion than that of historical imitation. This is like what happens here, although Ignatius does not explain it. Ultimately the two are the same and directly comparable." Cf., ibid., 214–16.

It should be noted here that, in our view, the eschatological and martyrological aspect of Christian suffering need not exclude an atoning quality (cf., n.4 above). In our understanding

Our examination should have shown that anyone who seeks to get rid of atonement (in the sense we have elaborated) as something insignificant or even non-Christian is tampering not only with a particular historically determined form of Christian piety, not only with the Christian phenomenon as a whole, but also with its nature and substance, with the Christian conception of what "God" is and what he is like. What is at stake here is nothing less than theo-logy itself, the Christian concept of Being, the Christian concept of God. Our Yes or No to atonement is a Yes or No to "Trinitarian ontology", to the "Father"-God of the New Testament.[261] To say No is to mutilate the form of the divine representative activity that springs from the roots of God's nature, permeating all his external actions.

To the extent that Christ, the great Atoner, enables us to atone and hence to be sons of God, he does more than locate the "place" where *man* can find his Christian identity: if it is true that, in this Christ and through his Spirit, God actually manifests himself to all, even to sinners, as Father (for within the Trinity he is Father), then Christ is also the "place" where *God* demonstrates his identity as the Christian God. The Cross can become the full revelation of the "Christian" God, the dramatic epiphany, shaped in response to sin, of the eternal mystery of the Trinity, only if the atonement of the Cross is applied pneumatically to the details of the Christian's personal existence.

To recapitulate: the inherent dynamism of the "representation" approach seems to drive us to these conclusions: our conviction that Christian existence has a satisfaction-expiation dimension is in no way inimical to the New Testament message, and "atonement" is an authentic and inalienable element at the heart of the New Testament; the fundamental patrogenetic principle, which inheres in all representation, not only guarantees in a radical way the grace-quality of Christian atonement and hence the absolute sovereignty of God in the process of atonement but also shows that "atonement" is the form of filial selfhood before the Father that is appropriate to the converted; and the atonement that is Christ, by its very representative nature, requires the atonement of Christians in order to fulfill its own meaning, in order to attain to the *one*, dynamic, total mystery of "Christ in you" (Col 1:27).

With this result we come to the end of our examination of the basic meaning

---

of atonement, martyrdom can be laid upon us in a concrete situation, to be endured, through grace, as a form of "sonship" in opposition to sin. This interpretation would make clear the specific "witness" quality of martyrdom: in the very midst of the denial of God the martyr witnesses to God's powerful nearness. Cf. N. Brox, op. cit., 236: "We are compelled to assume that, for the early Church, it was the event of martyrdom and the figure of the martyr that were decisive, not the martyr's verbal confession nor the personal ethical qualities evinced by his courage."

[261] Cf. n.18 above.

of atonement in the Christ-event (Christology and soteriology) and in the Christian (pneumatology and ecclesiology). It might seem that all this is no more than an extended prolegomenon to the topic under consideration. In fact we have tried to see what are the deep theo-logical issues involved in that topic. Thus we are now in a position very briefly to take up the question announced at the beginning of this study, that is, the relationship of "atonement" to "Sacred Heart" spirituality.[262]

4. Atonement and the Pierced Heart: atonement-spirituality in the context of devotion to the Sacred Heart

4.1 Limiting the question

As we seek to arrive at a theological evaluation of the idea of atonement in devotion to the Sacred Heart, we must ask whether this de facto connection between the two expressions of Catholic spirituality is simply the result of the history of piety, or whether it arises from revelation and salvation history. If—as we expect—the latter is the case, we shall then ask whether there is an essential salvific meaning behind the fact of this connection.

Therefore, following our existing procedure, we shall inquire whether there is such a meaningful connection (1) between Christ as "Heart" and the basic christological-soteriological picture of atonement (in the objective order of salvation) that we have worked out and (2) between devotion to the Sacred Heart of Jesus and atonement-spirituality (in the realm of Christian devotion).

From the methodological point of view it will be interesting to see whether the principle of "representation", which has proved its value so far, will be able to throw light on these questions too.

4.2 The Pierced One: the "Word" from the Father, addressed to us as atonement

If we look closely, we shall see that the "Heart of Jesus" does not come to us in the first place via the visions and contemplations of mystics, the profound meditations of saints and holy men and women, nor from the speculations of learned divines.

The "Heart of Jesus" comes to us in its primal sense in that the Father appoints his Son as the atonement for our sins. When the Father addresses his eternal Word as the word of forgiveness to sinners, when he sends the Son (in the Spirit) into the abode of sinners, so that those who are sinners can be

---

[262] We cannot, of course, deal with the whole topic of "Atonement and the Pierced Heart"; instead, we shall see how far the reciprocal relationship of atonement and the Heart of Jesus can be illuminated theologically in the terms of our principle of "representation".

reborn as sons, the Word is not only made "flesh": God is made into a Pierced Heart, that is, the ultimate visible form taken by his patrogenetic power of representation. We see the Heart of Jesus most of all in the decisive accomplishment of the saving event itself.

Guided by the principle of representation we may expect that what God does is not simply done *to* us, in an objective "for us", out of his absolute power to save, but in a "for us" that calls to us as partners, making it clear that all takes place in the area of personal communication between Father and "son". God does not simply "do" what he does: he "says" it to men with the intention of turning them, as sons, to himself, to the Father. True, his Word is not void: it is a deed; but each deed, too, is not only deed but Word as well. Finally God addresses us with that Word which is his Son. He speaks it to sinners: his Son becomes atonement: God's last Word is his Son in the form of the Pierced Heart.

Scripture shows that we are right to approach things in this way: it shows that God's salvation is not simply implemented but assumes the form of *revelation*.[263] The New Testament holds both aspects of God's action (work and Word) together in the concept of the μυστήριον τοῦ θεοῦ (cf. Col 2:2). It comprises "the real occurrence of the mystery" and the fact that "it is manifested and mediated *as such*", that is, that it is "both *done* and made *known*".[264]

Illuminated by this universal revelatory purpose on the part of the divine activity, certain New Testament texts, which initially hardly seem to support a "Heart-of-Jesus" theology, are in fact shown to point to the mystery of the Pierced Heart. Thus for instance the προέθετο ἱλαστήριον and the εἰς ἔνδειξιν of Romans 3:25f. become significant. Here it is said of Jesus Christ: "God put him forward *publicly*, exposed him *to view*, as an *expiation* [*atonement*] in the spilling of his blood, *in* his bloody death on the Cross",[265] with the intention of making "his righteousness . . . manifest in

---

[263] Cf. A. Deissler in MySal II: 226: "In the very development of its theology of the Word of God, the Old Testament itself sees Yahweh's speaking as the fundamental category of all God's activity *ad extra*"; H. Schlier, *Grundzüge*, 34–44 ("The revealed God").

[264] R. Schulte in MySal IV/2: 76; cf. ibid., 115: The "one μυστήριον of God" signifies "both reality *and* revelation at the same time . . ."; ibid., 76: In the Pauline and deutero-Pauline literature μυστήριον appears "intimately bound up with the kerygma of Christ; it has as it were become one with it. . . ."

[265] H. Schlier, *Der Römerbrief*, 111 [our italics]; cf. ibid., 110: προέθετο refers, not to the Gospel, but to the "event" which is made present in the Gospel; ibid., 110: "the shedding of blood is the event in which the προτίσθεσθαι of the ἱλαστήριον took place." Cf. S. Lyonnet, "De notione expiationis" in VD 38 (1960): 260: "Cum propitiatorium a nemine aspiceretur neque aspici posset, Christus *palam et publice a Deo exhibetur* coram toto humano genere, ut intelligendum esse videtur verbum προέθετο. Tunc enim misericordia Dei peccata condonans, vel potius auferens, sibique hominem reconcilians . . . sese manifestat non iam occulte . . . sed in loco omnibus patenti."

the cosmos",[266] so that "the whole weight of this affirmation lies in the proclamation of the saving event as such in relation to the world's situation prior to and apart from Jesus Christ".[267]

In 1 John 4:9f. too it is a case of the "self-revelation of God in his saving activity".[268] The "full revelation of what love is"[269] does not take place until "the Son of God is sent *to atone for sinners*", until "God in mercy overcomes the abyss that separates him from the world that, in its alienation from him through sin, is in such need of redemption":[270] this is not an "attribute of God" but "God absolutely".[271] Not until "the Son surrenders himself as an atoning sacrifice for sins" does "the love of God 'appear' among men". Only in this Son who has become atonement "do we really recognize the 'Father' and his unsurpassably loving disposition . . . toward mankind".[272] What God always was "has become tangible . . . 'among us' "[273] in the personal "appearance" of the Son of God as atonement.

Taken together with texts such as Romans 3:21ff. and 1 John 4:9f. the *locus classicus* of the Heart-of-Jesus spirituality (Jn 19:34ff.) would be significantly more convincing, in our view, precisely due to the revelatory quality and the divine intentionality manifest in the symbolic content of the scene of the piercing.

Johannine theology is "first and foremost revelation theology".[274] Thus it deserves special attention when it provides the Gospel at its climax (19:34ff.) with the "graphic illustration" of what is its whole aim (20:31):[275] "In the Johannine view Jesus is not recognizable as . . . Messiah and Son of God in the full sense until he is seen as the Pierced One."[276] What we have here is a theological picture "expressing the essence of the Johannine revelation, and hence all that man must believe",[277] "the conclusion of that revelation that

---

[266] Ibid. 114; cf. ibid., 111f.

[267] Ibid., 115. Cf. ibid., 104: πεφανέρωται in Rom 3:21 means that the δικαιοσύνη θεοῦ has been "made visible to our eyes and has been genuinely encountered. The form of the verb is perfect, indicating a unique event remaining operative as such in the present."

[268] R. Schnackenburg, *Die Johannesbriefe* (Freiburg, 1953 [HThK XIII: fasc. 3]), 204. N.b.: In what follows, we are combining quotation with an interpretation along the lines of our fundamental thesis.

[269] Ibid., 205.

[270] Ibid., 206.

[271] Ibid., 204f.

[272] Ibid., 207.

[273] Ibid., 205.

[274] J. Heer, *Der Durchbohrte*, 136; cf. ibid., 135.

[275] Ibid., 135. Ibid., XV: the image of the Pierced One is "the focus of all the fundamental strands of Johannine theology".

[276] Ibid., 135.

[277] Ibid., 139. Cf. ibid., 135: the Pierced One is the "sign par excellence"; 123f., 137, 159, 206, 273.

has taken place throughout the whole life of Jesus, yet that attains its climax in the death of Jesus".[278]

As we go on to see just *what* is being shown to us in the picture of the piercing (i.e., what is happening theologically), we shall find that the understanding of atonement we have developed will help us to appreciate the theological meaning and legitimacy of the Johannine symbolic realism.[279]

There can be no doubt that John's dynamic view, whereby the Passion ("the hour"), the exaltation (glorification), the piercing and the outpouring of the Spirit, are seen stereoscopically in one, is congruent, as a matter of fact, with the sequence we have established, that is, atonement, sonship carried through against sin, and the Spirit of sonship[280] sent out to pursue his work among the "sons" from him who has become perfectly "Son".

According to John 7:39, "As yet the Spirit had not been given, because Jesus was not yet glorified." And the glorification had not yet taken place; first there had to come the "hour" (Jn 13:1), first he had to perform the servant's task of representative atonement, symbolized by the washing of the feet (Jn 13:22ff.); first he had to become the Lamb who "takes away" the sins of the world (Jn 19:36; 1:29).[281] First he, *as* Son, must fulfill the "mandatum" (Jn 12:49) of God the *Father*, letting the latter's patrogenetic power exercise its full effect in him against the sins of those who are his; he must "endure" before this Father not only the sins of his brothers in the form of filial suffering, he must "endure" God himself, who desires to be "Father" even to sinners. First the Son must be pierced by the sin of the sons, their forsakenness by the Father: he must let God show himself Father toward the sins of his brothers in his own person. Only then, in this piercing, does his own sonship acquire such a pregnant fullness that the "Spirit of sonship"[282] bursts forth from his Heart, the excess as it were, of his filial atonement, the ecstatic and exultant power of love of his own being as Son, reaching out for the "sons" (cf. Rom 5:5); this is the Spirit who moves the hearts even of those who at one time were "enemies" (cf. Rom 5:5ff.), causing them too to cry out "Abba, Father!" (cf. Rom 8:14ff.; Gal 4:6).[283]

[278] Ibid., 123.

[279] In our interpretation of Johannine symbolism we are not claiming to follow John's theology in everything. Cf. J. Heer, op. cit., 109: in John the concept of atonement "does not occupy the central place it has in Paul, for whom it is axiomatic that Christ's death has blotted out sin and reconciled men with God". On the other hand see n.297 below.

[280] Cf. pp. 168ff. above.

[281] Cf. J. Heer, op. cit., 109f.

[282] On water as the image of the Spirit of the messianic age, cf. J. Heer, op. cit., 69ff., 106ff., 112ff.; H. Rahner, "On the Biblical Basis of the Devotion" in J. Stierli, *Heart of the Saviour: A Symposium on Devotion to the Sacred Heart* (Herder, 1957), 15–35; 34: "God himself in his redeeming humanity dispenses the living water of the Spirit; he pours it forth as the great 'Pierced One'. All this is accomplished, and the reign of the Spirit begins, at the moment when his Heart is opened." Cf. O. Casel, *The Mystery of Christian Worship* (see n.245 above), 17: "By his Passion the Lord became pneuma."

[283] On the Spirit and conversion, cf. R. Schulte in MySal V: 144, 150ff., 154ff., 172.

All this "speaks" to us from the fact of the piercing. That is why it becomes a "picture" expressing "a comprehensive theological reality";[284] its presuppositions are rooted in God himself. Before all history, out of the eternal and arcane depths of the Trinity, the mystery of representation in salvation history assumes concrete shape, over and above creation and Incarnation, under the conditions of sin, in the figure of the Crucified and Pierced One. The theological nature of atonement, as it unfolds in history, creates its own expression, its own sign. In this sign (picture), the event, the *work* of salvation, constitutes itself as "Word".[285] The "dogma" becomes "kerygma": in the piercing of Jesus, the "Logos" of John 1:1ff., who is with God as "Son", is addressed and delivered to the abode of sinners.

In the Pierced One the Father utters the Son as atonement for our sins. He is his final Yes and Amen to the world (cf. 2 Cor 1:19f.).

Since, however, this Word addressed to us comes from God the Father in order to turn sinners to himself as sons, it is in the nature of a claim upon us, calling for a response. The deed/Word of the piercing took place in order to fulfill the Scripture: "They shall *look* on him whom they have pierced" (cf. Jn 19:36f.).[286]

In what follows we shall show — in an equally brief and concentrated manner — that the particular atonement-spirituality practiced in the devotion to the Sacred Heart may be understood as a distinctive form of such a response.

4.3 *Devotion to the Sacred Heart of Jesus and atonement spirituality: the response to the Word understood*

4.3.1 *The "Pierced One" as the Word understood: the "Heart of Jesus"*[287]
If we did not know it already, modern semiotics would soon tell us that there are "*no* given natural signs . . . but only natural phenomena". The "sign as such" must "always be seen as a *propositional* construct". That is, "whenever a

---

[284] W. Thüsing, *Die Erhöhung und Verherrlichung Jesu im Johannesevangelium* (Münster, 1960 [NTA 21]), 267 (quoted in J. Heer, op. cit., 134).

[285] In this "Word", analogously to the three elements that have been identified in human speech, we can see an "informative", "exhortative" and "expressive" aspect (i.e., the presentation of a meaningful content relating to reality, the invitation to respond, and the self-disclosure of the speaker). Cf. T. Schneider, *Zeichen der Nähe Gottes, Grundriss der Sakramententheologie* (Mainz, 1979), 21; K.-O. Apel, "Sprache" in E. Braun, H. Rademacher, eds., *Wissenschaftstheoretisches Lexikon* (Graz-Vienna-Cologne, 1978), 541–49, esp. 547.

[286] J. Ratzinger, *Meditationen zur Karwoche* (see n.239 above), 5: " 'They shall look on him whom they have pierced' — the whole Gospel of John is basically nothing other than the attempt to concentrate our eyes and hearts on him." J. Heer, op. cit., 130ff., 159, 161, 164ff., 175ff., 189ff.

[287] We are by no means implying that the "Heart-of-Jesus" spirituality is the only possible or valid response, on the part of faith, to the Word of the Cross.

sign is introduced it is given a meaning" and "originates in the positing intention of a reflex consciousness".[288]

It pertains to its propositional nature that the sign cannot be simply encountered in pure "objectivity" but requires the mediating understanding of
the person who receives the sign. Like everything else, but preeminently so,
signs encounter in man an "interpreting existence".[289] Whether and how a
person understands some thing or event as a sign or symbol depends fundamentally on his understanding of the world and himself, on his own plan of
existence and, hence, on his freedom.[290] The sign is not always perceived as
such (cf. Jn 6:26). For this to happen it requires a special, puzzling and
mysterious agreement between the perceiver and the perceived, and that inner power of vision that goes beyond the dull, foreground, self-enclosed fact
to attain what is meant by it.[291]

This law applies even more strongly in the field of religious symbolism.
What governs the discovery and interpretation of the sign here, however, is
not pure thought but believing thought: only διὰ πίστεως does the external
fact become "accessible" and "present" to us as a saving event.[292]

If then the "inner structure of the Cross" — and thus the inner meaning of
the piercing — "cannot be simply read off from the external events",[293]
neither can that "looking on the Pierced One", which John commends to
us, be fulfilled by the mere act of looking, for such beholding is meant to be
"the response to the setting up of the sign of salvation"[294] and, hence, contributes the goal of the entire Gospel.[295] Rather, this beholding of the
Pierced One is "of a piece" with that typically " 'Johannine vision' in

---

[288] M. Bense, "Semiotik" in *Wissenschaftstheoretisches Lexikon* (see n.285 above) 524-29, esp.
525. In the present connection we are interested in the "triadic sign-relation" that arises out of
the propositional process: "Insofar as it is involved in representation, each sign must comprise
these distinguishable elements: a representational means, a represented object and an ex-
planatory, contextual representation of the represented object known as the interpretant." Cf.
also T. Lewandowski, "Zeichen", op. cit., 680-84, esp. 681.

[289] Cf. E. Schillebeeckx, *Christ: The Christian Experience in the Modern World* (London, 1980),
31: "Experience is always interpreted experience."

[290] J. P. Sartre, *Existentialism and Humanism* (London, 1948), 38, categorically states that
there are no signs in the world. Cf. J. Ratzinger, *Introduction to Christianity* (London, 1969),
141ff.; idem, *Die sakramentale Begründung christlicher Existenz* (Meitingen-Freising, 1966), 3–7.
Here we can only point out that the mystery of representation is also at work in the depths of
the (anthropologically significant) symbol.

[291] Cf. T. Schneider, op. cit., 17f. He quotes A. de Saint-Exupery's "The Little Prince": "It is
the heart which sees properly."

[292] Cf. H. Schlier, *Der Römerbrief*, 105f. (on Rom 3:22). Ibid., 106: πίστις here is to be
understood "as the act of faith, as *fides qua creditur*".

[293] H. Schlier, *Grundzüge*, 133.

[294] J. Heer, op. cit., 135.

[295] Ibid., 135, 133.

which man is confronted with the revelation in Christ and is summoned to faith".[296]

Only by a seeing in faith can the external event of the piercing of the side of Jesus be grasped as the accomplished self-surrender of the only begotten Son of God (cf. Jn 3:16); only thus can this "utterance *ad extra*" be apprehended. True, God has "put him forward publicly, exposed him to view, as an expiation [atonement]"; but "it is only faith that recognizes and understands him as such".[297] Only the believer "beholds" in the Crucified the mystery of atonement for our sins.

However, John summons not only the Jews of his own time but also people of all times to come and, particularly those who read his Gospel, to look in faith on the Crucified.[298] On the other hand it is the Holy Spirit who produces a faith[299] which is at work in the Church to "guide it into all the truth" (Jn 16:13).

Thus, in the Church's meditative womb and under the creative and initiatory power of the Spirit, the sign of the "Pierced One", too, has been transformed and developed into the even more profound image of the "Pierced *Heart*", a development that followed the growth in faith's appreciation of the atoning significance of Jesus' saving act.

We can illustrate the fact that atonement reveals its ultimate nature only in the image of the *Pierced Heart* by reference to the fundamental meaning of atonement as developed in our interpretation of it.[300] Substantially, "atonement" is filial love, acutely smitten by its extreme opposite, that is, the nature of sin; the Son's love, cut through, as it were, by the Father's No, and thus become utter pain; it is crucifixion, therefore, in the profoundest sense. The cold steel penetrates the most vulnerable part: in this atonement it is the "Heart" that is pierced.

Here too there is a deep symbolism: this Heart is at the "crucial" center of the Cross. The Pierced Heart is the "soul", the nerve-center where "Cross" is really experienced, the place where "Cross", in its theological nature, comes into being.

Consequently we are not dealing with two different symbols: in the "Heart of Jesus" the image of the Pierced One has attained *its own* true depth

---

[296] Ibid., 133; cf. 131ff. (on the meaning of "looking" in John), 172; R. Schnackenburg, *The Gospel according to John*, vol. 3 (Burns and Oates, 1982), 290–93.

[297] H. Schlier, *Der Römerbrief* III (on Rom 3:25). J. Heer, op. cit., 140–47, shows that, although the Johannine "revelation" theology lays less stress on representative atonement than the Pauline "community" theology does, nonetheless the atoning significance of the death of Jesus is "a substantial component of the Johannine view".

[298] Cf. J. Heer, op. cit., 133.

[299] Cf. ibid., 166ff.

[300] Semiotics would apply the term "interpretant" to the representation of this image in the context of our present approach.

and fullness: the "Heart of Jesus" manifests the meaning of the piercing: the accomplishment of atonement, the "bearing" of sin by the Son. Here, in the habitation of sin, in estrangement from God, the Son can no longer be anything else but the Pierced Heart.

And that is why this very Heart illustrates the primal meaning of all symbolism. If every symbol, "in whatever context", manifests "the primal unity of several fields of the real", if all symbols are working "toward a single goal" (i.e., "elimination of the 'boundaries' of the particular fragment that man represents in the bosom of the community and within the cosmos, and his integration . . . in the greater unity of brotherhood, of the universe"),[301] this means that Christ, specifically *as* the Pierced Heart, is *The Symbol* par excellence: not only does he unite all that is torn asunder; he overcomes sin, that abyss of separation and loneliness called "hell"; he is the "coincidence" of the holy God and the sinner, the sinner who, because he is a son, still needs the Father; who, deprived of that wholesome unity with God, his Father, would be eternally a metaphysical fragment, a torso, a broken shard of being. On the Cross sin is endured to its death; the sons are enveloped in love together with the Father and in opposition to their sin. But the price of it is *the* Son, as atonement, and that means as the Pierced Heart.

Devotion to the Heart of Jesus rightly sees Christ's physical heart as inseparable from the "Heart" which he is, personally: it sees his body's wounded Heart as an ontological datum of the first importance: it is the epiphany of the wound in Being itself. In the Heart of Jesus, Being—even in its denial by sin—is shown as love.

So we see that the image of the Pierced Heart has a greater representative and eloquent power than that of the Pierced One in itself. As a carrier of meaning it answers better to the intention behind the πεφανέρωται, the προέθετο and the εἰς ἔνδειξιν of Romans 3:21ff., and the ἐφανερώθη of 1 John 4:9. It expresses the internal theological disposition of the atoning Jesus more directly and explicitly; it "utters" more clearly what is involved in the process of atonement.[302]

If it is true that the meditative heightening of the biblical image of the Pierced One into the image of the Pierced Heart has a pneumatic origin, that is, that, in it, the *Spirit* is illuminating revelation from within, we can dare to say that ultimately it is the *Father* who fully addresses to the intimate subjectivity of the believer the "Word" already uttered by him in the piercing of Christ. He could not have found a more convincing way of demonstrating to us how much we are his "sons", how resolved he is to be a Father to us (cf. 1 Jn 3:1), than by showing us the Heart of his Son, pierced and broken on

---

301 M. Eliade, *Die Religionen und das Heilige* (Salzburg, 1954), 512.

302 Except, that is, to those who are no longer able to respond to the root concept "heart"—a frightening prospect.

account of our sins. Here we see "representation" at work, here we see "rebirth" taking place: we come to see how much this Father loves us, his children; we are begotten again into the awareness of sonship. When the Crucified and Pierced One dawns on us — in the Spirit — as the Heart of the Son pierced for us, the glory of the Father shines forth into our hearts:[303] God's last Word (cf. Heb 1:1f.), understood as the Pierced Heart, addresses the interiority of faith in the same way as the eschatological radiance of the New Testament outshines the "kabôd Yahweh" of the Old Covenant,[304] namely, as the appearance in history of the Absolute — which fundamentally means absolute *love*. Thus we can say that, in terms of the history of revelation, the Pierced Heart is at the point of convergence of the divine saving purpose.

All the same, understanding the Word and carrying it out are not the same thing. The inner dynamism of God's Word addressed to us impels us onward. Its perceptual form must be completed in the form of a response. This shows us the locus of the idea of atonement within the whole devotion to the Heart of Jesus.[305]

4.3.2 *Atonement as an existential response*[306]

The response is correct when it cor-responds to the claim put forward by the Word uttered and understood. In the Johannine presentation the response to the Word of the Cross occurs when man "looks up" to the Crucified, when in faith he recognizes the love expressed in the figure of the Pierced One,[307] lets himself be seized by it[308] and responds to it with an active love in his own existence.[309] However, understood as the Pierced Heart, as the Son who has become atonement, the figure of the Pierced One speaks with power and insistence of the love of the *Father*. Here it is *he* who speaks his final Word; he

---

[303] Cf. A. Lang, "Erkenntnis- und Methodenlehre, Theologische E." in LThK III: 1003–12, esp. 1005: ". . . God's real self-communication to men in the saving *event* implies, as an inner constituent, that man has a knowledge, facilitated by God, of this event." R. Schulte in MySal IV/2: 78: "Only when this μυστήριον is accepted in faith do we 'understand'. . . what God's grace has intended for us and imparted to us. . . ."

[304] Cf. H. Mühlen, *Der Heilige Geist als Person*, 254: "The kabôd Yahweh is a form of self-manifestation of the transcendent God (cf. W. Eichrodt, *Theology of the Old Testament* II: 29–35), which eludes further explanation." Cf. ibid. on the relationship of the Spirit of God and the theophany (2 Cor 3:6–18; Ex 33:18).

[305] See n. 262 above.

[306] On the "Heart-of-Jesus" spirituality and atonement, cf. K. Rahner, "Some Theses for a Theology of Devotion to the Sacred Heart" in *Theological Investigations*, vol. 3 (London and Baltimore, 1967); G. de Becker, *Les Sacrés-Coeurs de Jesus et de Marie*, 158–74; idem, *La Vie réligieuse et la spiritualité du Sacré-Coeur*, 301–25; H. Rondet, *Le Péché et la réparation dans le culte du Sacré Coeur*, 683–720; J. Heer, op. cit., 257–62.

[307] Cf. J. Heer, op. cit., 170ff.

[308] Ibid., 172.

[309] Ibid., 175ff.

can say no more. Therefore if the response is to meet *this* particular claim, it must be given to the Father *as Father*. But the name given to the response to the Father is — "Son". Thus an essential part of the believer's response consists in his efforts to *be* a son.

These efforts, of course, are opposed by the sinful condition of one's own "I" and the world. But the resolute surrender of the Beloved Son "for our sins" — even to his very piercing — makes it clear to anyone who looks in faith at the Cross just how determined God is to be a "Father", particularly in the case of sinners.

The form of response is plain to see: the believer must be a son in opposing sin and in "bearing" sin. This means, however, according to our fundamental insight into the nature of atonement, that he must himself be a person who atones. The elementary form of a lived response to the Father's Word, addressed to us in the Pierced Heart of his Son, would be to endure the manifold modes of God's absence (the result of sin and guilt) in one's own existence and in the world. Basically, "atonement" would be not something added to the faithful beholding of the Pierced One but an inseparable dimension of an existence lived in this beholding.

The basic form of atonement would be to be a son to the Father — in Christ, the great Atoner, pierced on account of our sins, and through the Spirit — in this world, marred by sin. And such a form of atonement exactly corresponds to the spirit of the devotion to the Heart of Jesus.

A basic understanding of this kind straightaway shows us that the concrete practice of atonement requires an objective multiplicity of dimensions.

It also shows that it is impossible to ask to whom atonement is made, to Christ or to God: subjectively there may be various emphases, but what actually takes place does so in reference to both. Atonement is a response to the claim, the deepest desire and wish, of the one to whom it is addressed. In the concrete this response is "being a son". However it is only in *the* son, not apart from him and his atonement, that the believer can be a "son" to the Father. *Christ* longs to be totally "Son" to the *Father* together with those who are his; the *Father* desires men to be sons to him in *Christ.*

So we cannot perform atonement to Christ without being *sons* with him *to the Father; we cannot atone to the Father without being his sons in Christ.* If we tried to atone to the Father and not to Christ, our atonement would not reach God at all, *the* God who wishes to be Father to us; it would be a response at cross purposes to the Word actually addressed to us.[310]

These remarks show the interpenetration of the "propitiatory" and "consolatory" aspects of atonement: atoning in Christ through the Holy Spirit (i.e., being a son by bearing sin) fulfills what is meant both by "softening the

[310] On the importance of our love of Jesus, cf. H. U. von Balthasar, *Elucidations* (London, 1975), 43–49.

wrath of God" and by "consoling the Heart of Jesus", for the atoning person yields to the ardor of God's saving will to be Father (in particular) to the sinner, and this fulfills the most fervent longing of Jesus, who came to restore to sonship what was lost.

The question as to what this "softening" and "consoling" means with regard to the divine affective intimacy of Father and Son quite naturally puts us at a great loss for answers.

We shall attempt an answer by pursuing our thoughts on a question already mentioned, namely, whether and how far God is affected by sins, that is, how far he "suffers" through it.[311]

The New Testament bears witness to creation in Christ, to the "sending" of the Son and the Spirit, to our involvement in the inner life of the Trinity, that is, the New Testament witnesses to God's dealing with the world and with man in terms of a representation with Trinitarian implications. It also affirms that all this has a real significance for God: to deny this would be to undermine the substance of the New Testament message.[312] This being the case, it is no longer sufficient to say that, for God, the evil deed merely signifies that the creature has failed its Lord and Creator; revelation, in fact, drives us to the conclusion that sin "taints" the relation of Father to Son in the Spirit within God—however incomprehensible this may seem.[313]

It may help at this point to consider whether the real meaning of "sending", "indwelling", and so forth, may not be fittingly translated by the following formula: God wishes to have his Son as Son *in his brothers*, that is, the Son wishes to be a Son to the Father *in men*. At any rate there can be no doubt that the mystery called "Christ" consists in the fact that the "place" where the Logos desires to be "Son", and *is* "Son", is the human reality of Jesus. "Christ" means this: the Logos is Son to the Father *in* Jesus and *as* Jesus.

But the whole mystery of Christ is that the Logos wishes—as Jesus Christ—to be Son to the Father *in all men*; God wishes his only begotten Son to be Son to him *in his brothers*, in me.[314]

Furthermore, does not what we call "Cross" mean the ultimate ratification and implementation of this very intention? Does not the Son show how

[311] See pp. 149ff. above. Cf. N. Hoffmann, op. cit., 165ff.; J. Galot, *La Realité de la souffrance de Dieu*, 224–45.

[312] J. Galot, ibid., 227f., 239ff.

[313] Cf. H. U. von Balthasar, *Crucifixus*, 33f.: if "the relation of God to the (sinful) world is taken up into the more fundamental relation of God the Father to God the Son, . . . the Father-Son relationship can be tinged with the God-world relation, and the eternal embrace in which Father and Son are turned toward each other can take turning away, alienation, into itself so that it can be experienced. . . ."

[314] Cf. Eph 3:17. On this, cf. H. Schlier, *Der Brief an die Epheser*, 169: "Faith causes our hearts to be Christ's dwelling-place. . . . The indwelling of Christ is not (only) a psychological phenomenon but primarily an existential one."

resolute he is in wanting to be Son in my place, in and through me, at the precise point at which I resist this wish on his part? For it is then that he takes upon himself his mission to "sinful flesh". In New Testament terms "sin" means *not* letting Christ be Son in me. And in the Pierced One on the Cross we see what happens when the person in whom Christ wishes to be Son is a *sinner*: when the Son is Son in the "place", the locus, of the sinner, it tears his Heart in two; the Son is torn from the Father, the Father gives up the Son. The Father is determined that his Son shall exercise his sonship in the sons; if they refuse, the Son enters this very refusal and combats it to the limit of his sonship, until all that is left of this refusal in the Son's Heart is that suffering that is the piercing of his filial love.

In this context "sin" means the denial of the relationship between Father and Son *to the extent that* the Son wills to take up his place, his locus, in the sinner; it means opposition to the reciprocal dependence of Father and Son in the economic Trinity. The sin of the "sons" is no longer simply something between the "rational creature" and "God": it affects the relationship of Father and Son *in* God. It affects God, because *in me* he wishes to be Father to his only begotten Son; it affects the Logos, because *in me* he wishes to be Son to the Father and has lovingly and obediently fulfilled the Father's will by living out his sonship in the place of sinners, representing them, to the very piercing of his Heart. Sin rises up against the God who wants to be a Father, in Christ, even to me; it opposes Christ, who desires to be Son to this Father, even in me; in God, sin thwarts the paternal will, the filial will. It tears apart Father and Son in the economic Trinity, that is, insofar as the world is meant to be the locus of the reciprocal love of "Father" and "Son" and to find its salvation therein. But since this can only take place in the *Spirit*, who both heightens in a personal manner what is most interior to Father and Son (their "*communio*") and also involves the world in this *communio*, sin positively "grieves" (cf. Eph 4:30) and "quenches" (1 Thes 5:19) the Holy Spirit, and thus—if all this is true—pierces the Heart of *God*.

If these remarks show that sin is something that affects God, they can also make it clear to what extent atonement—the countermovement to sin—has a real meaning for God. Atonement is the form taken by sonship in a world of sin. Thus it would affect God insofar as, through it, the believer responds to Christ's filial will (i.e., that of being Son to the Father in the believer) and to God's paternal will (i.e., that of being Father to Christ in the believer). And all this in the real world marked by sin, that is, with particular reference to that event in which Father and Son have exercised their fatherhood and sonship to the ultimate degree: in the Cross, in the piercing of Jesus' Heart, in the outpouring of the Spirit of sonship.

In conclusion we should like to put forward the following suggestion: atonement on the part of the believer has inner significance for God himself to the extent that, through it, the Divine Persons perform for the economy of salvation ("for the world caught up in sin") what they *are* for one another within the Trinity, namely, entirely "Father", entirely "Son" (the "first born among many brethren"),[315] united in the love of the Holy Spirit.

Our fundamental understanding of atonement, based on the idea of representation in a Trinitarian context, leads us on to consider a final dimension essential to the actual performance of atonement, namely, its own aspect of representation.

The Christian not only has his origin in the mystery of the representative "for"; he also receives his nature from it. "Representation" articulates the inner nature of love, which constitutes what is specifically Christian. This being so, the Christian in this world must be someone who atones in a representative capacity. For under the conditions of sin, love must necessarily take the form of atonement: atonement *is* the "for" mode of existence in a sinful world, it is the effectiveness of *caritas* in response to the most fundamental distress of our fellow men (i.e., their alienation from the Father), and hence it is the authentically Christian form of solidarity. The believer who knows that he *himself* has been redeemed by the Son from the evil void of sin and brought into the child's nearness to the Father will look up to the wounded Heart of Jesus, and in doing so he will "be for others" in such a way that he will help to bear and endure their own sin (cf. Gal 6:2; Eph 5:1f., Rom 15:1–3).[316]

He can only be truly a son if, concerned that his fellow men shall be sons of God, he practices atonement.[317] But if the question is asked, How can a man

[315] It is somehow constitutive of Jesus as Christ that his "being Son" is located in the real existence of the believer.

[316] Cf. F. Mussner, *Der Galaterbrief* (Freiburg-Basel-Vienna, 1974), 398f. Ibid., 399: The "burdens" that are "reciprocally" to be borne are "specifically the sins in which one has become involved". This bearing is "in fulfillment of the law of Christ. . . . Here the Apostle presents an interpretation of the commandment of love that even applies to sinners in the Christian community, thus revealing a depth in Christianity that is beyond comparison." H. Schlier, *Der Brief an die Epheser*, 230–32. Ibid., 231f.: The "imitation of God" takes place "in the way of love, which receives its origin and direction from the love manifested to us in the sacrifice of Christ. . . . The love of Christ, which he has shown to 'us', *is* . . . the sacrifice well-pleasing to God, offered to God on our behalf in his self-surrender. It makes possible, summons forth and provides the standard for a response of love in our lives. By loving after this pattern we act as 'beloved children', being 'imitators' of God, of the 'example' set before us in Christ." Idem, *Der Römerbrief*, 419: in Rom 15:1 "the required attitude is that of βαστάζειν, the weakness of the 'weak'. . . whereby βαστάζειν does not mean 'putting up with' but 'accepting' the weakness, 'taking it upon oneself' in love and thus lifting and taking it away (cf. Gal 6:2, 5)." Ibid., 420: the Christ presented to us as a model in Rom 15:3 is he who "did not live to please himself, but took upon himself the reproaches which men heaped upon God, bearing them away. . . ."

[317] Cf. R. Guardini, *Der Herr*, 358: " 'Redemption' means . . . not only something that happened then on our behalf: but from then on it continues to shape the essential form of Christian existence. We live by the redeeming act of Christ; but the form of this redemption has entered

really atone for another?[318] we must bear in mind — in view of the difficulty of theological intelligibility here — that what is being questioned is part of the mystery of Being itself. The principle of "representation" applies to everything that *is*, with an ontological power that is not totally available to reflection. Moreover, the Christian in particular must not try to measure the extent of his "being for others" ("pro-existence") by what is merely humanly possible.[319] Through faith and baptism the manner of his being and doing is revolutionized by the reality of his being "in Christ", by his existence in him who, through the power of the Spirit, wishes to exercise his sonship in many "sons".[320] Thus the Christian must not only believe in "God", "Christ" and the "Holy Spirit": he must also believe himself to be the habitation and locus of influence of the triune God, the (quasi-)sacrament of the universal intention of the economic Trinity "for" the world. It is Christ who, through his Spirit in believers, shows himself to be the great Atoner "for" sinners; it is the Father who, through the same Spirit, causes his Son to take effect in them as the first born among many brethren.

Thus, the Christian's personal existence in the world is totally dependent on the dynamism of the Spirit, who takes over this existence as the medium

---

into our existence as Christians and must express itself there. We cannot be redeemed unless the Spirit of redemption becomes effective in us. We cannot enjoy the benefits of redemption unless we collaborate in the act of redemption. To collaborate in Christ's redeeming work is to love our neighbor. And this love becomes forgiveness as soon as our neighbor's relation to us is like our relation to God, i.e., when he has done us wrong." Ibid.: "God's forgiveness did not take place as 'mere forgiveness' but as atonement."

On the picture of man as the "New Adam" (turning from oneself toward the other), cf. J. Ratzinger, *Introduction to Christianity* (London, 1969), 175, 185ff.; idem, *Meditationen zur Karwoche* (see n.239 above).

[318] We cannot go into the question in more detail. Cf. L. Scheffczyk, "Die heilshafte Stellvertretung", 115ff., 119ff.; idem, "Substitution (Representation)" in SM 5: 391f. [idem, "Sacrifice. II. Substitution (Representation)" in *Encyclopedia of Theology*, 1491-92]; idem, *Wirklichkeit und Geheimnis der Sünde: Sünde — Erbsünde* (Augsburg, 1970) 174ff.; H. U. von Balthasar, *Crucifixus*, 32-35; P. Eder, "Sühne", 132-44; R. Guardini, *Die Existenz des Christen* (see n.49 above), 169ff.

[319] Cf. L. Scheffczyk, "Die heilshafte Stellvertretung", 119f.: prior to any consideration of practical measures in terms of spirituality and pastoral work there must be faith's conviction, at the level of being, of the truth of representation in the mystery of salvation; "For representing others is not primarily a form of activity and a *system of things to be done* for them: it is deeper, as the word implies; it means to take responsibility for others *at the level of being*, sharing their destiny and being one with them before God." Faith that is alive, that is animated by love, "has already attained the highest reality of grace possible to us as pilgrims. Thus, once the Christian believes that he is a representative for others, this exchange, this taking of responsibility, actually happens." Cf. also H. U. von Balthasar, "Sich halten an den Unfassbaren" in GuL 52 (1979): 246-58, esp. 255: "The Church does her real work by saying Yes, by allowing things to happen through her, by being there and being used."

[320] See p. 165 above.

in which sonship is to be cultivated in opposition to the realm of denial. How then can the believer be unable to do what Christ desires to do in and through him by the power of the Spirit?[321] The sending of Christ to "sinful flesh", to each individual, takes place concretely and historically through the Spirit. Should the onward movement of this spirit come to a full stop in the very people who have been sealed and anointed by him *in order that* they should walk in this world, and hence encounter the sons of disobedience (cf. Eph 2:2), in the power of the same Spirit (cf. Rom 8; Eph 3:16; Gal 5:16,25)? What is at stake in the question whether Christians can atone in a representative capacity is this: have we the courage to affirm that most concrete of all instances of representation in salvation history? What is at stake is the ultimate consistency of God's self-affirmation *as* the mystery of representative "being for another".

Therefore we should not be surprised if, having taken pains to explicate theologically "how" representative atonement is possible in Christian existence, there remains an unsatisfactory area of obscurity. What we have come up against is not merely the impenetrability of some newly discovered, independent mystery, but the foothills, as it were, of *the* mystery par excellence: basically we are faced with the *mysterium entis* itself.[322] In the mystery of the Christian's "being for others" in statement we have a concrete instance, in salvation history, of the *mystery of Being as love*. In the end, to ask why and how the Christian can atone representatively for others comes back to the question as to how God is love, how he is triune, how he is "God". In the final analysis the mystery resists rational manipulation, and yet we must confess it; theology too must confess it. A theology that only says what it can grasp is an absurdity. In the final analysis, after all our attempts at an explanation, successful or not, Christian theology can be no more and no less than any other mode of Christian existence, namely, a μαρτυρία of the Ineffable.

5. Conclusion

With this recognition of the limits of theological reason we bring to a close our remarks on the theme of "Atonement and the Spirituality of the Sacred

---

[321] Cf. *Council of Trent*, sess. XIV, cap. 8 (DS 1691): "Neque vero ita nostra est satisfactio haec, quam pro peccatis nostris exsolvimus, ut non sit per Christum Jesum; nam qui ex nobis tamquam ex nobis nihil possumus, eo cooperante, 'qui nos confortat, omnia possumus' (Phil 4:13)." ["Neither is this satisfaction that we discharge for our sins so much our own as not to be through Christ Jesus; for we, who can do nothing of ourselves as of ourselves, can do all things with the cooperation of him who strengthens us." (*The Teaching of the Catholic Church*, ed. K. Rahner [Alba House, 1967], 319).]

[322] Cf. J. de Fraine, *Adam et son lignage: Études sur la notion de "personnalité corporative" dans la Bible* (Bruges, 1959), 220, on the idea of corporative personality: "Here we encounter one of the most profound intuitions of biblical metaphysics, namely, the dynamic and in no way static character of the notion of Being. . ." (quoted in W. Thüsing, *Per Christum in Deum*, 66 n.18).

Heart". It is a recognition that comes at the end of a considerable effort to understand, and is hence less liable to be thought of as a premature retreat into God's unsearchability. We have been made aware of these limits as our reflection climbed toward the towering heights of the specifically Christian reality of atonement, as it unfolded before us. The divine work of salvation allowed us to see, through it, the Divine *Being* as the primal mystery; this helped us to perceive the sovereign fact of the redemption in its transcendental meaning. Thus our study has resulted in a degree of illumination, to the extent that it has consistently pursued the path of a *"reductio in mysterium"*.

Our guiding light on this path has been the idea of "representation". It should have become clear at least that the principle of "representation", deepened within the context of the Trinity, is a universal horizon of interpretation manifesting great theo-logical penetration, and as such deserves critical attention and further testing on the part of theology.

We have suggested that in the light of this principle we come to see the paradoxical coexistence of God's absolute power to forgive and the unyielding insistence on historically performed atonement on the part of sinners (2.1), a parodox that is clearly present in the Old Testament and that rises to its stark climax in the *scandalon crucis* of the New Testament. It is the translation into the terms of salvation history of that unshakeable "logic" that resides in God himself, the eternal mystery of representation in Father, Son and Spirit; it is part of the logic of that mystery according to which Being is love; it is part of the onto-logy of love (2.2).

Atonement revealed itself to us as the mode of inner-Trinitarian sonship prolonged into the realm of the creature under the conditions of sin; as the form adopted by the son-Father relationship when the "sons" are sinners. In atonement God's power to forgive is shown to be the power of the "Father" to beget sinners "again" to sonship, respecting their dignity as persons by enabling them inwardly to overcome their sin, to "convert" it into the pain of filial love in estrangement from the Father. In other words, in atonement God shows himself to be Father by asserting the Son as Son—by the power of his Spirit—against the other sons' sinful denial: this takes place uniquely and unrepeatably in Jesus as the "Christ" (the Crucified and Risen One) (2.2.3); and hence it also takes place in those "for" whom Christ is, who are brothers to Christ and "sons" to the Father in the Son (3).[323]

In the light of the principle of "representation", grounded in the Trinity, the tension in salvation history between God's transcendental power to save and the demand for concrete atonement is shown to be the pneumatic

---

[323] The customary, rather formal definitions of atonement ("restitution for injury") here acquire a deeper, more personal dimension through their Trinitarian context: by lovingly bearing the sin and its consequences in the form of estrangement from God, the sinner becomes, in Christ and through the Holy Spirit, a son of the Father in opposition to sin.

transposition into terms of the economic Trinity, of the primal tension of identity and difference that subsists in the relationship of Father and Son in the immanent Trinity.

Those who share with K. Rahner the view that the "real problem" of Christian soteriology lies in the question why "this original forgiving will of God does not simply effect forgiveness . . . directly . . . but comes to mankind from a definite historical event, which itself is the 'cause' of forgiveness",[324] should find that our approach sheds some light on it, "redeeming" the doctrine of redemption to some extent from seeming arbitrary, external, forensic and positivist. What appears, in the fact of the Cross, as a certain ruthlessness on the part of God's righteous will is moderated by an ontology of the Cross, which renders it meaningful. In turn this ontology of the Cross is totally grounded in a Trinitarian ontology. The Cross becomes intelligible, albeit only as the reflected image of what absolutely exceeds intelligibility; the Cross becomes conceivable, but only as the inconceivable revelation of a God who, beyond all imagining, manifests himself as love so powerfully even against sin's refusal.[325]

It is the mystery of this love that is brought close to the believer in the cult of the Heart of Jesus under the compelling image of the Pierced Heart (4).

It appears, therefore, that this spirituality makes a distinctive contribution to the crucial task of Christian faith, which is to keep the "Word of the Cross" from slipping away into the existential remoteness and abstractness of the mere theological concept, as, for instance, in the impersonal idea of the "cause of Jesus". Its particular vocation, surely, is to prevent specific aspects of Christian faith and spirituality from becoming merely implicit and finally falling into oblivion; it is especially called to bring more convincingly, clearly and directly to the believing consciousness the profound content of the "Word of the Cross" (i.e., the wounded and yet merciful and powerful divine love) and its corresponding claims (4.3.1). Above all it could work toward making explicit — in a special atonement spirituality, that is, a form of Christian spirituality deliberately patterned on the mystery of atonement — that

---

[324] K. Rahner, "Salvation. IV. Theology" in *Encyclopedia of Theology*, 1525.

[325] Cf. H. Schürmann, "Jesu ureignes Todesverständnis", 305: "Understood at a sufficiently deep level, the 'pro-existence' of Jesus can shed light . . . not only on several dogmatic treatises but also on most theological disciplines." The present study may perhaps have explained why J. Ratzinger, in "Stellvertretung", in HThG II: 566, has occasion to regret that, although "representation" is "one of the fundamental categories of biblical revelation . . . it has had such a stunted development in theology."

It may be that our approach, i.e., representation in a Trinitarian context, can provide an element of mediation between the more moral and juridical conception of redemption in the Latin West and the more physical and mystical view of the Greek East; cf. F. Lakner, "Satisfaction" in SM 5: 433–43; R. Guardini, *Die Lehre des heiligen Bonaventura von der Erlösung: Ein Beitrag zur Geschichte und zum System der Erlösungslehre* (Düsseldorf, 1921), 72ff., 19ff.

aspect of atonement which, though inseparable from authentic Christian existence, is lived out, for the most part, in a merely unconscious way (4.3).

Clearly there is a need in our times for a work of actualization of this kind. Today, if ever, faith has stepped out of the security of straightforward performance into an almost hypersensitive self-awareness and critical self-observation; the question of the "nature" and the "essence" of faith has become pressing indeed. However, the answers being provided of late for the Church's public consumption show an almost total disappearance of the idea of "atonement", which is surely a remarkable and disturbing phenomenon. Does it not betoken a dangerously shattered relationship to basic dimensions of Christian faith-reality? Has not contemporary Christian consciousness been fatally affected, in that it no longer responds to the symbol (the Pierced Heart) nor to what is symbolized by it? Has the Cross, the event in which love goes to its atoning death, the Cross as the express word of this love, calling for the response of reciprocal, atoning love—has the Cross lost its power?

Our study has been intended as a theological reflection on the centrality, to the nature of Christianity, of what is contained in the symbol of the "Pierced Heart", that is, atonement in its christological/soteriological and pneumatological/ecclesiological sense.

"Atonement", it is true, is no longer a great and luminous word in the Christian world. It is hardly to be found among all the words so eagerly flourished by so many in the Church in their passionate efforts to speak the redeeming and liberating Word to the world in its distress.

The Cross is on the one hand "the locus of our identity and freedom under the conditions of history",[326] and on the other hand, in its innermost nature, it is the father's forgiving "Word" that has become atonement "for our sins" and *hence* delivers us from all evil. We have life insofar as we too carry out this Word[327] and let ourselves be "uttered" to our world by the Father, in the Son and through the Spirit, as witnesses to this Word—for this is what "atonement" means: being a "son" by grace in opposition to the baneful power of sin. This Word is the Word of truth and love, accomplished and effective, breaking untruth and egoism by a "bearing" that is by no means merely

---

[326] G. Greshake, "Erlösung und Freiheit", 345.

[327] Cf. J. Ratzinger, "Der Weltdienst der Kirche" (see n.238 above), 452: ". . . dismantling the battlements cannot mean" that the Church "no longer needs to defend anything or that she can live by any other power than that which gave her birth: blood and water from the open side of the crucified Lord (Jn 19:31-37)." Idem, "Bemerkungen zur Frage der Charismen in der Kirche" (see n.238 above), 272: "It is only from the opened Heart that blood and water stream forth. The mystery of this picture speaks to us, particularly in our time: it is a signpost, a challenge and a promise. Do not quench the Spirit—we can only really understand what this means if we are confronted with the Lord's open side, which is the source of the Spirit in the Church and for the world."

passive. If all this is the case, "atonement" is exactly what Christians need if they are to do what so many urgent, impressive, hopeful and yet ultimately empty manifestoes cannot do, namely, transform the world by the Word.

Leo Scheffczyk

DEVOTION TO CHRIST
AS A WAY OF EXPERIENCING HIM

1. Approaches to an Experiential Christology

Understandably enough, what Hans Urs von Balthasar has called today's "clamoring for experience" has even succeeded in pressing its claims at the very ground of our faith, Jesus Christ himself. Many proposed Christologies specifically give space to the experience of the person and work of Christ, while others endeavor (with greater or less success) to construct their understanding of Christ entirely upon the experience principle. An example of this is the work *Kontinuität in Jesus: Zugänge zu Leben, Tod und Auferstehung* by R. Pesch and Herbert A. Zwergel.[1] The latter author even attempts to use a deep psychological exegesis to uncover "the roots of Christian existence in Jesus of Nazareth", a procedure, however, which invokes all the dangers implicit in any psychological interpretation of Jesus. We find a somewhat different attempt in Georg Baudler's *Wahrer Gott als wahrer Mensch: Entwürfe zu einer narrativen Christologie*.[2] Here the author, a Catholic pastoral theologian, attempts to recall Jesus through narration and thus to make him the reference point for a new way of life — which immediately raises the question whether this is really an experience of the Person of Jesus Christ.

It is E. Schillebeeckx, however, who has become the most well-known advocate of this experiential Christology with his two highly successful books, *Jesus*[3] and *Christ*.[4] The very title of the first [Dutch original: *Jesus. The account of a living man*] manifests the most praiseworthy intention of presenting Jesus as someone alive now, relevant to today's man, someone "dangerous", who can give modern man new experience of salvation "in Jesus".

But in all these cases, if the results of the newly styled experience of salvation are subjected to a critical appraisal, one cannot avoid the fact that the contents of this experience seem remarkably similar to the common experience of contemporary awareness. Again and again we find the same

[1] Freiburg, 1974.
[2] Cologne, 1977.
[3] *Jesus: An Experiment in Christology* (London, 1979).
[4] *Christ: The Christian Experience in the Modern World* (London, 1980).

things: the implementation of justice and liberation, reconciliation with past history (*metanoia*) and confidence in the future. All this, however, is connected far less with the Person of Jesus himself than with his so-called *praxis*, the "*praxis* of the Kingdom of God". One cannot refrain from wondering whether here, under the aspect of experience, we have not the same phenomenon as that which characterized the critical Life-of-Jesus research at the turn of the century (and which led to Albert Schweitzer's resolute abandonment of it), namely, that all periods and individual interpreters find in Jesus their own ideas. The only difference is that now it is not a matter of ideas but of supposed experiences.

2. The Difficulties of the Concept of Experience

Our critique of this approach arises from the inadequacy of the concept of experience, particularly as applied to history and people in history.

Examination of the literature—very influential today—dealing with experience in relation to Jesus shows that there is no real awareness of the philosophical depths (and shallownesses) of the concept. In philosophy, at present, great stress is laid on the analysis, definition and differentiation of the concept of experience, while the psychology of religion is at great pains to describe the uniqueness of religious experience in particular. But the theological experiments we are referring to take hardly any account of this. However, our first task must be to find out what experience is. It may be of interest here that J. B. Lotz, in his splendid work on *Transcendental Experience*,[5] devotes no attention specifically to this kind of anamnesis or memory-experience, evidently because it is a special, internal problem for Christianity, not to be analyzed by the philosopher, but to be pondered by the theologian. All the same, this particular philosopher gives plenty of help with regard to the problems involved in this kind of memory-experience through his various definitions of the nature of experience. He describes experience as "the immediate, receptive appropriation of encountered reality". And he goes on: "In this way it approaches contemplation or intuition (not creative vision), yet without becoming identical with it" (p. 283). Similarly, Hans Urs von Balthasar defines experience as "the immediate awareness of reality".[6] Coming closer to the experience of Christ, which is of prime concern to the Christian, he observes: "From this perspective, Christian experience can mean only one thing, namely, that one's own existence grows into the existence of Christ, since Christ increasingly 'in-forms' the life of the

[5] Freiburg, 1978.

[6] H. U. von Balthasar, *Herrlichkeit*, vol. 1 (Einsiedeln, 1961), 354 [English ed.: *The Glory of the Lord: A Theological Aesthetics*, vol. 1: *Seeing the Form* (San Francisco, 1983)].

believer: 'until Christ be formed in you' (Gal 4:19)." Comparing this with the theologians referred to above, the incompatibility and direct opposition become clear. The gap which yawns here between the two approaches is no less than that, for instance, between mysticism and historical political interest. This in turn raises the question whether, for example, Schillebeeckx is right to claim the term "experience of Jesus" or "of Christ" for what he has in mind. Does it belong to the category of religious anamnesis-experience at all?

It is relatively easy to answer this question by referring to the explanation of the genesis of Christian experience found in *Christ*, by Schillebeeckx. First of all one notices the vagueness with which he uses the words 'experience', 'life' and 'thought', and the way he concludes by equating 'experience' with the present communication of revelation. Experience, for him, is always tied to intepretation, which is in itself a conceptual intrusion into the immediacy and receptivity of experience. For Schillebeeckx, the so-called context of experience of the modern world, "the framework of experience and expectation" is essential if there is to be experience of Christ or experience of "salvation in Jesus".[7]

It seems that experience of Jesus is only possible in such a context. But the question is whether this context is penetrated by a new meaning, whether new experience is genuinely possible in it, or whether there is only a reconfirmation of the old experience. Indeed, one must assume the latter, for Schillebeeckx goes on to say that the actual framework of expectation, or the basis of all experience, lies in the concrete situation of our history, containing "so much innocent suffering, injustice and injury".[8]

Jesus' message and life are addressed to this very life situation. Thus Jesus' message can be introduced as a component of the fixed framework of experience, but the question remains whether this is really experience, and not, as Schillebeeckx says elsewhere, a process of learning how to be truly human by having recourse to the story of Jesus of Nazareth. This, in brief, is our criticism: Schillebeeckx is not talking about a personal experience of Christ but about actualizing the memory of a human being against the background of the contemporary freedom of consciousness.

It can even be doubted whether this experience is religious at all, and not rather, for the most part, an experience of the present, supercharged with "Jesuanism". No kind of personal encounter with Christ occurs here, only the recalling of his example. As we shall say later, where the category of "devotion" disappears, there can be no personal experience in the form of a direct encounter. Here there are no grounds, evidently, for a real experience of the Person of Jesus Christ; unconsciously, perhaps, they are not even being looked for, for in doing so one would find oneself in the thick of theological,

[7] *Christ*, 62f.
[8] Ibid., 843.

and positively mystical, thought, which the author rejects as "the parrotlike repetition of a once-heard kerygma".[9]

But even as he does so, he indirectly points to the fact that the experience of the Person of Jesus Christ is of a unique kind: it is an anamnesis-experience.

3. The Nature of Anamnesis-Experience

In this connection we must observe once more that this mode of experience has been discussed very little by philosophy; indeed, philosophy can hardly be expected to deal with it, since it presupposes objective events and subjective attitudes that are not present in the natural realm and are not demonstrable. Can experience of an historical person or event ever be a verifiable phenomenon in the natural realm? All the evidence seems to show that the only way this can happen in the natural realm is by subjective recall, but in no way can this lead to the personal encounter and the personal exchange that appertain to the nature of the experience of Christ as previously described in the words of H. U. von Balthasar. Otherwise the person or event to be experienced would have to become real and present — which, for the historian, would be a pure miracle. But for the Christian faith it is a religious and theological possibility grounded in the uniqueness of the Person of Jesus and of the saving events. This anamnesis-experience, which is not merely a reduced form of a mere remembrance, is guaranteed on the one hand by the unique Person of the Christ who is to be experienced, who, as the God-Man, can be present because he is the spiritual Lord. Here the Person of Jesus Christ is not "spiritualized" in a human sense but "pneumatized". This means, in connection with 2 Corinthians 3:17, that Christ is now the Spirit-filled One in an absolute sense, and that as such he is also the One who is present in the Spirit, dwelling in his community and in its members. Faith can justifiably maintain the possibility of experiencing this pneumatic Christ, an experience that is unique since it is of the Son of God and of the man Jesus; for, quite apart from the question of whether these two should ever be separated from one another (e.g., in the search for the "historical Jesus"), in the case of the Risen Lord, exalted in the Spirit, they most definitely cannot. This means that the experience of the pneumatic Lord is also an experience of the man Jesus, who continues to bear the reality of his human life, suffering and death, and will never lose it.

But Christ's pneumatic mode of existence facilitates, on the other hand, this contact with man primarily because of his Godhead and his unique, Spirit-filled nature.

[9] Ibid., 846.

So we are confronted with the seemingly paradoxical result that, ultimately, it is only possible to experience the Person of Jesus Christ because he is a Divine Person; but, because the divine and the human are inseparable in this Person, the experience of the divine and the human is likewise indivisible; the experiences themselves "are inseparably divine and human".[10] This is what gives such depth and intensity to the experience of the human in Christ; for to experience the poverty and suffering of a man who is God, and in whom God "empties himself", is very different and much greater than to experience the poverty of a mere man.

What we have said here about experiencing the pneumatic Lord could be applied similarly to the way in which his saving deeds are made present. For they too, Spirit-filled and Spirit-borne, acquire such power that they burst the bounds of space and time and become accessible to the believer in anamnesis-experience. At this point we are in touch with lines of thought which are familiar to us from the theology of the "mysteries".

4. The Medium: Devotion

Naturally, if this anamnesis-experience is to come to fruition, it presupposes certain dispositions and attitudes on the part of the person concerned. What in general human experience is described as the element of passive receptivity must be given another, a higher meaning within the field of Christian salvation and with regard to the particular saving activity. Thus anamnesis-experience not only presupposes a special structure in the saving events and in the One who brings salvation but also, since it is an event that communicates, requires a particular disposition in the person experiencing anamnesis. So, on man's part, faith is required as a general structure, to quote a Pauline principle: ". . . that Christ may dwell in your hearts through faith" (Eph 3:17). "Faith causes our hearts to become Christ's dwelling",[11] and "heart" here is the emblem of the man characterized by inwardness and existential involvement. At the same time this faith and this "dwelling" must not be understood as something purely private and individual; first and foremost anamnesis involves the whole community, the Church, in which Christ and his saving work live on, and the Church is the all-embracing context of experience within which individual experiences of Christ and of salvation are made.

If we wish to trace this ecclesial faith, bound as it is to the Church's experiences and to the means at her disposal—such as word, sacrament and sign—to a single nerve, a nerve that must be touched if there is to be experience of Christ, we must see it as the living, whole faith that is expressed

[10] H. U. von Balthasar, op. cit., 311.
[11] H. Schlier, *Der Brief an die Epheser* (Düsseldorf, 1957), 169.

in devotion and in worship. Its form is that of complete dedication to the Person experienced, an expression of self-surrender to the Holy, and to the holy ones, the saints.

In structure this approach is essentially different from that of the experience of the human Jesus described above, which needs this Jesus only as a stimulus, as a peg on which to hang the experience of present life. It is no accident that Schillebeeckx remarks, in passing, that what he means by "salvation in Jesus" is still needed in the twentieth century.[12]

This ". . . still needed" is an illuminating expression: here we can see clearly that the relationship to Jesus is first of all limited to the category of "need" and then further restricted by the temporal "still". This means that a Jesus of this sort is to be encountered on human terms, according to human need, and possibly human caprice as well. Here man manipulates the present Lord and his Spirit, rendering experience or anamnesis impossible, for if it is to occur it must be under the control of the Lord himself in the divine freedom of the Spirit.

Experience of the pneumatic Lord can only be made in an appropriate, Spirit-given openness and readiness. It determines the human, subjective structure of devotion. It is a pneumatic attitude of unreserved openness and receptivity vis-à-vis the Lord pneumatically present — not some psychological state. Consequently, the results of an experience of Christ cannot be simply psychologized away. It is an attitude of the spirit and the will, and even today we do well, with Augustine and Pascal, to give the name "heart" to this intimate conjunction of spirit and will.

In more concrete terms, this Spirit-given openness is the faculty for meditation and contemplation. Nowadays, when Eastern practices of meditation are so popular, it should not be too hard to encourage the development of these charismatic, meditative and contemplative powers within the Christian ambit. But it must be remembered that the Eastern methods are aiming at an inner vacuum, whereas Christian contemplation is always ready for personal encounter, love, community, friendship with God in Jesus Christ. In a contemplation of this sort, a man can receive the Spirit's illumination, can enter into Christ. At this point forms of devotion can be helpful, provided devotion is seen, not as a subjective mood, but in the sense of the original "*devotio*", a form of worship of God in which the powers of the soul deliberately focus on some particular mystery.

Such focusing is basically an act of faith, which seeks to make sure of its goal by employing all the powers of the soul intensively. The goal itself, however, is that of a higher union with the Lord present in faith. The attention of spirit and heart to this goal acquires the character of inward prayer, in

---

[12] *Christ*, 63.

which contemplation of the mystery of Christ passes over into the spiritual motions of yearning, joy and love.

Furthermore, in a spiritual environment where devotion to Christ and a contemplative attitude are cultivated, the experience of Christ can also thrive. Contemplation is a spiritual receptivity for the experience of the presence of the pneumatic Christ. This experience, united with knowledge about the biblical Lord in his earthly life and suffering, will also embrace the human Christ, and indeed the whole Christ. Once human relations are seen in the context of the whole Christ, their incomparable meaning shines forth, radiating far more influence than some political Jesus reconstructed with the help of contemporary categories. To the extent that contemplative life is allowed to fertilize the active life and Christian *praxis*, the God-Man experienced in contemplation will also exert his shaping influence on the active life, and will do so far more profoundly than any human model designed to fulfill "needs".

ABBREVIATIONS

AAS: *Acta Apostolicae Sedis*

AHMA: *Analecta hymnica medii aevi*

AnGr: *Analecta Gregoriana*

AnMo: *Analecta monastica*

BAC: *Biblioteca de autores cristianos*

BBB: *Bonner biblische Beitrage*

Cath: *Catholica*

CChr CM: *Corpus Christianorum — Continvatio mediaevalis*

CSEL: *Corpus Scriptorum Ecclesiasticorum Latinorum*

Conc: *Concilium*

Div: *Divinitas*

DS: *Enchiridion Symbolorum* (Denzinger-Schönmetzer)

DSp: *Dictionnaire de spiritualité*

EE: *Estudios ecclesiásticos*

EuA: *Erbe und Auftrag*

EvTH: *Evangelische Theologie*

GCS: *Die Griechischen Christlichen Schriftsteller der ersten drei Jahrhunderte*

GuL: *Geist und Leiben*

GSCO: Geneva Series Commentary [GSC]

HDG: *Handbuch der Dogmengeschichte*

HThG: *Handbuch theologischer Grundbegriffe*

IKaZ: *Internationle Katholische Zeitschrift "Communio"*

LS: *Lebendige Seelsorge*

LThK: *Lexikon für Theologie und Kirche*

MCom: *Miscelanea Comillas*

MySal: *Mysterium Salutis*

NTA: *Neutestamentliche Abhandlungen*

PG: J. P. Minge, *Patrologia Cursus Completus*, series Graeca

PL: J. P. Minge, *Patrologia Cursus Completus*, series Latina

QD: *Quaestiones disputatae*

RF: *Rivisita di Filosofia*

RGG: *Religion in Geschichte und Gegenwart*

RThom: *Revue thomiste*

SC: *Sources chrétiennes*

SH: *Seckauer Hefte*

SM: *Sacramentum Mundi*

SPIB: *Scripta pontificii instituti biblici*

StAns: *Studia Anselmiana*

StAnt: *Studia Antoniana*

StZ: *Stimme der Zeit*

THAT: *Theologisches Handworterbuch zum Alten Testament*

ThPh: *Theologie und Philosophie*

ThQ: *Theologische Quartalschrift*

ThWNT: *Theologisches Wörterbuch zum Neuen Testament*

VD: *Verbum domini*

VS: *La Vie spirituelle* [series]

ZAM: *Zeitschrift für Aszese und Mystik*